the rhetoric of

AFFIRMATIVE RESISTANCE

H

Holbein: The Ambassadors.
(newly restored) The National Gallery.

the rhetoric of
Affirmative Resistance

Dissonant Identities
from
Carroll to Derrida

Julian Wolfreys

St. Martin's Press
New York

St. Martin's Press, Scholarly and Reference Division,
175 Fifth Avenue, New York, N.Y. 10010

First published in the United States of America in 1997

This book is printed on paper suitable for recycling and
made from fully managed and sustained forest sources.

Printed in Great Britain

ISBN 0–312–17330–X (clothbound)
ISBN 0–312–17331–8 (paperbound)

Library of Congress Cataloging-in-Publication Data
Wolfreys, Julian, 1958–
The rhetoric of affirmative resistance : dissonant identities
from Carroll to Derrida / Julian Wolfreys.
p.   cm.
Includes bibliographical references and index.
ISBN 0–312–17330–X. — ISBN 0–312–17331–8 (pbk.)
1. Carroll, Lewis, 1832–1898—Criticism and interpretation.
2. Derrida, Jacques—Contributions in criticism.   3. Criticism.
4. Identity (Psychology) in literature.   5. Narration (Rhetoric)
I. Title.
PN81.W56 1997
828'.809—dc21   96–50909
                                                      CIP

To

J.B. & R.R.

Il y a toujours quelque chose d'absent
qui me tourmente

Contents

vii

List of Abbreviations

AA Lewis Carroll. *The Annotated Alice: Alice's Adventures in Wonderland and Through the Looking Glass.* Edited by Martin Gardner. Harmondsworth: Penguin, 1987.

YW Charlotte Perkins Gilman. *The Yellow Wallpaper.* In *Four Stories by American Women.* Edited by Cynthia Griffin Wolff. New York: Penguin, 1990.

SH James Joyce. *Stephen Hero.* Edited by Theodore Spencer, John J. Slocum and Herbert Cahoon. New York: New Directions, 1955

U James Joyce. *Ulysses.* Edited and revised by Hans Walter Gabler *et al.* London: The Bodley Head, 1986. Citations are by episode and line number.

P Sylvie Germain. *La Pleurante des rues de Prague.* Paris: Gallimard, 1992.

W Sylvie Germain. *The Weeping Woman on the Streets of Prague.* Translated by Judith Landry. Sawtry, Cambs.: Dedalus, 1993.

Preface and Acknowledgements

To paraphrase Pierre Macherey, all the texts gathered here are related in that they belong to the age of what we call 'popular culture' (Macherey 1995, 7), whether they are immediately recognisable – determined or interpreted – as 'popular', or whether they can be comprehended as belonging to 'high culture'. Their gathering, seemingly heterogeneous as this is in its presentation, belongs in part, again in Macherey's words, to a 'study which elevates the disparate to the level of a principle' (Macherey 1995, 8). If the disparate is thus elevated, this is not so as to render what is disparate as a unified object, or to give it a homogeneous identity. And, furthermore, if the disparate *is* raised to the level of a principle, then this is not to say that the principle has behind it a programme already worked out or thought through, as a means of calming down the dissonance which is everywhere. Rather the disparate is celebrated for its own resistances – and its unceasing affirmations.

Thanks are due to a number of people whose names will suffice, and who also know who and where (and what) they are; they have contributed in a number of ways, over a number of years, directly or indirectly, to greater or lesser extents: James Kincaid, Jessica Maynard, Burhan Tufail, Peggy Kamuf, Vince Cheng, Jenny Bourne Taylor, Claire Jones, Virginia Mason Vaughan, Marcia Butzel, Geoff Ward, Mark Currie, Andrew Roberts, Marion Wynne-Davies, Jane Goldman, Charmian Hearne, John Nash, Alistair Davies, Jane Stabler, Moyra Haslett, John Abercrombie, Ken Newton, and *of course* those to whom this book is dedicated in friendship, gratitude and affirmative affection, and whose own dissonant identities, like those of the nameless others, are hidden everywhere in plain view throughout the surfaces of this book.

Chapter 5 is a substantially revised version of an essay entitled '*Meshes of the Afternoon*: Hollywood, the Avant-Garde and Problems of Interpretation', first published in *CineAction!* (December 1987, 11; 38–42). The author would like to thank the Editorial Collective for permission to republish this material.

Affirmative Resistances:
an Introduction, in passing

It is the essence of affirmation to be in itself multiple and to affirm difference.

Gilles Deleuze

Certain things such as mirrors, or language, have us believing that it [the body] is a coherent whole. . . . We would in fact love to be closed in ourselves. . . .

Bernard Cache

an undecidable scene or, resisting postmodernism

In Shinya Tsukamoto's film *Tetsuo: The Iron Man* (1993, 67 mins), Salaryman, the ambiguous 'hero' of the film, dreams of being bound naked on all fours and anally penetrated by a woman with a prosthetic device attached to her crotch. This comic phallus, which looks for want of momentary referents like a cross between a slinky toy, the baby monster from Ridley Scott's *Alien* or the ubiquitous conduit piping from Terry Gilliam's *Brazil*, is revealed in spread-legged close-up. The edit seems to imply that the viewpoint is that of Salaryman, that his is the gaze from which and to which the image refers. Salaryman's view would appear to be both constructed as, and constructing, ours also. As such, it seems akin to, or a possible parody of, soft-core pornographic photographs, The obvious difference is that engorged, lively and wayward phallus. Its writhing, semi-technological presence apparently dictates the direction of the viewer's gaze, as much as the gaze of its owner.

This entire dream replays the implied desires traced by a more or less complete range of pornographic scenarios, in certain given situations, in a seemingly 'postmodern' manner complete with industrial muzak. It follows hard on Salaryman's pursuit from a train station by another 'monstrous' female. Her hand has been replaced by a conglomeration of what look like pieces of machinery

1

and melting flesh. Or is it the machinery which appears to melt? There is an equivocal, even paradoxical, moment here. Things, events 'seem' and 'appear'. But as readers we cannot be definite in the meaning we construct. This doubleness, following the logic of paradox, confuses identities. A dissonance is in place as the text seems to have it both ways at once. Like the form of the film, characters are readable as being in the process of a constant becoming. We read a continual catachresis which informs process and affirms the catachresic in all identity, while indirectly resisting the reader's accession to stable meaning.

The woman just mentioned is but one example amongst several in the film of a 'cyborg', defined by Donna Haraway as a 'a hybrid of machine and organism' (Haraway 1990, 174). The notion of hybridity in the critical discourse relies for its possibility – as does the notion of the cyborg – on the reduction of figures to a culturally accepted binarism based on stable, knowable identities which are always implied. Hybridity and 'cyborg' also imply the notion of originary, single sources. As we shall argue in this reading, such definitions and identities are themselves troubled by the film. After Salaryman, who has himself begun to transmogrify into machinery, has apparently awoken from this apparent dream, we witness him in intercourse with his partner, he penetrating her from behind, first on the floor and then against the wall. Her pain and anguish is of no consequence to him. In what appears a classic Freudian reversal, the male, having lost control in his fantasy, feels the need to reassert his control, his mastery and his sexuality, all of which appear to be clearly related. Again, we read a possible play of certain pornographic images at work here. Yet the images are constructed in such a manner – incessant, intrusive and not always synchronous soundtrack, harsh lighting, the absence of (even faked) pleasure – which perhaps de-eroticises the sequence through what I would describe as a comic-book travesty, divesting the images in the moments of their projection of the power that pornography promises as the context of its constructions. I say 'perhaps de-eroticises' with good reason. To suggest that the scene does de-eroticise is to impose a reading which relies on an unacknowledged idea of what is , and what is not, erotic. That which is supposedly erotic is therefore somehow privileged over what is considered as not-erotic, given a quiet, hidden centre through the reading/translation/interpretive process. Difference is suppressed in the effort to produce a stable identity and calm down the troubling activity which *Tetsuo* can be read as affirming. Granted my reading does partake of certain assumptions and 'normalisations', albeit indirectly – more or less – but this is very much to the point of this introduction. The question is being raised, what is being read/interpreted/translated and what, if anything, is always already 'there', so to speak? Can we know, can we decide? Even in the moment that I attempt to describe what I see, I find myself caught out by reading/interpreting/translating. Not only are identities in the film questioned, but also those of the audience. Around terms such as 'erotic' there exist – or do we merely read this? – contexts for definition which have perhaps little enough to do with the erotic as such; we come to be aware of their imposition on us in evaluative ways through such a film as *Tetsuo* because no translation, reading or interpretation ever sits comfortably in the face of such wayward, yet conventional textuality.

Everything in the scene becomes helplessly ridiculous, grimly comic, in which Salaryman is seen as a feeble victim of his own excesses and desires. This is in marked contrast to the one other repeated sex scene in *Tetsuo*. In this other scene, Salaryman and partner/spouse/significant other/girlfriend are witnessed, again and again, a little more of the scene shown each time, 'making love' in the woods. The film quality of this *au naturel* scene is decidedly poor, film re-filmed, or an amateur home-video. The couple are leaning against a tree, her breasts and legs exposed, with no accompanying soundtrack, other than their own noises. They become aware gradually that they are being watched by whoever is doing the filming/watching. The 'natural' woodland context, the implied voyeurism, and the reflexive specularity all seem to play into porno-narrative, while playing with them and juxtaposing the sexual/dream sequences that I have already described. Pleasure and fear are explored and questioned in equal measure without attempts to reach closure in interpretive terms. Yet again, dissonant play is affirmed, the location of identity resisted.

The scene culminates in the moment, after (simulated?)[1] sex when, Salaryman having cooked for his partner, witnesses her in close-up parody of various food and lipstick advertisements (specific products don't need to be identified, you can all supply your own instances [I can certainly supply mine])[2] licking a fried sausage in a manner apparently implying oral sex. Set against this are harsh metallic scraping and rasping sounds every time her tongue caresses the sausage, juxtaposed with shots of Salaryman's sweat-covered, panic-saturated face, which assumes an ever widening look of disbelief, fear and awe, until the sausage is bitten in half, accompanied by visual and aural explosions. Orgasm and destruction simultaneously, as readings and identities collapse on one another. The binary on which we rely for our knowledge of what goes on gives way to the double logic of paradox and instability. Salaryman is back at the point of powerlessness, the moment of his worst nightmare rewritten in another form all over again. At which point, his phallus emerges through the table in the form of a spinning drill head (to which he will later refer as his sewage pipe, as if to deny or confuse the very identity which appears irrefutable), which seems to surprise him as much, if not more, than his partner. His sexuality has grown out of all proportion and is completely out of control, wrecking the furniture and provoking screams from his astonished partner. Oscillating drill head in hand, Salaryman runs screaming into the bathroom.

This little sequence of events plays between a number of textual and discursive situations and contexts, between a number of *what ifs* and *as ifs*, some of which I have already indicated, and most of which we have some familiarity with: the science fiction/stalker/horror movie, the commodified use of female sexuality and the displacement of the vagina onto the mouth in order to sell any number of products. There is also a range of possibly Freudian/Lacanian scenarios alongside the clichés of pornography. Pornography is cliché,[3] endless re-runs of the always already. Each of these scenes is, in itself, somehow connected or connectable to any or all of the others. Or at least, this is what our ability to read will tell us. In every case, each identity which we think we know or can read 'shatters singularity', to borrow from Bernard Cache (Cache 1996, 89). It does so by affirming not a different, oppositional identity but by resisting identity through the affirmation of the difference and dissonance of, within, the very idea of identity. All of these images, symbols, metaphors and narratives are initially comprehensible as being mercilessly – and, for me, humorously – exploited, played with, shuffled around, possibly parodied or pastiched in *Tetsuo*. It really becomes a problem deciding on how to read them or, indeed, if they are readable at all, as I have indicated by my own recourse to words such as 'seem', 'possibly', and 'appear'. Even terms such as 'pastiche' and 'parody' need something akin to ironic suspension. *Tetsuo* can be read as setting up narrative as anti-narrative, narrative as sampling, as digitised reconfiguration of all the commonest, commercially exploitable desires. This is a tentative reading, anyway. And what this provisional reading suggests is that the most constantly frustrated, fundamental de-sire is the desire on the part of certain readers to know identities absolutely, and without dissonance.

So what, if anything, can be said in the face of such a solicitation of figures? There is a sense in which the film text resists critical approximations or sadly inadequate précis. Such a film-text might well challenge the virility of some critics by its very affirmation of, well, everything. Or anything. And the rest. When I asked a group of students how would they explain such a film, one re-plied, quite rightly, 'what a stupid question!' She went on to explain that explanation was beyond or, at least, beside, the point; perhaps off the point altogether. *Her* point was, correctly enough, that explanation as a mode of narrative recuperation was simply inadequate in the face of such a self-consuming structure as *Tetsuo*.[4] Despite the mouth, the lipstick, the sweat, the sausage was, after all, a sausage. Wasn't it? The film seems to laugh in the face of all rational explanation or comprehension, as does the laughing head which appears throughout the film, apparently to mock Salaryman (but also appearing to mock the viewer). But, as we hope our précis of the scenario suggests, so much is potentially readable, regardless of the embarrassment of material concern-ing bodies,[5] despite the weakness of explanation, that, in the place of explanation, questions sprout, like the mechanical prosthesis of the Japanese yuppie. What are we reading? Is what we read already constructed, either partially or wholly? Do we perform the construction through acts of viewing? Does the act of view-ing become transformed – read/written – through the obvious necessity, as demonstrated above, of various contexts and dis-courses, which turn the viewing into a reading into a writing? And what is happening when those contexts, on which we like to lean, are made unstable themselves through a little rough play on the part of a seemingly knowing or coquettish 'text'? Slap and tickle indeed. As Berkeley Kaite suggests in *Pornography and Difference*, there are troubles 'in the spectator–text relationship' (1995, 9). These troubles are troubles within identity. They are the moments of projected dissonance which find articulation between supposedly stable identities.

If we could say anything at all for the moment about the examples from the film and about the levels at which the film's 'undecideables' work, it is this: they seem to support the view that meaning, if it is not 'in' the text or 'in' the play of the text's signifiers, is also meaning which is not determined solely by the reader. (This becomes apparent in the chapter below on Maya Deren's *Meshes of the Afternoon*.) Certainly there is plenty of potential for meaning to abound, albeit in a highly wayward fashion; an embarrassing excess, I'm tempted to say, were it not for the fact that this admission is somewhat embarrassing. But, if we learn anything at this juncture, it is the validity of a point put forward by Jacques Derrida in an interview; which is that meaning 'is determined by a system of forces which is not personal. It does not depend on the subjective identity but on the field of different forces, the conflict of forces which produce interpretations' (Derrida, in Easthope 1991, 238). The reader does not, cannot produce meaning alone. Concomitantly, the text does not, cannot generate meaning solely. Identity is always the result of negotiations of meaning, and the most brutal negotiations take place where identity is deployed in the service of power. Yet because identity is a projection, an event of continuous becoming, we can learn to read the dissonances within meaning as affirmations, rather than as negative or oppositional trouble spots. There is always the becoming of the constant double movement *between* reader and text, where comprehensibility can be resisted. In the context of the late twentieth century, Tsukamoto's film seems comprehensible if only because its comprehensibility is a carefully worked out play between tantalising modernist fetishes, relics, signifiers and the undecidability of such traces when placed in the given context of the film's 'narrative'. Comprehensibility is undecidability; the undecidable is what allows comprehension.

Perhaps the identity that is most furiously mocked by *Tetsuo* is that of postmodernity itself. The scene described seems to invoke a reading which would claim that machines and the technology which we are told are in danger of taking over our lives retain what Roger Luckhurst calls a 'subjectivist bias' (Luckhurst, ed. Brannigan *et al.* 1996, 175). Postmodernism as a critical discourse suffers from a retrospective anthropomorphising nostalgia for lost human identities, hence the need for terms such as 'cyborg' or 'hybridity'. Both are invested with the traces of originary humanity as a lost, though somehow comforting stabilising trace of identity in the face of the impersonal machine-text, the machine surface.[6] A certain depth is desired, so as to flesh out identity, and postmodernism in its technological obsessions, is little more than a scrabble to re-invent the illusion of depth as the meaning of identity in the face of the apparently impersonal.

Tetsuo resists the postmodern by laughing at it through a reading of postmodernism's own modes of representation. If the machinery of *Tetsuo* suggests liminal, dissonant entities as the affirmative identities *between* machine-identity and human-identity, between the stable binarism of human/machine, it also collapses the binary referent by suggesting over and over again that there is no 'natural' organism which is not technologically re-presentable or performable. Equally, we read the suggestion that there is no technology which cannot be anthropomorphised. Loving the machine makes our own identities certain. It gives human identity a purpose, a meaning. It serves the purpose of domesticating it, giving it an identity with which we can live (who hasn't seen those vacuum cleaners with eyes, or the award scene with David Niven's refrigerator in *Monty Python's Flying Circus*?), rather than having to acknowledge its otherness.

Tetsuo, however, can be read as undoing such dysfunctionalism in its play between the events of film sex, between the apparently natural and the apparently monstrous. Every act, every event of the film speaks of identity as always catachresic. Every sexual act in the text disturbs identities. And *Tetsuo* does not even offer a temporal comfort of a linear narrative, speaking of the once human which now is lost. Sex in the woods is only available on handy-cam, while sex in the home is unthinkable without prosthesis. *Tetsuo*'s narrative is not one 'in which the human body loses its specificity as "human" and becomes itself monstrously other' (White 1995, 244). The film is itself readable as an act of monstrous techno-human becoming which never ends. The dissonance of its identities is a multiple dissonance imprinted on all of us. What we read is that to be human is to be always monstrously other, without stability, without the unity of identity. We read the text as writing across itself what Derrida calls 'a certain emancipatory affirmation' (1994b, 54) concerning the secret of identity. Yet, if it is readable as affirming in this manner, it does so indirectly, in a kind of textual periphrasis, or what

J. Hillis Miller has described as 'presentation without presentation, that is presentation in an indirect form of something unpresentable by way of something that seems analogous' (Miller ed. Brannigan *et al.* 1996, 159). That 'something' which seems analogous is the tease of dissonant identity, and this, we might suggest, is a suitable provisional description of the workings of the rhetoric of affirmative resistance.

of sounds, sights and sites: reading other identities

In this book I read various texts for the complicating resistances to interpretive closure that they offer, and for the sounding, siting and sighting of dissonances in the presence of dominant modes of cultural logic which aims to produce stable identities that they apparently position; or which we can, at the very least, position, set up, sound and site, through our acts of reading. The terms 'sounding', 'sighting', 'siting' (with the ghost of a homonym, *citing*), help to recall to the process of reading the aural/visual elements of the process. However, we are not taking it for granted that the process of reading is an unambiguous one, hence the various flagging indicators above around terms such as 'pastiche', 'parody' and 'postmodern', and the proliferation of 'appears' and 'seems'. It is precisely the *alogic* of semblance and simulation where dissonant identities emerge, affirm and resist: *between*. Between reader and text, between one apparently stable identity and another. Sounding and sighting/siting seem to me to suggest some of this ambiguity, and the shaky ground we're on when we read, interpret or translate, in fact whenever we seek to construct an identity through some reading activity, whether for ourselves, the text, or for 'characters' in a text.

When we read, whether a book or a film, or, for that matter, a painting, photograph or piece of music, we hear the words and/ or images (we do *hear* images, as much as we see them) played back to us by the act of our reading. This hearing, which we take in part as a reflection, comes be translated as a facet of the identity for which we search. At the same time, or nearly the same time – which is not the same time at all but a different time, the time of difference – we locate, through whatever processes of revision we enter into, particular figures, some of which become keys, tones, keystones or cornerstones for us. Again, this is part of reading identity. 'Sounding' suggests a response to

what we hope will be there; we send out signals, waiting to receive back an image, reflection or projection based on the sounding
we are taking. We attempt to take soundings as a method of
location, recognising a familiar landscape or feature, although
the process of sounding requires the possibility of a place onto
which we can project in the first place. There is also the possibility in this of echoes, so that an alternative or eccentric sounding may be set off, even though this was not part of that for
which I was necessarily reading.

Sighting/siting, on the other hand, suggests a process of ac-
tive location of determinable referents effected by reading. This
is often accomplished by referral to a context or discourse, to
which the text more or less seems to be referring (or that is the
way we construct the referent). In *Alice's Adventures in Wonderland* (see Chapter 1, below), Alice seeks to sound and site herself, in terms of her knowledge of the world from which she
comes. She attempts to understand what she is witness to in
Wonderland by drawing on discursive and cultural contexts, citing
those contexts and discourses in the effort both to place herself
comfortably in this unknown place, to site herself through epistemological citations as it were, and to translate what she is in
the midst of by sending out soundings, in order that what she
sees – sights – and hears may come back a little more clearly.
And the joke is, of course, that she cannot. Alice, of course, did
not have the benefit of the words of Jacques Derrida, and so
was not aware that meaning and interpretation and identity are
dependent on the conflict of a field of forces. This is not, we
hasten to add, that Lewis Carroll was *not* aware of everything
that Derrida is (albeit in a very different fashion). Of course he
was. But this is precisely the difference of identities and the
knowledge which comprises identity with which Carroll has so
much fun, while Alice is always perplexed, never having much
fun at all, *because* she wants so desperately to be certain about
her identity.

Yet what I am trying to describe are basic processes in all acts
of reading, though my terms, sounding and sighting/siting, might
seem not wholly appropriate to what I am describing. The two/
three/four terms – reciting/resounding/echo chamber/projection
– do provide a sense of interaction however; they do imply that
we are read by what we read, as much as we think we read
what we have before us. Our identities come to be written as

responses to textual fields, and as a field of articulations of the other. The suggestion is there that we are already read by what we have previously read, or been read by. But I'll slow down, before this becomes all too much like a nightmare of Dodgsonesque proportions. The purpose behind this is to suggest, through the readings which are to follow, that we can respond through acts of readerly frottage to unveil textuality in a manner appropriate to the text in question, so as to incite/excite its own mobile, fluid space. The purpose is also to suggest that textuality can come to embody through its own technologies of rhetorical frottage a textile machinery of 'resistance', whereby dissonant identities emerge as the unpredictable event of affirmation. The resistances that are read and sampled throughout are not all of an order. Nor are they simply resistances of an obviously dissident or subversive kind. To posit this would be to imply a somewhat simplified dialectic structure which would, on the whole, not be necessarily relevant to the differences between the various texts in question. Moreover, to make out these resistances as belonging to a conscious, deliberate or inevitable strategy – which the dialectic model promises to effect – would be simply inappropriate as resistance is as much positioned by the reader in the act of reading as it is an effect of the text. Instead, I read for resistances which are affirmative; resistances which do not merely oppose a dominant discourse or practice, even though in some cases, as in the reading of Charlotte Perkins Gilman's *The Yellow Wallpaper*, such an interpretation must inevitably, it seems to me, occur, at least as an initial instance of looking for a way out, or in. But resistances are looked after which are of a more general and, simultaneously, a more specific nature by the very fact that, in the act of resistance, they – the figures, tropes, characters, images, metaphors, metonymies – affirm.

– What is it they affirm?

Many things. Perhaps most persistently the possibility of a heterodox notion of community developed as the affirmative response to an expanded notion of text, a rewriting of the concept which follows on from Derrida's own strategic generalisation of the term; also, the continuous resonance, the resounding dissonance of textuality *itselves*, whether that term implies the complication of identity, an institution or the idea of the institutional, or political or ideological situations and structures, in the face of mortifying structures of imposition which single, unified identities represent. Perhaps, most importantly, the tropes of resistance, the rhetoric of affirmative resistance, can affirm an on-going acknowledgement of the continued existence of otherness, by constant exposure to which, to paraphrase Gabriel Motzkin, one place's one's own identity in question (Motzkin 1996, 265) as the necessity of such reading.

– But is the act of reading, even of the kind you are proposing here, not a form of imposition?

We would hope not, though this is a risk which cannot be wholly evaded. The chance is always there, even though texts, we suspect, are often only constructed as repositories of old bigotries and complacent reading habits. Yet the chance is also that, to quote Motzkin once more, 'what is read, assimilated, and therefore remembered, hovers at the edge of identity, as something that is neither quite own nor quite other' (1996, 266). The space between allows for the chance of dissonant identity's affirmative resistance. And perhaps there is the possibility of establishing negotiations, of attending to, waiting on, and thereby liberating a dissonance in a manner akin to that of the narrator of *The Yellow Wallpaper*, whose reading of the wallpaper's textile serves as an inaugural moment in the liberation of the anonymous female figure, which is itself a possible projection of the narrator otherwise.

But to return to 'affirmative resistance', the idea and the possibility. It is not enough to say, if indeed this is even the place from which to start, that affirmation arises beyond opposition or resistance. Such a structure is still caught in the act of recalling and remarking the *geist* of an Hegelian continuity, invoking and whispering, somewhat smuttily (nudge, nudge, wink, wink) of the dialectic and its seemingly pornographic promise of transcendence, or even – and this seems even more *risqué* – *quasi-transcendence*. Instead, what we are seeking is an affirmation that is also simultaneously a resistance, not merely the consequence of one which emerges (quasi-)transcendently in the rags of the *aufhebung* as the step beyond. Instead, we want to imagine an affirmation as the possible side-step of the simple, dialectical resistance (a resistance which is also, merely, a response, a reaction); a 'textual' gesture, if you will, analogous to the *en passant* movement in a game of chess, whereby confrontation and hitherto inevitable opposition is side-stepped in advance of potential opposition by a positive gesture.

In chess, the *en passant* move is one in which the pawn, insignificant piece in itself, moves as if by accident. The gesture of *en passant*, made in passing, as it were, can only occur once a pawn has made its initial two-square move. The move is made so as to 'capture' another pawn (other pieces of higher value cannot be taken by the pawn in this fashion). The movement must happen, if it is to happen at all, immediately two pawns are side by side, otherwise the chance is forfeited. The pawn effecting the capture moves diagonally to the space beyond the pawn it aims to capture, thereby taking the desired piece without actually moving onto the square occupied by the opponent. The opposing pawn is lost, removed from the board, and the pawn making the move *en passant* has advanced. This move is, however, entirely optional. The whole thing has a careless, coincidental quality, which really establishes indirectly the ground for further movements and strategic gambits. The side-step does not even admit of the possibility that confrontation could have taken place. A textual gesture of affirmative resistance is similar. It is one that we apparently notice in passing, by the way, with the insouciance of the almost (but not quite) accidental.

– But how can this be demonstrated or explained?

It already has, in the opening gesture of this introduction, which has deployed a narrative without prior explanation, side-stepping the structure of concept prior to explanation through illustration (a small dissonance in the identity of 'the introduction'). But let's return to *Tetsuo: The Iron Man*. As has been suggested, there appear to be a number of visual and performative 'referents', to which we can respond by saying, 'oh, this is like this', or 'this reminds me of . . .', and so on. Standard intertextual referentiality, apparently. We've indicated a few such possibilities. We calm dissonant otherness down by stabilising the film's possible identities into a single identity. Also we assume the film to have properties supposedly intrinsic to its identity, in order to translate it into an organic whole and efface our acts of imposition. In doing so, we confirm our own cultural identities by being able to fix the text in place long enough to gain a sight of the identity we believe to be ours apparently reflected in the act of reading. The problem remains though. None of the images or visual tropes *quite* matches those other references or signifiers to which it supposedly points. 'Irony', we might say. 'Parody', 'pastiche', 'postmodernist reflexivity', etc. Yet for this process of 'making the pieces fit' to work at all, we clearly need terms, other signifiers which somehow match up, albeit approximately to what we witness, what we (think we) read. Ours is therefore an imperfect comprehension, a rough translation. As Gabriel Motzkin says of translation: '[t]he other's continued existence implies the continued existence of a different point of view. . . . The other poses a threat . . . to present identity' (1996, 267). The other is, precisely, the radically dissonant within identity. The images and tropes are largely metaphorical and metonymic in their referentiality; they don't 'mean' in exactly the way in which we think that they 'mean', should 'mean' or ought to 'mean' in a given context or situation. They are already marked by failure. The context to which we had referred is made improper. Corollary and concatenation are forestalled by the now skewed, 'de-normalised' foregrounding of the referents or signifiers. This foregrounding is, already, a rewriting, a re-inscription. The figure is no longer pure, if it ever was. It is now contaminated, while, simultaneously, it contaminates our point of reference. Artist Agnes Martin acknowledged this in 1967, when talking about her use of grids, squares and rectangles, in her paintings: 'My formats are square, but the grids never are absolutely square; they are rectangles, a little bit off the square, making *a sort of contradiction*, a dissonance, though I didn't set out to do it that way' (Lippard 1967, 55; emphasis added). Martin's language acknowledges the idea of a prior identity which is assumed but then troubled in the practice of painting, despite the artist's intention. After the act, she finds herself reading her paintings as affirming their otherness, despite what she 'set out to do'.

Thus a text is made to slip by us; it slips by us, *en passant*. In our attempt to capture the text, the text, through its figural play/gesture/gambit, has resisted ahead of our strategy, broken the square, affirming its own waywardness by side-stepping, apparently, what we might have to say, but saying it ahead of us, with a wry smile on its face. Like Alice on seeing the chess pieces actually moving and talking amongst themselves, we feel ourselves somehow as if we were invisible (Carroll 1992, 187).

'I' will, therefore, have been avoided. What we can read in the textual affirmation of its own textuality is an affirmation we have inadvertently effected, lured by the signs we thought were there all along, but which we constituted, despite ourselves, through the act of reading. We constitute the identities of texts, if I can put it this way, because our knowledge is informed by various textualities, discourses, practices and epistemologies. Our constitution is thus double. As much as we constitute the identity of the text we read through our prior knowledges, we are ourselves constituted, not only by the texts informing our knowledge, but also by the text we read, because it constitutes us, it reads us, according to the bodies of knowledge which it sets going in various ways in us, by the fact that we have engaged with it.

This all seems very slippery. What it does point to though is a certain desire that infects the act of reading, a failed desire announced above by Agnes Martin, when she says she hadn't set out to install the dissonance. Reading after stable identity (what might be called polite reading) is keen to get rid of the inauthentic, the contradictory, the dissonant. A well-taught and well-learned reading is eager to dismiss what it thinks it can determine as fraudulent, and so impose the stability of identity and meaning which it claims is merely *there* as textual property and what is proper to the text. In seeking to effect this dismissal, reading believes itself capable of suppressing difference. This is an old desire, a Platonic desire no less, as Gilles Deleuze has acknowledged (1994, 265). To read in such a fashion, after such a desire – to subject ourselves unquestioningly to the mastery that such desire can have over us – is to condemn, directly or indirectly, what Deleuze calls the 'state of free, oceanic differences, of nomadic distributions and crowned anarchy' (1994, 265). What is being read after in the name of reading is a sense of sameness.

Tetsuo is but one instance of affirmative resistance, of the gesture which does not acknowledge its simulacra solely as simulacra, and which seemingly refuses to be counted within the Platonic schema as composed of copies and debased representations. It seems to play with such representations in order to refuse the privilege of the historical, cultural and political concept of the individual body (and the idea of representation in general), and its neatly articulated homogeneous identity. Indeed, the film is so readily recognisable as a 'bricolage', 'pastiche' or 'portmanteau' film that it has already given up all possible acknowledgement of itself as unique, individual, discrete as a 'work of art'. Yet, paradoxically, it is this 'giving up' which tips us off to its irreducibility and undecidability. To suggest that it copies is to miss the point, or still to be enthralled by the Platonic desire. For the film-text is not composed of copies but constitutes its nature through annotation, something quite other than copying. The film is readable as a constant event of affirmative dissonance. It affirms the dissolution of bodily and psychic identities, whether through performance or representation. The film makes conglomerations of its contexts and references ahead of its own narrative.

Its footnotes are more privileged than its main text, if we can even determine where such a thing as the 'identity of the main text' lies. It goes further than this. The law of textual hierarchy, to borrow from Derrida's essay on the function of footnotes (1991d, 193), has been subordinated to a principle of re-marking textual marginalia. The film knows that if there is a law, then there must also exist the possibility of 'all deceptions, transgressions, and subversions' (Derrida 1991d, 194), and it has answered the call of the secondary material in order to deny its own authority, ahead of the very fact that such authority might ever have been read as existing. To quote Derrida again, speaking of *Glas*, '[a]ll modes of secondariness are tried and mimed and made parasitic and grafted, tattooed (inserted in the body) . . . [t]he text is a continuous annotation . . . [t]he text plays on play' (Derrida 1991d, 204). Thus the film's composition appears to 'mime' – imperfectly, distortedly (these are not failures of representation but readably deliberate distortions and dissonances) – the grafting of machinery onto flesh or flesh onto machinery, as it has apparently grafted onto itself in supposedly parasitic/parodic ways the snippets of films, commercials, cultural referents, images and illusions, all of which pretend to have to do with the idea of the individual body and the cultural identity which determines that body's representation.

Tsukamoto's film seems to play with the possibility of the impossibility of representation, when representation is always an act of citation, the image being drawn or copied from elsewhere. It takes the conventionally secondary or contextual, foregrounding the secondary as all there is, without origin in and through the dissonance of monstrous contextualisation. The film plays as its textual gambit the frustration of identity's supposed uniqueness. It can be read that the film-text draws not on a stock of referents, so much as our desire to search out those referents as so many confirmations of our 'unique' identities. It has placed within it the already self-acknowledged figures of other discourses, other contexts we think we know, believe we read, only so as not to copy them merely. For, to return to the idea of the copy, the very idea of the copy implies a failed fidelity, and the constantly frustrated desire for such verisimilitude. *Tetsuo* mocks the very idea and possibility of fidelity. In doing so it enunciates failure as the affirmation of difference. It also mocks our knowledge of the knowledge we believe mistakenly that we 'possess', and the limits of our knowledge concerning who we are, who I think I am, for example. A 'copy' of the Mona Lisa with a moustache or goatee beard is no longer a 'copy'. It never was. It was, is and will be something other, it affirms its own vitality through the dissonance of the 'departure' which we perceive from an original we have in mind, and through the resistance to the idea of the original which the affirmation puts in place.

So *Tetsuo* is something other, composed of non-dialectical otherness, which never appears to allow itself to be read as merely a series of copies, even though we might be tempted to pursue such readings. I began with such readings, only to leave off, thereby marking their limits. The film thus affirms its own vibrant identities through its *en passant* resistance to being read in any constraining manner. It is not merely a 'postmodern' version of some age-old narrative or myth; it is its own, but without boundaries, without (the need to construct) the illusion of being a discrete entity. We can only read in its wake, reading for a departure from what may have been copied, while having to acknowledge a departure being made incidentally, ahead of the prospect of a copy being created, and all this *in passing*.

– Where then does *Tetsuo* situate itself?

In a position which is not a position in the conventional sense. The idea of the position conventionally has been made to correspond to the idea of the subject, discrete and isolated. The position imagined through the reading of this film resonates in, through, a space for which there is no single subject. The space which affirmative resistance acknowledges is a space beyond any possibility of a single identity.

paradoxical identities and surfaces of reading

Each instance of affirmative resistance has then to be read according to the terms which we must attempt to read it in the process of dictating. It is not that there is something characteristic of certain texts which can be defined as affirmative resistance. This would be to construct an identity for 'certain texts' and not others. Reading would be made safe. On the contrary, there is no text, no identity, which is not troubled by affirmative resistance and its rhetorical dissonance. No given set of texts can be said to exemplify affirmative resistance. If I have chosen to focus on certain properties which I read in given texts, this is not to assume that these properties are constant across texts and identities. To reiterate a certain point. We just cannot be sure whether it is a case of a text having a property or whether the reader invents or perceives that property. This is undecidable. It is the undecidable event of reading. The space between identities – in this local argument the space between reader and text – is where certainties about acts of reading as reassertions of identities come to be troubled. Also troubled are suppositions about properties of texts *as* characteristics of an identity. This book sets out to explore a set of disparate, wide-ranging texts, rather than a group of texts which seem to share an identity, precisely because I wish to explore how one reads and how one wants to read. If this is an example of a 'mode of reading', it is the example of a mode which does not have determined limits or a fixed identity. If this is a 'mode' at all, it is one which constantly breaks its own frame of reference. The rhetoric of affirmative resistance is involved in intimate ways in unpredictable acts of reading, therefore. Like Agnes Martin (or even Alice) I may set out with the desire to read certain figures, but all too often there is something for which the act of reading cannot account. This something troubles not only my reading, but also *me*. This might in certain contexts be said to be the aporia of theory, the aporia between the articulation of a theoretical programme or code and the proof of that theory through example.

The rhetoric of affirmative resistance is then readable as installing the aprogrammatic within the possibility of the programme. It partakes of doubling, paradox, catachresis, projection and semantic torque, all of which challenge and resist indirectly readings which aim to produce the illusion of depth, while affirming textuality as a multiplicity of surfaces. Across these surfaces are projected the traces of innumerable identities. And affirmative resistance is, importantly, not equivalent with polysemy. Beyond polysemy, affirmative resistance is the trace in excess of any formalisable codification or programmaticity. I indicated earlier that affirmative resistance was not a two-step programme, relying initially on the establishment of an opposition which invoked or promised a return of the dialectic. Affirmative resistance differs from dialectic in terms of its own resistance to any possible theorisation of itself as simply an opposition in the first place.[7] Also, to say that affirmative resistance is reducible to any one definable concept or 'thing' which always resists in the same fashion – or affirms in the same fashion – every time is to miss the essentially idiomatic (affirmative, resistant), improvisatory quality of affirmative resistances. The example of *Tetsuo* is one of a range of images apparently half-known from elsewhere. It is this half-known quality which resists appropriation through the affirmation of the dissonance set up in the dissimilarity from what is supposedly known. Something, some projection emerges between identities and 'it must be confessed', in Philippe Lacoue-Labarthe's words (in his reading of the subject in Theodor Reik) that

> the figure is never *one*. Not only is it the Other, but there is no unity or stability of the figural; the imago has no fixity or proper being. There is no 'proper image' with which to identify totally, no essence of the imaginary.

> (1989, 175)

These images or figures are themselves never only themselves; they are never single. They vibrate slightly out of tune with the figures that they appear to be imitating. Their dissonance is not a general dissonance which opposes a particular reading, but is dissonant locally, within the frame of reference already dismissed. Such dissonance unsettles the frame. In this dissonant sounding is the denial of the possibility of an absolute frame of reference to which the critic can refer unerringly every time. The rhetoric of affirmative resistance readable in textual forms is what makes interpretation problematic from text to text and between one identity and another, especially if one were to attempt to build up a global theory of interpretation. There is always in such a textual vibration, to quote Geoffrey Bennington, 'the possibility of recitation outside the "correct" context' (Bennington 1994, 25). This is readable across the paintings of Agnes Martin.

Martin's paintings may be understood as returning to us as their audience an infinite range of recognisably repeated lines, spaces, intersections, shapes, planes, none of which are exactly the same. Yet they return, implying a continual remarking which makes possible an act of reading which desires the endless repetition of the same and the suppression of difference. The possible misrecognition of the similar as the same and the paradoxically infinite possibility of reiteration which affirms the singularity of every line and mark suggests the Nietzschean notion of eternal return. Of the eternal return, Gilles Deleuze has commented:

> The eternal return is a force of affirmation, but it affirms everything of the multiple, everything of the different, everything of chance *except* what subordinates them to the One, to the Same, to necessity, everything *except* the One, the Same and the Necessary.
>
> (1994, 115)

Martin's paintings are readable as playing with a desire for the same while sounding the resonances of the different. Indeed, resonance can only be possible because of difference. We read Martin's paintings in their use of repetition-in-difference affirming the dissonant resonance of the eternal return. The dissonance arises out of a comprehension in her paintings of non-equivalence. Her textile meshes do not give way to the Same or the One; they avoid becoming-similar, and thus, in their own dissonances, affirm their vibrancy and their community, a community of reiteration and non-similar recitation, where difference is understood as making possible what Deleuze calls 'a complex of affirmations always coextensive with the questions posed and the decisions taken' (Deleuze 1994, 115).

Given this we can read through the repetition-in-difference of Martin's paintings, the gesture of disappearance in repetition. The disappearance is that of unified identity, such an identity having vanished within and between the sounding and sighting of dissonance. The repetitions of Agnes Martin's paintings are not part of some structural closure pointing to the absolute or ideal Structure. Each repetition has, in Deleuze's words, 'no in-itself' (Deleuze 1994, 70), no absolute identity. Strictly speaking, there is no repetition in Martin's paintings for each 'repetition' is irrevocably altered in the context of the painting as a whole. This sense of alteration should not be taken to imply that there is some original. This would miss the very nature of the radicality of the difference sounded in Martin's repetitions, and would reduce her grids, lines, bands and flows of colour to the function of signifiers (which they have always already escaped, avoided), with the prospect of some anterior signified, whether transcendental or otherwise. This in itself would speak of the possibility of closure, thereby calling a halt to the radical affirmation of which Deleuze speaks at some length. The affirmation of Martin's repetitions-in-difference are themselves constitutive of non-oppositional resistance in that they avoid in passing the imposition of an interpretation of their 'function' as of the order of signifiers. Their resistance is non-oppositional because they never allow for the reading of either a signified or a position-in-opposition from which they are situated. Positions are dissolved, fluid, contingent on the chance, multiplicity and discontinuity which each painting is readable as being in the process of affirming, within its own highly provisional and mobile structures, and from painting to painting. Each painting affirms every other painting as part of, and discontinuous from, the textuality of the paintings as a non-totalisable, non-absolute whole. The whole is neither absolute, nor totalisable for two reasons: first, signification is never simply available as part of interpretation, dependent on the act of interpretation to bring it into being. Second, the 'whole' is always contingent on the possibility of being altered by the subtraction or addition of another painting, or other paintings. To borrow from Geoffrey Bennington's discussion of the question of idiom, Martin's paintings are always *'event[s] to be nego-tiated in [their] singularity'* (Bennington 1994, 34). The singularity of which Bennington writes is not the singularity of a unique identity; it is the singularity of the other irreducible to the One. The context of each mark, each space, each line or wave has to be considered in its particular context. And this must be done in order to comprehend how repetition is difference.

Which leads us back to the possibility of the repetition or recitation, to recall Bennington's word, outside the 'correct' context. If Martin's paintings are readable as articulating apparently their own deconstruction; if they are readable as being deconstructive *events* shifting their grounds from painting to painting; and, if there is a resistance, a side-stepping of the possibility of the signifier-signified binarism (which is, however, echoed in the *im*possibility of such a relationship), then what can we ever construct as the 'correct' or, for that matter 'incorrect' context within which the traces of a particular painting occur? If *Tetsuo* had affirmed, amongst other things, a context-excess as a condition of its resistances and dissonances from which there could be read position-without-subject-to-itself, then Agnes Martin's paintings appear to play with the dissonance of the im/proper context and the singularity that the premise of eternal return affirms. Positions can no longer be spoken of properly in these readings. Rather, they are presentations without presentation, to recall Hillis Miller's words, situations without situation. They are situations always on the way, to come, 'always *coming*', in Jean-Luc Nancy's words, 'endlessly, at the heart of every collectivity'. Such an endless becoming, Nancy adds, 'never stops coming, it ceaselessly resists collectivity itself as much as it resists the individual' (Nancy 1991, 71).

Situations on the way, always coming, are what come to be affirmed endlessly, in a multiplicity of ways, voices, soundings, sitings, and sightings. Departures of which we spoke earlier are also the possibility of the 'to-come', looked at – or looked *for* – from other directions. What we are trying to read for and to think through, amongst other things, is the idea of the limit, and the possibility of thinking on the limit which traces the condition of difference. The two 'texts' so far commented on or, at least, *around* have brought to bear in ways that mark, affirm, their singularity, and, through the reiteration of singularity and the idea of the singular repetition, this question of thinking the limit of identity, dissonance arising as its radically other expression.

enabling texts

Texts cannot be understood if we stop short at a presumed meaning. They must be allowed to continue their discourse. Only when they continue speaking can they survive as the expression of what has been expressed and as the *irreducible relationship between the two*. A reader is not primarily a receiver of content. A reader enables a text to speak.

(Frey 1996, 7; emphasis added)

We do not stand before a subjectivity already given, fitted or packed; rather, we are called to produce it – being is above all becoming, event, production.

All dominant subjectivity is constructed to prevent this alternative . . .

(Guattari 1996, 214)

Between these two citations we can read the projection of affirmative resistance, along with an expression of the interests of this book, written in other words. Irreducible relationships *between*; constant becoming; the unpredictable event. These are the places where we cannot settle on a fixed identity, even though conventional acts of reading would like to assert themselves the possibility of such places, and against statements such as those above. This introduction has, in passing, introduced what is already known; or, at least, accepted about acts of reading. Like any act of writing or text, it only has its chance when read *in the relationship between*, when it becomes other than it is, when its other comes to speak and be spoken. What is accepted about reading, or that which is known (whatever we may think we know when we use the word 'know') belongs to an identity dependent on certain non-reflective ways of interpretation and in equally non-reflective situations of reading. The texts referred to have been borrowed from in order to determine for the moment certain terms, structures, habits and, of course, the thinking of limits of identity. Talking about the terms as though they were, for the instance, absolute or actual, is – equally for the instance, the instance of the thought, the limit of the thought, and the thinking about a particular limit of any term, structure or habit – a demonstration or performance of what Derrida calls 'operating from the inside

borrowing all the strategic and economic resources of subversion from the old structure, borrowing them structurally.
(Derrida 1976, 24)

Derrida does go onto say in this provisional definition of 'deconstruction' that its enterprise 'always in a certain way falls prey to its own work'. And this is precisely what has been happening here. But this is the chance we have taken. However, the texts to which I have referred have been acknowledged in a certain fashion, if only so that, in Derrida's words again, the erasure of particular determinations (terms, structures, habits, economies, whichever you will) can be effected. This introduction thus exemplifies what Derrida describes as 'the necessity of *passing through* [in passing] that *erased determination*' (Derrida 1976, 24; my emphases). The structure, the 'determined signifying trace' (Derrida 1976, 23) is always faintly visible; but as visible are the erasures in the process of being perpetrated as part of a certain necessary affirmation. This doubleness is, in Félix Guattari's words, a 'double movement, on the one hand of closure, and on the other of opening, of a bursting of co-ordinates that risks unbinding, madness, disorder' (1996, 216).

The doubleness, and the risk it entails may be read in a text outside the immediate frame of reference of this book, in Hans Holbein's *The Ambassadors* (see frontispiece). One of the most familiar paintings in London's National Gallery, perhaps the most familiar element of Holbein's painting (before we even see it, so to speak) is the obliquely projected skull in the centre-bottom of the painting. This can be viewed as a skull only if the viewer stands to the right, or crouches to the left, of the painting, and glances either down or up at the skull so that its proportions appear to reform themselves, so that the skull appears for the viewer as a skull. Standing, or sitting, directly in front of the painting, you cannot tell that the skull is a skull, exactly. Of course, so many viewers come to see Holbein's painting precisely because of that skull-projection. They know it is supposed to be a skull, that it will reveal itself as a skull as the viewer or reader of the painting positions him- or herself in relation and in response to the demands made by the painting. The text thus seems to dictate the act of interpretation on the understanding that if that reading act is to become one which acknowledges the constraints of skewed representation it must bend itself to the resistance to representation which is installed in the image.

The text of Holbein's painting thus affirms its own textualised nature. A condition of its identity is that part of the painting always remains at odds with the majority of the painting's representations. Seeing the skull involves the viewer/reader in a degree of awkwardness, perhaps even physical discomfort. As viewers, as readers, we must shift our own perspectives. In doing so, we must renounce the certainty of our own positions as viewers, giving up to the painting our identities as readers or viewers. We can only ever be partial readers of this text, we can never construct a complete, stable identity for Holbein's enigmatic, playful image. However, it is not only the painting which is incomplete in its identity. The painting offers to challenge our identities as readers. And the image returns our gaze as inadequate, our identities incomplete. As Kaja Silverman points out in her own reading of the painting, the anamorph prevents us from 'effecting an imaginary mastery' (1996, 177) over the painting because it appears to dramatise a gap in the gaze; developing and paraphrasing Lacan's own reading of *The Ambassadors*, Silverman suggests that the painting 'effects a deconstruction of normative vision' (177); and with that, of course, any normative position or identity is also resisted.

This playful image has been taken so seriously, principally because of that *memento mori* which disturbs representation, reading and identity. Humanist readings of the painting insist on an attempted incorporation of the death's head into the overall image, despite its anamorphic distortion and dissonance. The humanist urge is to calm the catachresis of anamorphic projection into a mere metaphor, the troubling dissonance of identity subsumed into a normalised, domesticated function. The key signifier and symbol of human *vanitas*, the death's head becomes a reminder of 'our' mortality. I mark off the pronoun with good reason. Humanist readings would insist on containing the frightful textual play of projection which so disrupts the painting's mimetic realism by connecting the humanity of the audience of the early modern period with that of the audience at the end of the twentieth century: 'we' in the 1990s understand the painting in a manner similar to its first and subsequent viewers, once we see the death's head for what it is, once we see the skull as others have seen it over the last four hundred-plus years.

This is no accident, as Lacan lets us know. The conventional perspectival position, whereby the gaze appears to emanate from a single, unique position, emerges at a cultural and historical moment close to the appearance of the Cartesian concept of subjectivity (Lacan 1994, 86). The painting, we can be convinced allows us insight into a common human condition which is shared, and which, like the skull itself, can be viewed anamorphically down through the centuries. Even Kaja Silverman's reading, in its efforts to mediate against the 'dominant fiction' of the painting – that part of the painting which passes for 'reality' because it is painted according to the rules of conventional perspective – goes so far as to assert as a dialectical and oppositional gesture that Holbein's image shows us not only his world but our own (1996, 178). Even in the gesture of oppositional criticism, the reading conforms in its gesture of opposition to a form of shared identity. Similarly, every visitor to the National Gallery who encounters this image is thus able to construct a comforting identity for him/herself, if s/he only puts him/herself out a little (both physically and metaphorically), the reward being that the viewer in the 1990s is connected intimately to the ambassadors, to those for whom this painting was made, and even to Hans Holbein the Younger. And what are we connected by? Death.

It's all about reading and a supposed commonality of identity, a universalising of the reading process which occurs because decisions about identity have already been made. We read in a certain manner because such a reading conforms for us the identity we believe is ours. Yet, stand in front of Holbein's painting, refusing to move to either side in order to make sense of the projection, and read the projection as a projection across the text, as a textual device directing reading in another manner, a manner which disturbs commonality and coercive universality.

The anamorph cuts into the illusion of the real created by conventional perspective, as both Lacan and, after him, Silverman acknowledge. It disturbs the purely representational and mimetic condition of the image, calling attention to the act of painting as a textual act concerned with itself, concerned with textual painterly and inscribed effects which resist appropriation, mastery and unification. It extrudes and intrudes, simultaneously projecting itself from the margin, from the frame. It reminds us that all images are somehow framed. This is what makes them images, texts to be viewed, to be read, to be interpreted. The frame alerts us to the necessity of responding to an identity through an act of reading which seeks to construct identities. The bottom left of the anamorph is dark shade, out of which the details of the distortion emerge. What the projection projects towards is a vertical-textual rhythm which is affirmed everywhere in the painting, and to which multiple order even the ambassadors themselves are subjected.

Immediately above the skull is the lower table, with its lute, its book with the intrusive marker, the folio of music, open and folded back, the globe out of its frame, decentred. A pair of compasses lay on the table, while the lute, doubled by another, dark instrument, face down and forgotten, on the intricate mosaic of the floor, has a broken string (presumably readable as another figure for human mortality).

Above the lower table is yet another table, covered with an intricately crafted cloth. On this are various scientific instruments, devices for measuring the land, sea and sky. The heavens themselves. In proof of this is the astral globe, securely mounted, unlike its earthly counterpart, below.

Above, behind, and around all of this is the sumptuous and intricately worked green drapery, which leads back to that floor, with its equally intricate tiling, laid out in highly complex patterns, like the drapery, like the table covering, even like the robe of the right-hand ambassador. Patterns, surfaces, weave and fold, whirl, dive and surround throughout the surfaces of the painting. Patterns incorporate the ambassadors who have become mere framing devices themselves, a pair of columns at the margins of the texts and textiles which are so important to this painting. They frame the double tables. They serve as inner frames to the left and right of the painting, even as they are framed, their identities defined by text and textile, by textuality. Like the sheet music, the book, the reading of which is interrupted by painting, the astrological and geometrical devices, the ambassadors are there to be read. Their identities are only constructed through acts of reading, even as the world or the heavens can only be known through reading and interpretation. The two globes suggest acts of reading, interpretation and mapping as crucial textual precursors to the act of identity-formation.

Thus Holbein's painting implicitly resists interpretation and translation, even as it resists the attempts to read a single identity for it, from the supposed perspective of a single identity. It simultaneously affirms identity as radically textual and radically multiple, interrupting the interests of Cartesian oriented systems and discourses. The artisanal activity necessary in the making of draperies, cloths, clothing, floors (all those devices in the painting which are conventionally ascribed to a representational background) connects and interweaves between the textual surface, the textile weave of the paint, to the devices for reading and interpretation which abound everywhere in this single image, breaking into and fragmenting the supposed unity of the image. Whether globe, compass, musical instrument or written text (music, map, or literary/philosophical/theological), whether for geographical, astrological, geometrical or aesthetic purposes, all the devices we read are there as a reminder that there is no reality, there is no identity which is merely given. All such devices are not merely products of a prior reality but instruments which make possible the discursive and textual knowledge of what we choose to term reality. Textualising tropes within the painting, such devices can be read as preceding reality, or even marginalising the real, showing it to be merely one more textually produced identity. The real is, then, itself textual, a writing always formed or produced – always *becoming* – in relation to reading.[8] This being the case, no one identity can ever be produced as a single, homogeneous identity, because, as Holbein's painting can show us, there are always multiplicities of identities, possible multiple readings. *The Ambassadors* is a clearly historicised text. History is itself affirmed as a textual affair. Holbein's text is marked off and appears to mark itself off from any universalising desire or tendency, any interpretive will in a distinctly dissonant fashion. Thus it resists indirectly, and it does so from within the 'dominant fiction'. It plays a constant double movement between identities, taking its chance with both closure and openness. It disorders order.

The doubleness spoken of here, which is also the doubleness of the limit, the double-limit marked by both determination and its erasure, is commented on elsewhere. In his commentary on his String Quartet No. 2, 'Hunting: Gathering' (1994), South African composer Kevin Volans writes:

> I decided to try and write a piece which included as many different musical fragments as possible, strung together in a pseudo-narrative. To keep the fragments separate, each is written in a separate key. As I wanted the different pieces to come and go in a random fashion like images or events from an unplanned journey, my principal problem was how to move from one key to another without any sense of development (i.e. without modulating) . . . I made reference to several different pieces of African music . . . [t]here are also several more private references to Scarlatti, Handel, Stravinski and my own earlier pieces.
>
> (1994, 3)

The quotation usefully highlights the idea of the determined signifying trace, the ways in which the 'enterprise of deconstruction always in a certain way falls prey to its own work', and the attempt to resist closure while acknowledging the necessity of the reference, however private or provisional. What Volans's words seem to testify to is the fact of the absence of any absolute signified, and the affirmation of a certain refusal to privilege referents. The music confuses, reinvents and effaces particular identities as keys to the music (ways of reading it) in favour of the affirmation of multiple, dissonant identity of the music-text. What is it that is being sounded? Do we know? Do we think we know? Or do we know that we don't know, and, in not knowing, come to know – find ourselves on the way to knowing, a 'knowing without knowledge' if you like – that the music in question does affirm irreducibly the time of difference, the spatio-temporal irreducibility of the difference of identity, and, with that, freedom from the 'order of the signified'? (Derrida 1976, 18) And this is indicated in the mute figure of the colon, which equally separates the terms 'Hunting: Gathering' in Volans's title, without giving privilege to either one. Both are signifiers, without modulation, of the other, without being reduced to an opposition. What goes on here as the gesture of affirmative resistance is the collapse between a certain, private reference and a 'public' or performative iterability, a collapse which is, too, the opening of the aporia between the positions. We may think we can hunt – or, alternatively, gather – the references, Volans may acknowledge for us some of those, and others for himself, but this does not lead to a resolution or closure of possibility of iterability within the structures of Volans's composition, a serial composition which undoes the narrative gestures of motifs, themes and so on. Even if we were to identify all the figures, all the elements of citation, recitation, what we name pastiche, and so on and so forth, there would always be an excess beyond citationality which neither we nor Volans for that matter could identify, recover, situate. Volans' title, 'Hunting: Gathering' nicely figures in its colonic torsion both the processes of conventional reading/writing, and the aporia in the activity.

The issue of affirmative resistance is, in many ways, about an articulate freedom and the articulation of freedom, as referred to by Jean-Luc Nancy (1993). Nancy argues that philosophy attempts to enclose 'freedom' by formulating 'freedom' as a problem within the logic and discourse of philosophy. Yet freedom is *not* a problem, as Nancy points out. For Nancy, freedom is freedom *of* thinking and freedom *as* thinking, where thinking, in these formulations of Nancy's, escapes the limits and definitions of philosophy. Thinking is *not* philosophical, it avoids philosophy, being at the limit, being *the limit* of philosophical comprehension: hence freedom as/of thinking.

If this is the case, and if we accept Nancy's thought on philosophy as indicating what he calls throughout *The Experience of Freedom* the other thinking, such a concept of the other thinking *must* also be applied to what is called literature, what is called art, what is called music, what is called film; in short, to all textual 'formations'. And this is so if only so that textualities' affirmations can be understood to question (the question of) limits, thereby being readable as being on the way to exceeding and escaping 'literature', 'music', 'art', 'film' or whatever, in order to be part of what Nancy describes as the 'form-lessness' (Nancy 1993, 60) of the other thinking. The other thinking is that thought, thought-as-affirmation, which does not oppose itself to 'philosophy' or 'literature'. For to set up an opposition is, still, once again, to put or place one's thought within a system which encloses and forecloses, which is governed by the economy of closure, and which initially and ultimately imprisons. Rather, the other thinking, what is being called here affirmative resistance, thinks in a space 'beyond' the thought of the system as the structure of all thought and Absolute Knowledge. This is not to suggest any simple 'beyond' as though such a thing were possible, but to argue in another way, *on the way* to the otherness of affirmation. To borrow from Nancy's argument on philosophy (Nancy 1993, 63–5), 'Literature', 'Film' or whichever textual name we propose as an example of the textuality of which we are thinking, does not produce or articulate this alterity I am naming affirmative resistance. It does however make possible the reading of such otherness in a 'beyond' which is 'within' (see the earlier remark of Derrida's on 'deconstruction'), sounded and sighted/sited, as non-identical reiterations, dissonant identities as a signal of return which does not obey the laws of the structure which is named variously 'literature', 'philosophy' or 'film'. And that this is so is possible because affirmative resistance is not subject to such laws, even though it seems that it cannot help but refer to them. As if to acknowledge this, we must always read a relentless unfolding of textual surfaces in the attempt to by-pass a merely dialectical reading.

In consideration of the question of what we read and what is 'there' (or seems to be there), and the insistence of an irreducible opening of difference between the two which makes the answer unknowable even in advance of the question, the texts in question – those already mentioned and those to come – appear to us to let us see. Apparently, they unveil what (we believe) we read. Yet this 'unveiling' is not of the order of bringing the truth out of the closet, bringing before us a certain presence or the promise of a presence. Rather, what we think we see or hear, what we believe is given to us to see and hear, is obtained through implied (although never simply present) 'structures' of negation. Texts of affirmative resistance are best understood as *apophanic* (*apo* = off, away, away from, other than; *phanai* = speak). They read as speaking away from the subject, from the truth. In speaking so, they affirm an opening always on the way to arriving, always open with/to the possibility of the speech of otherness, a non-locatable resistance. What is at stake is nothing short of the struggle for the ground of representation, the ground which is also that of the question of interpretation, and the power that the control of representation and identity can wield (which we can see opened by readings of Holbein's *The Ambassadors*).

Representation, like the concept of philosophy in Nancy's articulation of freedom, has the power to subject and enclose, to imprison. To return to Deleuze on this issue, who draws from the work of Michel Foucault, he argues that representation dominates our perception and imprisons the very idea of difference: 'difference is not and cannot be thought in itself, so long as it is subject to the requirements of representation' (Deleuze 1994, 262; thus any possibility of freedom, difference, affirmation must always already have side-stepped, in passing, as part of the evasion of being put into a simple oppositional situation, if it is not to be mastered). Elaborating his theory of representation, Deleuze points to the following four categories as keystones – he calls them 'iron collars' (262) – of representation: identity, opposition, analogy and resemblance (262). 'These are', states Deleuze, the 'four roots of the principle of reason' (262). The texts to which I have so far referred bring to bear, or can be brought to bear, a degree of pressure on reason and its keystones, as they themselves are readable as being in the process of toying with the premises which support identity, opposition, analogy and resemblance.[9] Yet, Deleuze argues, representation, despite its appealing power, *'does not acquire the power to affirm either divergence or decentring'* (263; emphasis in original). Such alternative power belongs without appropriation to the difference or affirmation that textuality is in the act of always moving towards. There is no reason this should be so; and that it is so means that there is no reason – as a repressive, imprisoning structure – which cannot be dismantled from the inside through an intoxicated utilisation of the structures of reason. This involves the affirmation of the difference which such structures keep quiet about, but on which they are dependent. Such affirmation thus articulates resistance, and can be heard, seen, situated, read as resistant affirmations.

Now it has been argued that 'predominant in postmodern theories of representation are approaches that locate "the body" within systemised networks and circuits' (Fraiburg 1993, 39). However, as initially appealing as such a relocation of the body within the postmodern may seem, the problem is that, despite the seduction of the fetishistic tag 'postmodern', the argument relies on all sorts of recuperative and dialectical language in order to work its magic of a promised radicalism. The idea of the 'Body' (as a possible identity) no matter how much re-mapping it undergoes still recalls the classical, discrete, humanist body with its limits, against which networks and circuits are positioned. The very term 'postmodern' implies an opposition of the order of the dialectic in that it is opposed to the modern, in a more or less simplistic, and even reactionary or antithetical, fashion. And finally (for now at least) there is the arch-taboo word against which Deleuze has warned us so eloquently: representation, which in many cases can be concerned with nothing other than the re-presentation of identity to the self. To have a postmodern theory of representation is still to have an idea of representation which must always in some way refer back to other theories of representation, and into which the supposedly 'postmodern' theory is recuperated. Representation reintroduces the metaphysical, the order of the desired, yet absent signified. Postmodern theory has not yet escaped the inescapable nature of Representation, which is as a 'site of transcendental illusion' (Deleuze 1994, 265).

Representation as this site maintains its power through the ability to position the illusion of an 'identical thinking subject'

(Deleuze 1994, 265). But in the *en passant* gesture of a reading of the kind I am proposing, whereby resemblance is subordinated to difference rather than the other way around (as Deleuze outlines; 1994, 266), difference comes into play and resemblance is seen for the shabby copy it always was, rather than the shining projection of presence from the magic lantern of truth. What we are therefore arguing for are what Deleuze has called (note the double plural) *'affirmations of differences* as a consequence of the multiplicity which belongs to each Idea' (1994, 267). Such multiplicity, the multiplicity of the idea, is no mere polysemic wealth; it is the affirmation of the aporia at the heart of knowledge and the desire for knowledge. Non-knowing is on the way to us as the resistance to closure and as the affirmation of the other.

I have patently failed to name that about which I am talking; and for a very good reason: because that which is being spoken of cannot be named, not 'properly'. Hence the constant recourse to exposition. Hence the 'failure' (recalling an earlier term) to introduce – to introduce 'properly' – what might otherwise have been named the 'subject' of affirmative resistance, which is clearly not a subject at all, given this failure, which is apparently deliberate; and given the avoidance, the side-stepping, which has been remarked, if only in passing, so as to notice where the 'subject' is not. Affirmative resistance is a form of speech which doesn't directly address the subject. It speaks and writes away from the subject, away from 'itself'. It is announced here only so as to 'designate that which is first of all [to be] abandoned or "given over to the outside..."' (Kamuf 1991, 15). We might suggest that the rhetoric of affirmative resistance is that which is expressed in the following words of Jean-Luc Nancy:

– Il s'agit ici avant tout de l'interprétation

(1982, 9)

Notes

1. Isn't that the point? What do we as viewers/readers know, or think we know? We have the evidence of our own eyes, but cannot even trust as to whether what we witness is an image of the real or an image of a simulation.

2. The advertising campaign that springs most readily to my mind – and which sprang to the minds of my students on seeing *Tetsuo* – was a series of British commercials for Cadbury's 'Flake' chocolate bar. The most recent of which (as I write), is worth commenting on for the laughable lengths to which it goes to equate crumbly chocolate with sexuality, eroticism, phallic-oriented satisfaction, and oral sex. A young, dark-haired woman reclines in a free-standing bath, in a large, tiled room which would not look out of place as a set in a Peter Greenaway movie. The music is vaguely operatic, though not ostensibly so. The scene is almost diaphanously rendered, as swirls of steam curlicue around, most notably from the crystal water which allows for glimpses of skin. As the woman reclines, water oozes – suggestively? – over the edges of the bath and across the floor tiles. The woman's toes are seen playing with the quaintly old-fashioned taps. Her mouth (bright red lipstick, camera from the side and from overhead) bites down on the chocolate flake. . . .

3. The term 'cliché' is appropriate at this juncture, given its various meanings, such as snapshot, photographic negative or typesetter's plate, all of which suggest endless reiterability, as does pornography itself.

4. Showing the film to different communities of students -- for a Women's Studies course entitled 'Images of Women', and for an Interdisciplinary Studies course focusing on the topics of Power and Sexuality – evoked similar responses. Despite the initial sense the students had of being repelled, they mostly found the film liberatingly comic; over the trajectory of the film's narrative group-laughter grew or diminished according to gender, women finding the film funnier than men. The potential multiplicity of meaning liberated the students to reject critical authority.

5. Drawing from Donna Haraway's essay already mentioned, we can construct a reading of *Tetsuo* along the following lines: the dissolving bodies/machines of the film are readable as repeated rejections of the discrete body/identity in humanist discourses/readings, which effect and process containment, mastery and closure. The cyborg-bodies evade the traditional pleasurable/sensual/erotic/secrecy networks, even while they appear to hint at such meshes, to reject them in apparently 'parodic' representation of the networks in question (although even this reading is merely oppositional, and is situated in terms of a normative discourse of the body against which it is located). But the bodies of the film go further. In implying that the parodic (as one form of identity) is *all* there is, there comes the whisper that any idea of a prior or pre-eminent 'legitimate' discourse was only ever itself an illusion or fantasy projection of a voyeuristic kind.

The point here is that there is no identity which is not already dissonantly troubled.

6. Both *Terminator* films address the question of 'subjectivist bias' in their 'what if' scenarios: what if the machine built by humans assumes the trace of human identity in the ability to think? What the films suggest is that once the machine can think, once it takes on a human characteristic, it will become 'inhuman' enough to desire the destruction of all other humans, to assert its own identity, and to prevent humans destroying it. Just who is being inhuman to who, and why?

7. On the articulation of the difference between deconstruction and dialectic which has informed the commentary above, see Geoffrey Bennington, 'Deconstruction and the Philosophers (The Very Idea)' (1994, 11–61).

8. Jean Baudrillard puts forward the idea that the map precedes the territory in *Simulations* (1981, 2). See also Geoff King's marvellous study of cultural cartographies, *Mapping Reality* (1996), for a lucid development of Baudrillard's ideas.

9. Keystones in this passage is used as a purely provisional term, not suggesting final grounds, even though Deleuze's own language does give the impression of the four concepts in question as being somehow fundamental or originary. What I have sought to indicate are hidden keystones which serve Deleuze's four concepts, even as those four serve the functions of representation.

1

Alice: an architecture of knowledges? or, identities in dispute

As the subject is quite inexhaustible, there is no hope of ever coming to a regular finish

Lewis Carroll

'When I use a word', Humpty Dumpty said in a rather scornful tone, 'it means just what I choose it to mean – neither more nor less'.

'The question is', said Alice, 'whether you *can* make words mean so many different things'.

'The question is', said Humpty Dumpty, 'which is to be master – that's all'.

Through the Looking Glass and What Alice Found There

What is a dream but the erased writing of a book that writes itself in this erasure, and that we read with closed eyes: the lack – lacuna, omission, deficiency – of a book?

Edmond Jabès

the problem of the house

The first part of the title of this chapter appears to carry a number of claims, or, at least, implications and insinuations (as does the second part of the title, but we'll come back to that). It appears to imitate in part Michel Foucault's *The Archaeology of Knowledge*. The term 'Architecture' suggests moreover definable structure, knowable pattern or construct. It implies a classical form, a monumental, perhaps even phallic structure, of the kind discussed in some psychoanalytic readings of *Alice*, about which there is

35

more to say, further on. Such implications are no doubt there, in the title, although they are installed with a certain awareness of how these terms, echoes and possible meanings might possibly be read as providing a context for these readings of *Alice's Adventures in Wonderland* and *Through the Looking-Glass*. The title of the chapter thus has something to say about perceived identity, and the way in which that identity carries with it some other possible identifications not wholly consonant with what one appears to see. This is not merely an observation about the title but, in a way, suggests this reading of Lewis Carroll's *Alice* books. We would ask the reader to indulge the title a moment longer.

Some simple observations: Knowledges. A plural, clearly. Knowledge no longer in the abstract, no longer some amorphous gathering as the possible goal of inquiry and research or questioning. And 'an Architecture': note the indefinite article, which implies the possibility, if not the certainty of a structural plan, blueprint or design each with their illusions of depth. Elision in speech also allows a new term to affirm itself, against what seems there so obviously. We hear 'anarchitecture', which names surface and unpredictable event without order or identity. Aside from the obvious possible installation (another architectural term) within this of 'anarchy', there is also the suggestion of that which is outside or beyond architecture, that which has passed by architecture. This is not the same as non-architecture, not a direct opposition, but rather an *en passant* gesture, signalling an affirmative resistance at the very heart of architectural structures. All structures are, in some measure, architectural, not least those structures which we employ and impose in order to define 'Knowledge', and to create in the name of knowledge a rigid hierarchisation of values. An architecture of knowledge no less. Yet there is still the affirmation of *anarchitecture* within the expression of an architecture.

Why all this talk of architecture in relation to Lewis Carroll's writings, and the possibility of *anarchitectures*? Houses, dwellings, furniture, domestic trappings are to be found everywhere in both *Alice's Adventures in Wonderland* and *Through the Looking Glass*. The narratives of both texts are the result of Alice entering and emerging from houses, domestic and internal spaces. Yet we read in the textual use of such supposedly familiar figures a constant delegitimating mockery of our knowledge of the architectural, that knowledge of the domestic space by which

Fig. 1.1

we orient our identities. The spaces are transformed as identities and they transform Alice's identity, making possible the affirmation of her otherness.

The burrow or well into which Alice falls on following the rabbit is immediately other than a rabbit's burrow. It has its 'cupboards and bookshelves' (*AA* 26). Alice tries to make sense of this estranging encounter by recalling her experience of institutional architecture in the form of the school-room (*AA* 27). On landing, Alice's first experience is of a passage, 'a long, low hall. . . . There were doors all round the hall, but they were locked' (*AA* 29). Problems grow greater because the key she finds is too small for the doors. And, while the locks of the doors are too large for the key, the door to which the key belongs is too small for Alice to pass through, as Tenniel's illustration demonstrates (Fig. 1.1). One interesting thing about this illustration is what it seems it has to tell us, or what we can read there, concerning Alice's identity in relation to the architectural feature. It is not that the door seems small necessarily, but that Alice appears too large. Already, it would seem, she has become bigger than she should be, although she has yet either to eat or drink. Alice's identity is already problematised in relation to the architectural feature. Architecture, while affirming its waywardness, estranges our view of Alice. Perhaps even more than this, Tenniel's illustration is marked by an undecidable quality. We need to use our gaze to make decisions about the identity of the image, yet we cannot wholly be sure, according to the gaze alone, what is true or accurate. This is important in relation to the text as a whole, because vision is one of the two primary means (the other being memory) by which Alice makes assumptions about others' identities. However, as we know about Alice, seeing is very rarely believing, and sight alone cannot provide complete knowledge of the world.

In Chapter Four of *Alice's Adventures*, 'The Rabbit Sends in a Little Bill' (*AA* 55–67), Alice becomes far too large for the house, her bodily limits threatening to burst the house at its seams. To reiterate an earlier point, entrance to Wonderland is through the house, as we see here (and as we see in the first chapter of *Through the Looking Glass*). One must navigate the domestic structure in order to gain access to the other place, the place of the other, but these houses and architectural features are never quite as we would expect them. The supposedly familiar domestic details prove troublesome for Alice. And this is not only because Alice grows large or small. She expands and shrinks as a response to being in these particular houses. Her transformation into identities other than who she takes herself to be is a condition of strange architectures, of the *anarchitectural* within architectures, whether those architectures be concrete, discursive or epistemological. In Wonderland, architecture is never quite what it should be; it is never comforting or familiar, its identity being dissonant within itself. Alice's knowledge of the architectural space, and her relation to it – and her own identity – is troubled from the outset.

Later, Alice encounters the Duchess's house, which she believes to be 'four feet high' (*AA* 77). She is immediately troubled by the presence of the frog- and fish-footmen (*AA* 79–80). After her meeting with the Cheshire Cat, Alice sees the March Hare's house; or, she takes it to be the hare's house,

> because the chimneys were shaped like ears and the roof was thatched with fur. It was so large a house, that she did not like to go nearer till she had nibbled some more of the left-hand bit of the mushroom . . .
>
> (*AA* 91)

Even though Alice makes an assumption about the house's ownership (or at least this is an assumption about whose identity is determined by the house, by belonging to that structure), she only has her own eyes to go on (we know how unreliable these are). And seeing, as we have already suggested, rarely confirms assumptions about identity in Wonderland. The house, we read, is not conventionally constructed. Odd materials (for a house) and equally odd shapes are incorporated in the building. Thus the identity of the house is confused. Furthermore, it is not – apparently – on the same scale as the Duchess's house. Architecture is estranged from itself, as the text once again resists the idea of architecture in affirming *anarchitecturality*. In Chapter Seven, the Hatter's tea party takes place out of doors, where there are repeated cries of '"No room! No room!"' (*AA* 93), and this is also the place of the famous riddle about the similarity between the raven and the writing desk (*AA* 95). Of course the cry of 'No room' is absolutely correct in one sense: there is no room, no architecturally delimited space, because, quite simply, the tea-party occurs out of the house.[1] But Alice assumes the more obvious sense of the words, misunderstanding the *anarchitectural* nature of this anarchic scene.

The visit to the Hatter's – which for Alice had been a decision about the choice of whose house to visit, the Hare's or the Hatter's – is followed by another odd moment of *anarchitecturality*. Working her way through the woods, she notices 'that one of the trees [has] a door leading right into it' (*AA* 104). Here we have architecture so displaced that only the synecdochic door presents itself in what we would assume to be the wrong place. It *is* synecdochic inasmuch as we take it to be the representative, the symbol for the house, however absent that structure might be, But the important thing to notice is that, however we read the door, its relationship to a greater identity is never fulfilled; it leads only into a hallway which Alice takes to be the hallway of her first Wonderland encounter.

And then there is the opening chapter of *Through the Looking Glass and what Alice Found There*, which is appropriately entitled, and concerned with 'Looking-Glass House' (*AA* 175–99). In this chapter, Alice tries to show off her understanding of architectural spaces. She tells her cat in her typically knowledgeable fashion, and in a tone implying the identity of the school room, about the room in the looking-glass:

'Now, if you'll only attend, Kitty, and not talk so much, I'll tell you all my ideas about Looking-glass House. First, there's the room you can see through the glass – that's just the same as our drawing-room, only things go the other way. I can see all of it when I get upon a chair – all but the bit just behind the fireplace. Oh! I do so wish I could see *that* bit! I want so much to know whether they've a fire in the winter: you never *can* tell, you know, unless our fire smokes, and then smoke comes up in that room too – but that may be only pretence, just to make it look as if they had fire. Well then, the books are something like our books, only that the words go the wrong way . . .'

(*AA* 180–81)

Alice's identity in both books is dependent on her knowledge of the architectural space: her sense of her selfhood *should* be confirmed by the house, the home; instead of which, her encounters with architecture and its spatial dimensions are anything but comforting, and might best be described as *unheimlich*. Her involvement with estranging architectures always renders Alice's identity as other than it is. We read the event of dissonance in her identity as a result of her Being becoming homeless, as her sense of her identity is dislocated in the world. The problem for Alice is that architecture, furniture, the domestic space, just don't conform to her expectations. The architectural won't be read as it should be and, consequently, her identity – *who* she is defined by *where* she thinks she is – is troubled. Clearly there is available to us a reading of Alice as a being who inhabits, or who desires to inhabit, who seeks to belong, as part of the definition of her identity, to a particular dwelling. Carroll's text then may be read as asking the question later asked by Heidegger in relation to being: what is it to dwell? (1993, 347). Alice, it seems, can be read as striving to answer such a question, but the dissonance within her identity may be said to affirm itself in the fact that she always finds her identity challenged in being away from home, being un-homely. Nothing in Wonderland lets Alice dwell, even though she dwells upon the most fundamental of questions in asking herself who she is (*AA* 37–9; 67–8; 76; 225–6). And of course it is not just Alice's condition which is read as being in a constant process of becoming-homeless; Carroll's text may be understood as resisting the possibility of identity-as-dwelling, while affirming the homelessness of all identity, even its own. *Alice's Adventures* and *Through the Looking Glass* are texts which we suggest are never at home with themselves.

But to return to the scene just mentioned. Alice's speech to her cat suggests that the identity of Looking-Glass House is not only undecidable and unstable, but that also, as the other of Alice's home, it installs a continual dissonance within the home's identity for her.[2] Home is always destabilised, and with that destabilisation which resists knowable identity comes the destabilising of Alice's identity. This is revealed in the gaps of Alice's knowledge, when she says the looking-glass fire's looking-glass smoke may be only a pretence. She cannot be sure, although she suspects the simulacrum for what she thinks it might be. Also her knowledge is revealed as having limits, which are the limits of the frame, the limits of a projected identity. Some things can never be sited, they are out of sight, and therefore out of knowledge. Gaps in knowledge amount to the aporia of identity's certainty's about itself. These gaps are what we might read as affirming the inexhaustibility of Carroll's text on the subject of identity.

Ambiguities and simulacra are constituent elements of the dissonance within identity, *anarchitectural* elements installed in the architecture of meaning. Like paradox, they destroy, in Gilles Deleuze's words, 'common sense as the assignation of fixed identities' (1990, 3). This destruction involves the destruction of the illusion of depth, of which activity the mirror in *Through the Looking Glass* is readable as emblematic, figuring as it does a play of surfaces. Thus this text takes up where, as Deleuze argues, *Alice's Adventures* had left off. If we agree with Deleuze's assessment, that there is the movement away from depth and its abandonment (initially figured by the underground into which Alice emerges), in favour of surface (as represented by the playing cards), then the second book is a book made entirely of surfaces, such as the mirror and the chess board. The nature of the text's affirmative resistance is such that, while Alice may not be aware of what her actions entail, all her events affirm what Deleuze has described as the 'disavowal of false depth' (1990, 9). Thus Alice can be read as being in the act of affirming, as an affirmative identity which mediates unknowingly against her own apparent desire for stable identity. In being homeless, Alice comes to reveal to us the affirmation of identity's dissonance. The text is read in the event of passing Alice by, putting her to use as a dissonance within, and a resistance to, the frame, the house of identity. As the mirror shows us, Alice's moving through the surface is rendered as other than she thought she was, becoming a textual effect (and Carroll's secret is that Alice has always been such an effect).

The mirror reveals from the projections of its surfaces the possibility of asymmetry. Asymmetry may be said to break the frame. The surface of the mirror troubles the neatly ordered composition of identity, even as it appears to frame the subject, giving identity a finite and knowable limit. Thus the mirror can be said to be one figure of affirmative resistance. Resisting depth, it affirms identity's dissonance and the pure surface effect of an identity reflected as other than the self, and from which there is always something 'out of true' or hidden, something which remains unknowable (for example, the other side of the glass reveals the laughing faces behind the clock and the vase; Fig. 1.2). Alice typically makes the assumption that seeing produces knowledge; the gaze equates with the knowable for Alice, and yet the seen is not all there is. As Martin Gardner observes in his excellent note on the theme of the looking-glass (*AA* 180–3), the mirror inaugurates the constant movement of 'going the other way', which constitutes for Gilles Deleuze the event of '[b]ecoming unlimited' (1990, 8), exemplified by the *Alice* books. This ceaseless movement undoes identity. Left–right reversals and inversions are everywhere across the surface of the text, as Gardner reminds us (*AA* 180–1). They disrupt the closure which absolute reflection promises. Inversion haunts not only structural forms and architectural designs and devices, such as the home and its objects, but also the double identities of the text, such as Tweedledee and Tweedledum. Doubling, inversion, dissonance, all asymmetrical otherness is readable in language itself. When in *Alice's Adventures in Wonderland* Alice wonders whether 'cats eat bats' can be the same as 'bats eat cats' (*AA* 28), she exposes and affirms the asymmetrical within the structure of language which prevents the possibility of identity's self-sufficient reflection, of itself, to itself. This effect becomes more marked as Alice's adventures continue. Having just asked '"[d]id you say 'pig,' or 'fig'?"', the Cheshire Cat begins to disappear, until only his grin is left (*AA* 90). This event, which makes Alice feel giddy and unstable, leads her to remark while she has seen a cat without a

Fig. 1.2

grin, she has never, until this moment, seen a grin without a cat (*AA* 91). What is read at first to be merely a language game involving asymmetrical inversion becomes an a-structural or *anarchitectural* feature of perceived identity. What we read then in Carroll's confounding of the architectural is that its identity is dependent on that which most troubles it: *anarchitecture*.

It is well known that in Wonderland the anarchy of seemingly useless knowledges reigns. *Knowledges* is stressed in the plural once again, for Wonderland is comprised of a wide-ranging and heterogeneous collection of epistemological models and discourses, none of which are able to communicate or agree with one another. It is this impossibility of consensus or even communication which installs the anarchy in *anarchitecture*. Disorder is the order of the day. Anarchy reigns, furthermore, and affirms its knowledges' uselessness repeatedly, in complete ignorance of that which Alice brings to Wonderland, the dream of order, which Alice dreams as a condition of her being asleep. In falling asleep, Alice attempts to put in place structures of what she takes to be meaningful knowledge as a way of making sense of Wonderland. Yet Wonderland is resistant to such ordering, such architecture, and we read that Alice is herself subject to such anarchy, such *anarchitectural* movement in her identity.

And it is not that Wonderland is merely a representation of the movements of the unconscious, as some psychoanalytic readings of the text have suggested. Wonderland is not the *identity* of the unconscious tamed to some metaphorical or metonymic order. To read the text in this way is to misunderstand, misread, the nature of both Wonderland (to read as does Alice) and the unconscious (which is unorderable and unknowable as such). We can read that Carroll's texts affirm a resistance to acts on the part of the reader of ordering taxonomy, and they do so through a knowing revelation of themselves as principally textual. Caught up in this revelation is the possible unfolding for the attentive reader (as we come to understand indirectly through Alice's incomprehension in the face of Wonderland) of her/his identity *as* 'a reader rather than... a user or observer' (1993, 30). This phrase, which sounds like one possible description of Alice's experience, is taken from an essay by architect Peter Eisenman, in which he describes the shift from classical architecture to what he calls:

> a not-classical architecture [which] begins actively to involve an idea of a reader conscious of his own identity as a reader rather than as a user or observer. Such a reader brings no *a priori* competence to the act of reading other than an identity as a reader.... The competence of the reader ... comes from the capacity to read *per se*, to know how to read ... architecture as text. Thus the new 'object' must have the capacity to reveal itself first of all as a text, as a reading event.
>
> (1993, 30–1)

Wonderland does nothing other than affirm itself as the constant 'becoming', in Deleuze's sense, of a reading event, a textual *anarchitecture* in search, not of an author, but of a reader who comprehends his or her identity as constituted through acts of reading. Alice, for all her literal-mindedness and attempts to impose a tyrannical order of knowledge on Wonderland, is an imperfect reader, an observer in Eisenman's sense, unable to comprehend that she too is a textual trace. Her identity is involved in the textual event and determined by it, as is any identity.

the inexhaustible subject

The 'trend' towards 'psychoanalytic interpretations' observed by
Martin Gardner in his introduction to *The Annotated Alice* (*AA* 8),
is guilty of the same kinds of mis-reading as Alice, although her
guilt is one of ignorance, rather than the desire to observe, construct an identity, and impose an interpretive methodology, at
the expense of the textual event. William Empson began this trend
in 1935, in his *Some Versions of Pastoral* (1935). While Empson's
reading is no doubt more subtle and, certainly, more tentative
than a number of subsequent readings, such as Martin Grotjahn's,
John Skinner's and Phyllis Greenacre's, nonetheless, the desire
to read Carroll's playful assertions of Alice's moments of falling
asleep and waking as quasi-epistemological parameters determining *how* the Alice books are to be read, is to take moments
of textual play, as structural-interpretive indicators. The logic seems
to be: Alice falls asleep, Alice wakes up and (we read) we're
told she was dreaming between these two points, *therefore* these
texts are to be read as dreams, and we need to impose the appropriate framework in order to read properly and to construct
an identity for *Alice*. Events within the textual *anarchitecture* are
misread and obeyed. Instead of little cakes and bottles, the critic
finds labels, which seem to say, 'psychoanalyse me', *avant la lettre*
as it were. Perhaps it's the best joke of all of Carroll's books,
and the moment of laughter whereby the texts both affirm *and*
resist, unleashing, as James Kincaid puts it, 'possibilities for new
configurations of being' (Kincaid 1995, 93). When Martin Gardner
says of Greenacre's analysis that, although 'her arguments are
most ingenious, possibly true, . . . one wishes she were less sure
of herself' (*AA* 9), we find ourselves thinking of Alice's responses
to so many events in Wonderland.

It is interesting and instructive to look at one recent reading
from a Lacanian perspective of Alice, which shows how, while
psychoanalysis can never exhaust the subject of *Alice*, Alice certainly exhausts psychoanalysis. The essay in question is by Richard
Feldstein, and is called 'The Phallic Gaze of Wonderland' (1995,
149–75). My criticism is not directed at Feldstein but rather at
Feldstein's anlaytic rhetoric which cannot but help but ignore
the 'literary' in favour of pursuing its own truth. This essay allows us to understand how the desire to assert an identity for a

text is inextricably linked to a question of mastery over that text, and being sure of one's own identity.

Feldstein's reading makes a number of statements concerning Alice similar to my own, but the moments of divergence, where Feldstein pursues the interests of Lacanian psychoanalysis, are telling. We would agree in our readings of Alice at those points where we discuss identity. For example, Feldstein suggests that:

> Alice's attempt to make sense of what the animals say and to compose significance from the strange sequence of incomprehensible situations is tied to her perceived identity. This identity is a construct created from experiences on the surface world that have been transposed to Wonderland, a nonunified field of signification. . . .
>
> (152)

and,

> . . . *Alice* presents an emblematic study of the representation of the representational process itself as it relates to the reconfiguration of Alice's identity.
>
> (152)

Feldstein also states that Alice

> gropes to understand it [Wonderland] by applying previously learned principles to her present experiences . . .
>
> (153)

and,

> . . . it is [the] relationship of the subject to the intersubjective network that Alice confronts when comparing her experiences from one world to another in a desperate attempt to reconstruct an identity for herself in relation to these new surroundings.
>
> (153)

And there are other statements of a similar kind, such as:

> So when she asks 'who am I,' she really means 'who am I in this world' . . .
>
> (154)

or

> In Carroll's emblematic story there is the problem of how to situate the subject in relation to the lack of knowledge produced by nonsensical events that subvert an understanding of Alice's situation.
>
> (154)

and, finally,

> Any previously perceived unity dissolves when her body begins to take on strange, incoherent, even unrecognisable shapes that are unrelated to her internalised self-image.
>
> (159)

Given some minor variations, these statements on Feldstein's part and others like them throughout the essay too numerous to quote express, more or less, allowing for a few differences of perception and interpretation, how I, and many other readers of *Alice*, see the narrative. Much of what Feldstein states in remarks such as those above are a given of *Alice* criticism, and I reiterate certain contours of such statements in the section which follows. If I have a quibble over such statements, it is that they may be read as giving Alice too psychologically coherent a character in the first place, which subsequently becomes disrupted by the nature of her encounter with Wonderland. Certainly, I think that Alice is disrupted in her sense of her identity by Wonderland. But this is not the same as saying that I read Carroll as having endowed Alice with any particularly coherent personality or identity which is then turned topsy-turvy. If anything, while I read Alice as measuring what she takes to be a unified self or coherent personality, this is not to say such a personality was ever in place. Alice may not be sure of her *self* in Wonderland, but then, what is there to suggest that her *self*, her *identity* – an identity 'emblematic', to borrow Feldstein's word, of all our identities – is ever fully-formed or guaranteed as dissonance-free?

Yet this is only a minor disagreement. It does, however, point to the way in which a psychoanalytic reading can ignore the contours of the text, bringing to that reading of the text a previously constituted identity, on which stable structure it is itself reliant in order to prove its point. Psychoanalysis *finds* Alice ahead of reading. It observes her, seeking to make her its subject, by making it subject to its highly ordered gaze, and what follows, at least in the case of Feldstein's reading, is the attempt to construct a quite different identity for the text: the identity of Lacanian reading in all its phallic selfhood. And it's not that Feldstein performs his Lacanian reading badly. Within the parameters of his discourse, his reading is particularly effective as an example of Lacanian psychoanalytic thinking applied to the field of literature. In terms of his chosen institutional and academic/discursive identity, he's very sure of himself, to recall Gardner's phrase. Indeed, to go further, given what has already been said in the introduction to this book concerning what we think we read, what we think we see 'in the text', a Lacanian reading – or indeed any other reading which emerges from a specific set of rules and within a discipline or discourse – seems perfectly reasonable up to a point. But that point is reached in the contest for the identity of the text, where the dissonances of the text's identities are not read as troubling moments or blind spots for the discourse in question. The problem is the contest between psychoanalysis as a discourse and identity and the affirmative resistance of *Alice* it-*selves*. If *Alice* is readable in terms of a rhetoric of affirmative resistance, it is precisely because, from the perspective of this work, it seems to anticipate all the possibilities of a Freudian or Lacanian reading, not only ahead of those readings, but ahead of the codification and regularisation of the discourses and disciplines from which such readings spring. It is readable, from our present vantage point and after the Freudian and Lacanian scenes, as anticipating, confirming, playing with, resisting and passing such readings. In being so readable, it affirms its dissonant identities, and the possibility of reading it at all, as otherwise than psychoanalysis.

But let's turn to the specific problems which Feldstein's Lacanian reading positions. Feldstein reads *Alice's Adventures in Wonderland* as revealing 'a structure of fantasy based on the romantic quest for sublime completion in the Other followed by the mocking of that fantasy' (1995, 170). What binds together Alice as desiring subject to the Other, according to Feldstein, is the Lacanian *point de capiton* or Master Signifier. As a paraphrase of an aspect of Lacanian thought this is fine. The trouble comes when Feldstein makes decisions for the text, assuming that Wonderland, as a representation of the unconscious, 'presents the discourse of the Other' (1995, 150). Once Alice has entered Wonderland, she '*begins*

to suture herself to a master signifier that retroactively quilts all
other signifiers to it, and thus enables her to begin the process
of making sense of this nonsensical dimension confronting her'
(1995, 150). The problem is that we cannot say for sure that this
is what Alice does, can we? What we read in such a remark is
the desire of the psychoanalytic critic to suture (in this case) his
institutional discourse and authoritative identity onto a text of
non-unified, mobile events, so as to find that identity asserted.
Making the text fit the theory involves the subjugation of all
wayward and dissonant signals, the Other to the desiring subject, in the self-representation of a cohesive identity.

Another comment of Feldstein's concerning Alice's interpretive practices highlights the same transformative and transfer-
ential dilemma: 'Although Alice uses the precepts learned from
her mother, father, school, and society to read the spatial and
temporal implications of the desiring text, it proves to no avail
until nonsense itself emerges as a cohesive signifying function'
(1995, 163). Can nonsense, being nonsense, be said to emerge?
Can it be said to do anything, in fact which rids it of its diverse,
self-differentiating identities. Becoming a cohesive signifying
function would erase from nonsense its identity as nonsense; it
would become something else, but as soon as the signifying function is calmed down and perceived as 'cohesive' then there is
no longer nonsense *qua* nonsense. What we see is the imposition
of an identity on the part of the critic onto a random field, in
order to damp down the dissonance which troubles the interpretive act. Of course, this can always be achieved, while seeming to maintain nonsense in its nonsensical 'form', by suggesting
that the text belongs to a 'fantasy' paradigm. This explains and
excuses that which is within identity and that which troubles
the identity of the interpretive mode. Ironically, Feldstein suggests
in passing that '[s]omething in the story will always evade the
impulse toward conceptual mastery by confronting it with
unassimilable phenomena that cannot be geometrically placed
and intellectually assimilated' (1995, 162). The irony is at Feldstein's
– or at least psychoanalysis's – expense. While he reads Alice's
inability to comprehend 'textual relations', there is no sense that
the critic could apply his definition of textual slippage and epistemological failure to the act of reading *Alice* psychoanalytically.

This means that something has to be imposed on the text, in
order to prevent all that slipperiness from getting even more

slippery, or else to allow the unassimilable to be quietly excluded from the house being built. Sooner or later, of course, the phallus rears its head. As Feldstein tells us:

> In Carroll's emblematic story there is the problem of how to situate the subject in relation to the lack of knowledge produced by nonsensical events that subvert an understanding of Alice's situation.

> (1995, 154)

Is this a problem, and, if so, for whom? There's a curious and quite comical effect in process in this passage. You'll notice that the reader's understanding of Alice's 'situation' (what her identity is in relation to the text as a whole) is subverted producing a *lack* of knowledge. The text has a lack, and the reader has a desire, to fix the subject in place. The problem is thus one not necessarily for Alice, nor for Lewis Carroll, nor for any reader other than a reader with a particular structure to put in place, to erect a certain epistemological architecture. What's missing is the keystone. For Feldstein, the Other is conveniently 'a pre-given structural site' (154; again, this is not to say that it's not, but that the gestures of the critic with regard to the reading of Alice proves a little too forced in its constructions). Thus between Alice-as-subject and Wonderland-as-Other, the critic projects a lacuna awaiting closure, awaiting the tie of the 'master signifier', so that 'floating signifiers' (164) can be made to mean something for the critic. For Feldstein, the master signifier is 'Rule Forty-Two', an unwritten rule wielded by the King in an effort to assert his authority. Rule Forty-Two attempts to fill a certain lack and, in so doing, assumes the phallic function, standing in for the absent master signifier. The problem here is of assuming unequivocally a particular function for *anything* in Wonderland, as Richard Feldstein does. To do this, to fix a metaphorical meaning for Rule Forty-Two (or indeed anything), is to miss the *anarchitectural* anarchy of Wonderland nonsense. In seeing the phallus in this position, and in attempting to fix the text's identity on this problematic location, is to be passed by the text. The master signifier or phallus never was 'in' this text, indeed it seems a text amazingly free of phallic functions. The only phallus being inserted is that of the psychoanalytic critic being too sure of himself. As if to acknowledge this problem at some level, Feldstein then goes on to assert that Alice herself is the 'turgid phallus of nonsensical Wonderland' (1995, 167). At the moment of being sure, he's not quite so sure. If everything is so nonsensical, what power does the phallus have exactly?

Being sure of oneself reveals a desire to be seen to test one's knowledge and one's identity in order to prove its truth, the goal of such a reading having been already predicted from the start. In doing this, one imposes, projects, or transfers one's identity onto the other. This is not only what we read in Feldstein's interpretation, it is also what we might predict as the readable trajectory of the psychoanalytic reading straining towards its climax. One's identity supposedly becomes assured in an act of reading which will guarantee that identity through what Deleuze calls 'the permanence of *savoir*' (1990, 3). Now, he is talking here about Alice's knowledge of herself and the world and the effect the loss of her name has on her personal identity. Losing her name the wood,

> She very soon came to an open field, with a wood on the other side of it: it looked much darker than the last wood, and Alice felt a *little* timid about going into it. However, on second thoughts, she made up her mind to go on: 'for I certainly won't go *back*,' she thought to herself, and this was the only way to the Eighth Square.
>
> 'This must be the wood,' she said thoughtfully to herself, 'where things have no names. I wonder what'll become of *my* name when I go in? I shouldn't like to lose it at all – because they'd have to give me another, and it would be almost certain to be an ugly one. But then the fun would be, trying to find the creature that had got my old name! That's just like the advertisements, you know, when people lose dogs – "*answers to the name of 'Dash': had on a brass collar*" – just fancy calling everything you met "Alice," till one of them answered! Only they wouldn't answer at all, if they were wise.'
>
> She was rambling on in this way when she reached the wood: it looked very cool and shady. 'Well, at any rate it's a great comfort,' she said as she stepped under the trees, 'after being so hot, to get into the – into the – into *what*?' she went on, rather surprised at not being able to think of the word. 'I mean to get under the – under the – under *this*, you know!' putting her hand on the trunk of the tree. 'What *does* it call itself, I

wonder? I do believe it's got no name – why to be sure it hasn't!'

She stood silent for a minute, thinking: then she suddenly began again. 'Then it really has happened, after all! And now, who am I? I *will* remember, if I can! I'm determined to do it!' But being determined didn't help her much, and all she could say, after a great deal of puzzling, was 'L, I *know* it begins with L!'

(*AA* 225–6)

Alice's identity becomes erased in *Through the Looking Glass*. She slides into what Deleuze calls 'the paradox of infinite identity' (1990, 3). This is the result of the a reading act founded on the supposed permanence of knowledge. As we see from this scene, and what follows with the Fawn (who may also be a pawn, though we can't tell), is that the condition of losing one's identity is not peculiar to Alice, but a risk involving all naming, all memory, all knowledge and all identity. The wood/chessboard serves as a topographical and spatial reminder of spacing within identity itself: there is always an unnameable space of forgetting, the space where identity cannot resolve itself, where reading cannot complete the circle. The tree does not have an identity *for-itself*; only Alice can provide its identity for it. And, in a similar manner, as Alice speculates, were she to lose her name (which is to say her identity), 'they' (whoever *they* are) would have to name Alice otherwise. Identity is not what one gives oneself, but what one is given by the other. As we see from Alice's reference to the advertisement, identity is an affair of writing. Her next comment can be read as showing us how identity as a written trace is not unique. It has the possibility of being endlessly iterable. Here, we read that Naming is what one awaits passively as a condition of identity being given from outside the self (see the final chapter on Derrida and Daniel Deronda, below). The act of answering proves for Alice that one's identity is never self-sufficient, never self-generated, but a response to a call from another place than one's identity, which causes her to remark: 'Only they wouldn't answer at all, if they were wise'. We read the possibility of resistance here, a resistance to the imposed architecture of identity. This resistance is dependent on a wholly other kind of conditional knowledge – 'if they were wise' – which operates as, and thereby affirms, the other to identity. Resisting certain forms of identity keeps affirmative dissonance in play. It also suggests the inexhaustibility of the subject.

The question remains, how then are we to read the *Alice* books? As readers who believe we are certain in our identities and knowledge of our identities? Are we to observe as Alice observes, mistaking observation for interpretation? or are we to give up the dream of identity, to resist it indirectly by losing 'ourselves' in reading and writing, becoming other, becoming *anarchitectural* readers? The Alice-effect can be read as showing us how what Foucault called the 'problem of discontinuity in discourse' (1972, 114) is one possible means by which one is written as less sure of one's identity. For Alice, being less sure of oneself emerges through the inability to cite properly. The Alice-effect is readable as always already located *in* Alice's identity, which, dependent on citation, becomes troubled by citation always coming out other than one thinks it should. Being less sure of oneself – or one's other – than Richard Feldstein, one would open one's identity to the reading event, and the questions which such an event engenders. Questions such as 'Which dreamed it?', the final chapter of *Through the Looking Glass*, in which Alice realises finally that she may have been part of the Red King's dream (*AA* 344), as part of anarchitectural otherness allow us sight of the dislocation of identity. Or there is the question with which Carroll closes the book, affirming in the event of writing the opening of identity: 'Which do *you* think it was?' (*AA* 344).

a dissonant dynamic or, anarchitecture's trembling

As an opening gambit in her discussion of post-modern urban spaces and the condition of psychasthenia ('a disturbance in the relation between self and surrounding territory'; 1992, 1), Celeste Olalquiaga offers a telling paraphrase/analysis of *Alice*, which is worth repeating:

> [Alice] is suspended in time so that she can freely explore space – the limits of her body – until she is ready to grow up. In the narrative guise of a dream, Alice goes through a series of adventures that confuse her sense of physical identity, in an experience similar to postmodern culture: she floats among domestic objects that fail to give her any hold . . . and is later completely lost in Wonderland, where signs are deceiving,

animals and plants talk and transmute themselves, and she grows or shrinks at the arbitrary will of mysterious mushrooms, cakes, and potions.

Complete with a compulsive repetition of time . . . and a voluntary simulation devised to please the fooled senses . . . reality and appearance merge into one . . . time and space are highly evanescent and can only be reconstituted through repetitive linguistic riddles. . . .

(1992, 3–4)

While Olalquiaga concentrates on the confusion of *physical* and *bodily* identity that Alice undergoes, her acknowledgement of issues of representation, verbal, semantic and textual dislocation in Wonderland also points to the partial dissolution – or at least oscillation – of the epistemological boundaries of identity. This is also acknowledged by Gilles Deleuze in his reading of *Alice*, through a focus on paradoxes of pure becoming and surfaces. In terms of the construction of a stable identity through reliance on epistemological competence and the attendant recall of structures of knowledges upon which Alice relies as the means by which she situates her identity (a reliance which is always frustrated because of interference from within), there is also a continued undoing of Alice's phenomenological identity. Olalquiaga goes on to make the distinction between Alice's world and the post-modern world, by pointing out that Alice's 'recourse to language' as the means to stave off the symptoms of psychasthenia is not as effective today, 'where verbal language is being gradually displaced by the visual' (1992, 4). This assertion is questionable to the extent that it relies on a principally phonetic, rather than written comprehension of language. Arguably, written language, written signs, logos and other pictograms, maps – all writings – rely on their visual element for the purposes of reading, interpretation and the situation of the self in relation to the performance of a discrete identity.

Understanding the question of Alice's identity beyond purely bodily terms, and seeing it as a question of reading and writing brings back to the reader the conventional textual architectures which Carroll's dissonant dynamic of *anarchitecture* makes tremble. It is not that Alice suffers from psychasthenia (Olalquiaga is not suggesting this but uses Alice as an analogical example of the experience and symptoms of psychasthenia). This is to rush to-

wards seeing Alice as having a presumed reality of a different
order to the realities (or otherwise) of Wonderland and its in-
habitants, and to put her back on the analyst's couch. What I
want to suggest is that the phenomenological experience of being-
in-the-world is always an experience of being-a-reader, being
within the textual movement or event suggested by Peter Eisenman
and explored by Carroll in the *Alice* books, where identity is
always presented with the limits of its own perceived separation from its others, where boundaries are always in the process
of dissolution and fictive reinvention or narrativisation, erasure
and rewriting. It is this which Deleuze, in drawing on Plato (as
part of the continuation of the project begun in *Difference and
Repetition*), describes as the dimension of 'pure becoming without measure. . . . It always eludes the present' (1990, 1–2).

'Alice' then – and *Alice's Adventures in Wonderland*, as well as
Through the Looking Glass – is readable as the expressly played-
out dissonant dynamic of affirmative resistance. The reader, like
Alice, can be tricked into deciphering those numerous rhetorical
figures and signals which seem to be telling us something. Such
signals, we are assured, mean something, we can construct an
identity which is stable and therefore reassuring. Yet the rhetoric of affirmative resistance is that trace where 'Alice' can be
read not as a 'character' with a psychological and bodily unity
and identity, but as a written character, an identity composed –
written – by a range of knowledges ordered into an architectural whole. Carroll's text can be read as an indirect militation
against such an architecture. Psychological 'character' is indirectly
resisted (passed by) in the reading event that affirms the waywardness and dynamic of the text's *anarchitecture* through the
exposure of the paucity and limits of what Alice thinks she knows.

Particularly, Alice 'with her all-too-common perceptual apparatus' (Kincaid 1992, 288) relies on and tries to recall maxims,
truisms, and commonplaces given the aesthetic gloss of verse,
the sugar to coat all acts of poisonous self-surveillance, the magic
potion which supposedly stabilises identity and corrupts the child
into an adult. All such commonplaces 'speak from the heart of
her adult culture' as Kincaid puts it (1992, 288), and Alice is so
far gone that she seeks safety in these trite little texts in order to
convince herself – to convince her of the solidity of her self –
that she's more grown up than child. Knowledge, we read, is
employed in the effort to damp down the 'becoming' effect of

unfolding textuality which Alice encounters, not only in Wonderland but from within herself, within her own identity. Yet we can take heart in the fact that every time Alice tries to measure Wonderland according to her 'knowledge of the real world', she finds herself lost, her identity confounded, through the affirmation of nonsense which is not opposed to sense but which inhabits the very heart of logic, reason and knowledge. James Kincaid observes that, when 'Alice is distressingly disoriented . . . [she] turns for the stability of conventional moorings' (Kincaid 1992, 288). But it's not just Wonderland which confounds Alice's identity every time, it's the child within her, that hidden trace.

It is this hidden trace which projects itself affirmatively across Alice's identity which leads Jean-Jacques Lecercle to suggest that '[p]oor Alice is reduced to the state of a tape recorder' (1994, 118). Claiming that Lewis Carroll anticipates the debate between Jacques Derrida and John Searle (1994, 124–8), Lecercle highlights Derrida's critique of Searle in terms of interference on a radio set (128). It is precisely this interference which comes between Alice and her desired identity. Her identity becomes altered through remembering and recitation; and, as Lecercle reminds us with reference to Borges' 'Pierre Menard', the 'alteration of the text is due to its iteration' (129). In Alice's case, her alteration, her becoming other, is due to her citations and recitations which, because they are radically transformed, becoming other than Alice had supposed them to be, transform Alice's identity also. It is such self-troubling that causes Alice, in response to her own rhetoric or to the questions and statements of others, to make comments such as:

> 'Oh dear, what nonsense I'm talking!'
>
> (*AA* 36)

> 'I – I'm a little girl,' said Alice, rather doubtfully, as she remembered the number of changes she had gone through, that day.
>
> (*AA* 76)

> 'I don't know what you mean,' said Alice.
>
> (*AA* 97)

Or we might turn to two scenes, like that in the chessboard forest, where Alice is forced to call into question exactly who she is. The first occurs just after Alice has arrived in the hallway at the beginning of the adventure:

Alice took up the fan and gloves, and, as the hall was very hot, she kept fanning herself all the time she went on talking. 'Dear, dear! How queer everything is today! And yesterday things went on just as usual. I wonder if I've been changed in the night? Let me think: *was* I the same when I got up this morning? I almost think I can remember feeling a little different. But if I'm not the same, the next question is, "Who in the world am I?" Ah, *that's* the great puzzle!' And she began thinking over all the children she knew that were of the same age as herself, to see if she could have been changed for any of them.

'I'm sure I'm not Ada,' she said, 'for her hair goes in such long ringlets, and mine doesn't go in ringlets at all; and I'm sure I can't be Mabel, for I know all sorts of things, and she, oh, she knows so very little! Besides, *she's* she, and *I'm* I, and – oh dear, how puzzling it all is! I'll try if I know all the things I used to know. Let me see: four times five is twelve, and four times six is thirteen, and four times seven is – oh dear! I shall never get to twenty at that rate! However, the Multiplication Table doesn't signify: let's try geography ... no *that's* all wrong I'll try and say *"How doth the little –"'* ... but her voice sounded hoarse and strange, and the words did not come out as they used to do ...

....

....

....

....

....

....

....

'I'm sure those are not the right words,' said poor Alice ... 'I must be Mabel ... if I'm Mabel, I'll stay down here! It'll be no use their putting their heads down and saying, "Come up again, dear!" I shall only look up and say, "Who am I then?

Tell me that first, and then, if I like being that person, I'll
come up: if not, I'll stay down here till I'm somebody else" . . .'.

(*AA* 37–39)

The second scene involves Alice's conversation with the Caterpillar (Chapter Five):

'Who are *You*?' said the Caterpillar.

This was not an encouraging opening for a conversation.
Alice replied, rather shyly, 'I – I hardly know, Sir, just at present
– at least I know who I *was* when I got up this morning, but I
think I must have been changed several times since then.'

'What do you mean by that?' said the Caterpillar sternly.
'Explain yourself!'

'I can't explain *myself*, I'm afraid, Sir,' said Alice, 'because
I'm not myself, you see.'

'I don't see,' said the Caterpillar.

'I'm afraid I can't put it more clearly,' Alice replied very
politely, 'for I can't understand it myself, to begin with; and
being so many different sizes in a day is very confusing.'

'It isn't,' said the Caterpillar.

'Well, perhaps you haven't found it so yet,' said Alice; 'but
when you have to turn into a chrysalis – you will some day,
you know – and then after that into a butterfly, I should think
you'll feel it a little queer, won't you?'

'Not a bit,' said the Caterpillar.

'Well, perhaps *your* feelings may be different,' said Alice:
'all I know is, it would feel very queer to *me*.'

'You!' said the Caterpillar contemptuously. 'Who are *you*?'

Which brought them back again to the beginning of the conversation.

(*AA* 67–8)

The effect on Alice of becoming other is that she finds her identity
always poised at moments of imminent dissolution into an *other
identity*. It is not that Alice either knows or doesn't know. She
often knows that she doesn't know: She knows she doesn't know
her tables, or her geography, or her cautionary verses.[3] However, she knows there is a gap in her knowledge, her memory,
her identity. But from the position she occupies, one of knowing
that she is non-knowing, she comes to understand how knowl-

edge is not all there is to identity. She is able to understand that the great puzzle is her identity, who she is *in the world*, as she puts it, or who she is for others, the *they* already mentioned who name Alice as Alice, and who, she supposes, will come to reclaim her. In the passage in the hallway, Alice comes to the conclusion that she'll stay put until she gets any identity which is not Mabel's. Being 'Alice' becomes less and less important, as long as one can avoid the imposition of a particularly unattractive identity (in this case poor Mabel's, who, from Alice's perspective just has nothing going for her!). Multiplication may not signify, but in Alice's case, neither does her name, at least not to her. We read in this passage then, the separation of identity from itself, with Alice coming to occupy a liminal space between identity and non-identity, a liminality which always becomes another troublesome space, rather than settling into an identity, however undesired.

The scene with the caterpillar doesn't rely on memory and institutional forms of knowledge, but addresses the relationship between perceptions of identity and the contest within language over identity's instability and the desire for fixity. When Alice says that she cannot explain *herself*, she's not joking, although, funnily enough, Carroll seems to be, by playing the word *myself* in italics (as he does with the words *you*, *your*, *me*, and even *was*). Everything in italics in this scene addresses the problem of identity, of what one can say about one's own identity, and about how language, fraught as it is with dissonance and the signs of otherness, only serves to defer, rather than construct, knowable versions of identity. Alice may have known who she *was* but, when she was knowable, then she was other than she is. Identity is thus seen to be a question of temporal spacing, as well as semantic equivocation. And between the space of *was* and *is*, laughter can be read as emerging.[4]

Elsewhere in this collection of essays I suggest that laughter is the sound of affirmative resistance (Ch. 3). If this is the case then, with *Alice*, the laughter is that of a child, of *becoming-child*. The child within Alice is the event of becoming-child within all adult readers, the radically other of both Alice and the adult. In reading Alice – as a supposedly unified character – as being 'committed to aping grown-up responses' (Kincaid 1992, 293), we are able to read the cultural writtenness of her desired identity. In reading this, we are able to comprehend how the structures built out of knowledges are repressive in their efforts to stabilize. The two passages above show how Alice is in fact freed from repressive knowledges and identities. In the event of becoming-child, affirmative resistance is found as the dissonant possibility within the cultural imposition of identity. Alice loses herself – a self which *they* have imposed – only to become other.

Alice, then, can be read as trying to hold onto the identity given her, to master her surroundings by measuring their traces according to what she has been taught. Not only is this a typically adult gesture, but it is also a typically institutionalised gesture (another structure where the architectural, the epistemological and the ideological coalesce). Behind all of Alice's thoughts, responses, questions and annoyed statements are 'norms', 'rules' and 'systems', suggesting a discourse of mastery coming from some other, hidden identity which is not Alice's own, not essential to her. Alice tries to install a separation between consciousness and representation in an effort to maintain her received identity, but such an effort breaks down constantly, as we have already suggested in reference to cats, bats and grins. Alice's desire for a knowledge of Wonderland (a knowledge brought about by an act of reading which produces an identity) is predicated on the possibility of that knowledge being separable from the object of its enquiry. Thus, as Foucault has shown us, the definition of identity is a form of power practice, made possible by a certain relationship between, in this case, Alice's power practice and its relationship to knowledge of Wonderland. Yet Wonderland just will not conform to Alice's *a priori* assumptions. The power/knowledge relationship will only work if the object of enquiry conforms in each instance the parameters of the framework being applied to it. The 'order of things' in the text of Wonderland is that there *is no order of things*. This leads us to state, once more, that there is no depth, only surfaces, more or less obliquely angled and refracting infinitely. Alice cannot impose what Michel Foucault has termed a 'new describability' to the textual *anarchitecture* (Foucault 1969, 191). And neither can we as readers, other than as readers who give up the desire for identity in the face of the text, in the face of the other. Carroll's text can be read as a constant urging to us as readers to lose face in the other. Wonderland affirms its dissonant dynamic of childlike textual play in its indirect resistance to all forms of categorisation, taxonomy, law-making or other acts of discursive disciplinary methods. And what we understand from this, and from Alice's failed acts of interpretation as discipline, is that her identity has been formed only through the power of others' disciplinary acts in the form of lessons – and possible punishment. Wonderland, on the other hand, resists punishment. It remains, to draw on Foucault's description of the condition of 'ordinary individuality', 'below the threshold of description' (Foucault 1979, 191). Alice is unable to lower the threshold, and so, we feel, are critics such as Phyllis Greenacre or Richard Feldstein.

Yet this is not to imply that *Alice* affirms individuality. Instead, what is affirmed is endless writing; endless writing as an uncategorizable '"poethics" of the text' (Ward 1995, 168).[5] In the case of the *Alice* books, the texts are inscribed by a 'poethics' because they speak constantly and affirm from the place of childhood, the place of the other, in the face, and resistant to, rules, norms, systems, discipline, punishment, order, hierarchy; in short *the* architecture of knowledge. Carroll's writing posits the affirmative possibility of a 'poethics' by its being haunted by what Jacques Derrida has called 'the ghost of the undecidable' (Derrida ed. Cornell *et al.* 1992, 24), even if it never articulates a programme of poethics (given what I have already said about Alice's reading practices, such a programme is clearly undesirable). The undecidable, Derrida tells us, is not merely the

> oscillation or tension between two decisions [as in the argument over semantics between Alice and Humpty Dumpty and the possible meaning of *Jabberwocky* in *Through the Looking Glass;* (*AA* 261–76)]; it is the experience of that which, though heterogeneous, foreign to the order of the calculable and the rule, is still obliged ... to give itself up to the impossible decision, while taking account of law and rules (24).

Carroll acknowledges this obligation at the close of *Through the Looking Glass* by turning his final question to *you*. What the meaning might be is undecidable. Asking the question, Carroll exposes the reader to the writing of the undecidable as the experience of reading. The experience of reading *Alice* involves giving oneself up to impossible decisions, as an ethical act which is also an act of reading not governed by the determination of a meaning, or the decision to decide on an identity. Carroll asks the question in order to decide on the undecidable, in order to decide *not* to decide.

We should then read the figure of Alice not as a privileged agent but as merely one more figure-in-writing belonging to the undecidability of the *anarchitectural* event. At the end of *Through the Looking Glass*, after Alice has apparently woken up, her identity remains undecidable, subject to an impossible decision. As the quotation above shows, she is not even sure if she was part of another's dream. At the end of *Alice's Adventures*, just prior to waking up, Alice has learnt to challenge the authority of the law, refusing to recognise its cultural identity and power by shouting 'Who cares for *you*? . . . You're nothing but a pack of cards!' (*AA* 161). Alice has learnt not to decide, it would seem, and we read Carroll giving her this statement as a way of affirming that which Wonderland had sought to suggest from the first: that identity is only ever constructed out of the chance movement of surfaces. By the end of *Through the Looking Glass*, Alice appears to salvage a vestige of childhood, otherness and undecidability. For a moment, she appears to do this in the earlier text. However, Alice's identity at the end of *Alice's Adventures in Wonderland* is not of her own governing. She is woken by her older, apparently more adult sister, returned to a supposedly stable selfhood within a discernible hierarchical structure. Alice's sister decides on Alice's identity, first by waking her, then by giving her orders:

> 'Wake up, Alice dear!' said her sister. 'Why what a long sleep you've had!'
> 'Oh, I've had such a curious dream!' said Alice. And she told her sister, as well as she could remember them, all these strange Adventures of hers you have just been reading about; and when she had finished, her sister kissed her, and said, 'It *was* a curious dream, dear, certainly; but run off to your tea: it's getting late.'
>
> (*AA* 162)

The emphasis in the sister's second statement seems to back up Alice's assessment of the dream and serves to impose a definition on the experience of the undecidable. Wonderland it appears must give way to tea, as a trivial and temporal order is asserted as a mark of reality, the knowledge of the world, and one's identity as a place within that reality being constructed through temporal order. Tea-time will return Alice to the house, her house. Alice would seem to be homeless no longer. Interestingly however, Carroll can be read as attempting a subversion of the elder sister's authority (which her identity as *elder* sister allows her to assert), by having her half-dream or day-dream a much simplified form of the narrative which Alice has re-told in other words, until she, the nameless sister, is called back to 'dull reality' (*AA* 163). The sister is thus readable as becoming other as a result of taking in Alice's narrative. Part of the sister's corrective to this day-dream is to project her sister into a grown-up future, surrounded by children (*AA* 164). The sister we see cannot dream completely because she is already more grown-up than Alice (this having already been indicated at the beginning of the narrative through the sister's reading matter which, we are informed, 'had no pictures or conversations in it' [*AA* 25]), and even as she thinks of Alice having grown, she cannot help but imagine that Alice in the future will remember her own 'child-life' (*AA* 164). The sister's thoughts are thus traced by the movement of becoming as defined by Gilles Deleuze, with its ability to 'pull in both directions at once' (1990, 1), to affirm the paradox of pure becoming through becoming-past and becoming-future, while never remaining present. The child-life thus affirms itself even at the distance of a projected memory imposed as a possible narrative or identity on one person by another. Although the older sister tries to provide a narrative coherence to life, her projection of her sister's identity into the future oscillates with temporal displacements, and the affirmation of the becoming other which is the *anarchitecture* of the Alice-effect.

The Alice-effect is something which troubles not only Alice's identity, but also the identity of both *Alice* texts. In conclusion to this part of the chapter, we will read three particularly pronounced examples of this from *Through the Looking Glass*.

The first is not Carroll's, strictly speaking, though it is readable as a sign of the text's displacement of identities. If we recall the double illustration of Alice moving through the surface of the looking-glass (Fig. 1.2, above), we see at one lower corner, the following symbols (appended by Tenniel to all the *Alice* illustrations, in addition to his signature):

Fig. 1.3

Outside the narrative, at the margin of the text and the illustrations, we find these images for which reading cannot account as
part of Alice's adventures and yet which we may take nonetheless as emblematic of the dissonance within identity which we
read Carroll's texts affirming. The dissonance is readable and
appears to occur because the figures are not symmetrical. This
is not merely a case of the printer reversing the entire image as
part of the reproduction and printing process. The left-hand figure is the one we find on every illustration. The right-hand figure is an asymmetrical, dissonant ghost, the imperfect other of
the figure's already enigmatic identity.

   This is though still only a minor textual figure which serves
as a momentary example. Our next example is from the end of
Chapter Three. Reading, we find the last sentence incomplete
(its identity as a sentence unfinished and improper):

> So she wandered on, talking to herself as she went, till, on
> turning a sharp corner, she came upon two fat little men, so
> suddenly that she could not help starting back, but in another
> moment she recovered herself, feeling sure that they must be
> (*AA* 228)

(Alice recovering her*self* aside, as though the sight of twinned
identities[6] could somehow cause a momentary rift in one's own
identity,) readers of *Alice* will know that this sentence can only
be completed by joining it to the title of the next chapter, which
is 'Tweedledee and Tweedledum' (*AA* 229). Importantly, the identity of the text as an affirmative and dissonant identity is traced
in Carroll's playful movement across borders. This is readable
as one of Deleuze's moments of pure becoming. The identities
of the chapter ending and sentence ending transform, as they
are transformed by, the title-identity, while the event of becoming, in moving in both directions simultaneously means that reading leaves neither identity stable or intact. Furthermore, the
movement has within it yet another 'literary' identity, bringing
about the confusion of genres. As Martin Gardner puts it in his
note on the above sentence, the sentence-fragment and title re-

write themselves when placed together into a rhymed couplet (*AA* 228). In Carroll's wonderland, no textual identity is safe.

The last example of identity's soliciting across the surfaces of the text can be read as movement yet again, this time between Chapters Ten and Eleven of *Through the Looking Glass*. As these chapters are short, their movement is worth observing in full:

Chapter X
Shaking

She took her off the table as she spoke, and shook her backwards and forwards with all her might.

The Red Queen made no resistance whatever: only her face grew very small, and her eyes got large and green: and still, as Alice went on shaking her, she kept on growing shorter – and fatter – and softer – and rounder – and –

Chapter XI
Waking

– and it really *was* a kitten, after all.

(*AA* 337–9)

As we can read, it is not only a question of the Red Queen's transformation into a kitten. This is not merely the narrative of the exchange of identities, as one becomes the other through an act of agitation. Once again, chapters themselves transform, from their titles to their contents. Once more, we read Carroll carrying the sentence across from one chapter to the next, as writing spaces itself out. This act enacts the writing of identity otherwise, which we read in the transformation of chapter titles, where the change of a single letter affects the identity named by the title. One chapter quite literally becomes the other, becomes other than itself. Identity's dissonance is affirmed, as stability becomes by-passed, by the chance which involves the completion of the sentence. Narrative movement implicates the disturbance of identity in its passage as it resists *en passant* the laws of literary organisation and the identities which such laws determine.

identities in dispute

In conclusion, back to the title. The second half of this chapter's title recalls another title, as much as the first part had done. In the case of the second phrase, 'identities in dispute', I am acknowledging the subtitle of Jean-François Lyotard's *The Differend: Phrases in Dispute* (1988). Lyotard's attempt to articulate a post-modern philosophy involves the theorisation of the impossibility of making a decision, reaching an agreement without creating a wrong, between *énoncés*, different 'phrase regimens [such as] reasoning, knowing, describing, questioning, showing, ordering, etc.' (1988, xii). 'Phrases', remarks Lyotard, 'from heterogeneous regimens cannot be translated from one into another' (1988, xii). I think the applicability of this statement to a reading of *Alice* sensitive to the rhetoric of affirmative resistances and the gambits of dissonant identity becomes immediately clear. None of the disputes between Alice and any of the other Wonderland creatures is ever resolved. The discussion concerning identity between Alice and the Caterpillar leads only to the point of departure. Discussion between Alice and the other participants in the Hatter's tea party leads to frustration and misunderstanding. There cannot even be agreement in this particular case about the rules of riddles or the correct pronoun by which Time should be designated (*AA* 95–7). The court case breaks down into puns in the face of the complete disagreement between parties concerning not only evidence but also correct terminology (*AA* 153–61). The almost immediate breakdown of order in the court renders the court's identity *qua* court apparently farcical; yet the farcical dissonance within the 'proper' identity we assume is all we ever see. If we assume the 'proper identity' as having been, prior to the Wonderland identity, we do so only as a way of reaching some form of agreement with ourselves as readers, as a means of identifying the text and calming down its playfulness. Much of the narrative movement of *Alice's Adventures* and *Through the Looking Glass* is dependent upon the absence of commonly agreed criteria for judgement or the formulation of stable identities. Very often, what we read is a dispute not only between phrases, between discourses or epistemologies in *Alice*, but also a constant dispute about the grounds of the representation or expression of identity itself. This gives us much to consider concerning the impossibility of any agreement about the identity of Carroll's text.

This marks the *Alice* books as being available to us as strategically *anachronistic* texts from where we read today, even as they are strategically *anarchitectural*. For they can be read as anticipating in so many ways so much of the movement of late-nineteenth-and twentieth-century thought and aesthetic/literary concerns. Artaud claimed a certain kinship, albeit problematised, with Carroll's writing, as a gesture of identification. And, similarly, there is readable across the texts the apparent anticipation of Freudian or Lacanian scenarios, which identities the psychoanalytic critic has sought to reclaim. There are readable also what William Spanos calls the '"anti-formal" imperatives of absurd time' (1995, 23). There is also an argument for suggesting that *Alice* seems to anticipate what Spanos describes as the symbolists' 'aesthetic reaction against the humanistic principle of utility, the imperative that man's role vis-à-vis the material world was to control or, more accurately to manipulate Nature . . .' (1995, 18). The identity of *Alice* as modernist precursor, perhaps? This is too hard and fast an oppositional identity, though certainly we can read Carroll's text playing with the dilemma which is raised by Alice's inability to control or manipulate the world around her. And we might take this further to suggest from our readings of improper sentences and the other textual challenges to 'proper textual identity' that the text seems available as a reaction against the humanistic principle of utility. Whatever Carroll's text may or may not do, we, as readers aware of its dissonant movements which counter the imposition of identity, may wish to situate it indirectly resisting humanist principles.

For example, we may wish to read *Alice* as an attempt, as a gesture of affirmative resistance which indirectly articulates a 'critique of and an alternative to modern self-subjugation' (Bernauer 1990, 9), if by 'self-subjugation' we understand the acceptance of an imposed identity. Carroll's writing makes resistance at least imaginable as a possibility of dissonant identity. It does so all the more slyly because it never suggests we take that resistance seriously. Thus we can read it as slipping past us, even as we read that no identity is, or ever can be, absolute, and that there is no 'normative designation', to recall a Foucauldian phrase from somewhere, which cannot be denied. It is not that Carroll writes of a breaking of limits, a movement beyond them; no such movement is ever possible in terms of the constitution of one's cultural or personal identity. However, we may read Carroll's texts as critiques of, works on, the limit, whereby the limits of the limit are exposed. The limit of identity is not absolute, and becoming unlimited is not the same as the desire to be absolutely without limits but to play at the edges of the limit.

Alice is used to take language to the limit, to the limits of sense, of meaning, of its ability to function in order to create subjects or to produce stable identities for subjects through the utilisation of discourse. Wonderland word-games strip language of its utility. Because of their disputatious particularity, such games affirm their rhetorical heterogeneity and the idea that '[t]here is no "language" in general' (Lyotard 1988, xii). Each event in Wonderland, each movement of the text, involves another type or genre of discourse, which in turn provides what Lyotard describes as 'another set of possible phrases' (xii), which cannot be linked except by the stabilising of an identity which inevitably does some kind of wrong to the phrases or identities concerned. 'What is at stake in a literature', writes Lyotard, 'is to bear witness to differends by finding idioms for them', the differend being 'the unstable state and instant of language wherein something must be able to be put into phrases cannot yet be' (1988, 13). This unstable state appears to be affirmed most repeatedly by Carroll's writing; or at least this is what I read there. Alice feels she has to put things into words and yet cannot, adequately. I read the dissonant identity of the *Alice* books affirming the differend, and resisting application in the name of identity. I read identity in play against and within itself. Carroll, I would like to suggest, can be read as refuting indirectly what Lyotard calls the 'prejudice anchored in the reader by centuries of humanism' that language is merely something used by '"man"' (1988, xiii). The languages which articulate identities in dispute play with us; like the books of Looking-Glass House, Carroll's phrases 'go the wrong way', as Alice puts it (*AA* 181). They go against the grain of our reading prejudices and habits, they deny utility, control and mastery, telling us to give up our*selves*, and play and play some more.

Notes

1. This reading of the phrase may well annoy some readers, I imagine. However, with a text which is as radically destabilizing with regard to its own identities as *Alice*, to suggest that a phrase has a particular meaning more so than another, seems to misunderstand the very nature of what occurs in reading this text.
2. It seems important that Carroll's writing can be read as always insisting that identity is never complete, for itself; identity is always identity for someone else, as one's own identity is always dependent on identity's relation to some other, and determined by that other.
3. There seems a cautionary tale for reading from institutionalised positions here, which is that the identity of the act of reading may, at any time, become faced with its own inadequacy.
4. Of course, this 'between' space can also be a space for other unpredictable articulations. *Alice* is very much a text of the spacing – and spaces – of identity.
5. The term, 'poethics' as used by Ward, is taken from Richard Weisberg's book of the same name, *Poethics* (1992), in which Weisberg coins the term 'poethics' in order to give attention to the communications of the other in legal discourse, and thereby re-establish and 'revitalize the ethical component of law' (Weisberg cit. Ward 1995, 168). I am not seeking to compare or contrast Carroll's writing with legal discourse or its analysis, but the term clearly operates powerfully in the face of all transactions in the name of identity between power and knowledge.
6. These twins' names – Tweedledee and Tweedledum – announce identity's difference from itself. Each name obviously suggests the other, but the resemblance or identity is only ever partial.

2

The writing on the wall or, making a spectacle of yourself: projection and *The Yellow Wallpaper*

project: a design or pattern according to which something is made; a mental conception, idea or notion; speculation; something projected or thrown out; a projection, an emanation (of some being); something projected or proposed for execution; a plan, scheme, purpose; a proposal; a projectile, a missile; to throw forth, stretch out, expel, reject, give up; stretched out; extended; given up, abandoned; of mental operations; to plan, contrive, devise, or design (something to be done, or some action or proceeding to be carried out); to form a project of; to present to expectation; to put before oneself in thought; to conceive, imagine; to cast, throw, hurl, shoot, impel, or cause to move forward, or onward in any direction; to place so that it protrudes or juts out; to throw or cause to fall (light or shadow) upon a surface or into space; to cause (a figure or image) to appear or 'stand out' *on* or *against* a background; to draw straight lines or 'rays' from a centre through every point of a given figure, so that they fall upon or intersect a surface and produce upon it a new figure of which each point corresponds to a point of the original. Hence to represent or delineate (a figure) according to any system of correspondence between its points and the points of the surface on which it is delineated.

This speaking will occur, and for feminist reasons, it must; the category of women does not become useless through deconstruction but becomes one whose uses are no longer reified as "referents," and which stand a chance of being opened up, indeed, of coming to signify in ways that none of us can predict in advance. Surely, it must be possible both to use the term, to use it tactically even as one is, as it were, used and positioned by it, and also to subject the term to a critique which interrogates the exclusionary operations and differential power-relations that construct and delimit feminist invocations of "women."

Judith Butler

Who speaks writing?

Susan Stewart

In this chapter I attempt an articulation of a poetics of projection as one expression of affirmative resistance through a reading of Charlotte Perkins Gilman's *The Yellow Wallpaper*. This poetics is, however, a poetics without programme, without installed code or structure which dictates how we should read. With this in mind I seek to open up projected images, fold them back upon themselves, so as to imagine a gap between the spectral immateriality of representation and the materiality of lived experience which projection represents otherwise. This gap, I argue, is the space where the affirmative resistance of a poetics of female projection comes to be articulated; projection is a speaking, a continuous speaking as a broader act of writing always on the way to articulation. Therefore this chapter seeks, as the announcement of affirmative resistance, to voice through the act of writing a poetics open to the unexpected, a poetics awaiting the unpredictable, the unprogrammable, which will arrive as its necessity and which will obligate the reader to comprehend the projection of the material conditions of women's existence, projected as textual constructs.

This project also indirectly addresses what has recently been identified in a textbook on the subject of literature and gender as 'a common critical problem which is often associated with certain kinds of Anglo-American feminist literary criticism' (Goodman ed. 1996, 132).[1] In discussing readings of *The Yellow Wallpaper*, Lizbeth Goodman, identifies the problem as a 'temptation' to read 'too much into the autobiography/fiction connection', so that the text merely serves as an example in the history of women's writing rather than speaking for itself. Goodman is right to address the problematic status of such a teleological gesture, especially given that the gesture itself seems complicit with the kind of patriarchal politics which Gilman's text is at pains to foreground and side-step. Goodman assembles a number of the key feminist arguments concerning *The Yellow Wallpaper*, such as Gilbert and Gubar's, Mary Jacobus's and Elaine Hedges' (1996, 109–144) in the context of this text's and others' (such as *Alice*) relation to perceived female disorders, such as madness and hysteria. Such acts of contextualisation, while valuable (as valuable and valid as, say, psychoanalytic approaches to the text), may have a tendency to reduce the text to a case study, and thereby inadvertently 'treat' the text in precisely that manner which the text seeks to resist and avoid through its very inscription and affirmation. The very appeal of *The Yellow Wallpaper* as a text of affirmative resistance is in its self-aware attention to acts of writing as acts of affirmation *and* indirect, non-dialectical resistance. As Robert Shulman notes in his 'Introduction' to the Oxford edition of the text,[2] there is the 'sense of the painful qualified liberation' of the narrator (1995, xxxii), and this emerges specifically through the act of writing itself, through an illicit, proscribed act of writing. What the character writes becomes the text of *The Yellow Wallpaper* and to diagnose the character or read the character's representation and identity through her own strategically resistant, affirmative acts of inscription is to take insufficient account of rhetoric and its carefully manoeuvred dissonances, in favour of a psycho-mimetic approach. The text itself is suspiciously wary of teleological structure, the desire for a knowable identity, and the closure of narrative, and this is most readily apprehended in its performance of writing which is most densely, aphoristically expressed in its very title (as I shall explore below).

This chapter thus takes as its focus the projection of the female as a non-essentialist affirmation of a female trace, a female writing, whilst attending to, and commenting on, materiality and the material conditions of female experience and social existence. The idea of the projection is one which resists static control and appropriation through its being, of necessity and by its very condition, a process, an event, requiring for its possibility the ability of the reader to recognise in the event of projection a moment yet to come, through the calculated chance of writing's ability to carry in it the trace of a counter-position which is not ever simply an opposition. Projection requires both space and time and involves implicitly through the event of signification a number of always changing subject positions. Projection also requires a certain 'throwing-out', a 'moving-away-from', in its being-projected. This figures the mutability of the catachresic trope, announcing a refusal to be completely confined through definition. Projection announces the catachrestic feminine, the troping of the feminine as an agency of 'improper sense', and the transformation of meaning in order to reveal the marginal-isation and exclusion of the female from meaning (where mean-ing is assumed to be equivalent to truth). One possibility of projection is that it throws out the feminine voice, text, trace, in a ventriloquial pantomimesis which exposes and resists the limits of masculine discourse, whilst also affirming a dissonant sounding and citing/sighting of a possible site for the feminine inscrip-tion. This chapter and those on Maya Deren and Sylvie Germain looks at the strategy of working with, and through, what can be understood as projections or *projected traces*; shadows, patterns, flickering lights, multiple images, resonances, visions, spectres, aphorisms. Each of the texts in question 'project' the female, of-ten seeming to mime masculine constructs for the framing of 'Woman', whilst utilising many, if not all, of the definitions at-tributed to the term 'project' above, drawn from the *Oxford English Dictionary*. Each of the texts construct, project, elusive, illusory, allusive figures, potentially figures of catachresis, figures offer-ing to change radically our comprehension of the female and feminine 'in' textuality. Their catachresic tropes ultimately deny the material/immaterial binarism, by playing, and altering, by-passing, the meaning of such a pairing.

The figures are material inasmuch as they are potential signifiers, but otherwise immaterial in their being-projected, breaking with the constraints of materiality through acts of projection. The act of projection itself can of course transform through its potential for generating other writings, other traces. It can also transform through its being part of a project of tracing the instability of externally imposed meanings (an instability not to be stabilised through rendering catachresis as merely metaphor). Projection, in the case of these texts, 'deconstructs' what Judith Butler de-scribes above as the reification of women as solely referents (Butler 1993, 29). As Butler points out, the opening up of 'women' in this manner – what I am terming 'projection' and, in the case of these three texts, the differential project of projection, which is also a projection of a certain project, articulated differently each

time according to the chance of place and context – makes possible future significations, 'coming to signify in ways which none
of us can predict in advance' (Butler 1993, 29). The texts being
read also figure forms of affirmative resistance in their projection of women because they cannot be read (from certain so-
called poststructuralist assumptions), either as simply rejecting
the material condition of being-female, or, on the other hand
(from particular feminist positions), as simply privileging the
material as some essential or foundational condition of being-
female. Such readings replicate the body/spirit dichotomy, along
with attendant binarisms already mentioned above. Instead, in
each case, the texts in question offer figures for understanding
the transformation of material conditions through immaterial
tactics, tactics and strategies of affirmative projection which insists that a critique is performed of material conditions, whereby
materiality becomes the pre-condition of, in Judith Butler's words,
'a principle of *transformation*, presuming and inducing a future'
(Butler 1993, 31). The projections in question project towards a
future, through memory of material pasts. Such projections are
by their very nature incomplete, because they project towards,
on the way to, a projection of non-essential, non-unified, identity. In such incomplete projections the female affirmation resists
enclosure by the very condition of being-incomplete. Incomple-
tion does not suggest absence, lack or inferiority. It does suggest survival and the resistance to being enclosed, defined in
what Luce Irigaray calls 'an order of forms inappropriate to'
women (Irigaray 1993, 109). Gilman, Deren, and Germain all
question such inappropriate forms, through acts of affirmative
projection.

In her study of the female grotesque and the risky possibilities
female excess might have for a feminist politics and aesthetics,
Mary Russo recalls from her childhood an elder female voice
commenting on some other woman's behaviour that the other
woman was 'making a spectacle' of herself (Russo 1995, 53). As
the older Russo comments, projecting back to her memory of
her younger, other self, '[m]aking a spectacle out of oneself seemed
a specifically feminine self' (Russo 1995, 53). The idea of the
spectacle, suggests Russo, belongs to 'radical negation, silence,
withdrawal, and invisibility, and the *bold affirmations of feminine
performance*, imposture, and masquerade' (Russo 1995, 54; emphasis added). The idea of the spectacle offers the possibility for

imagining 'models of transformation and counterproduction situated within the social system' (Russo 1995, 54). Silence, withdrawal and invisibility are all non-locatable places from where projection can be imagined. They construct an alternative identity from a possible range of alternatives perceived as dissonant. In order to make a spectacle of oneself one has to project a performance of oneself knowingly, as one supposes others might imagine the hitherto unprojected or hidden self. Identity is rewritten as other than itself in the spectacle of projection. Effecting the projection as spectacle says 'yes', as a response to a demand to reveal oneself, show one's hand. But it is an act of saying 'yes' which is an apparently acquiescent affirmation of the other's point-of-view. Yet in the act, the spectacle and projection, the way in which one affirms, apparently so acquiescently, posits an implicit resistance to giving up knowledge of one's identity to another; identity is always hidden in the act of spectacle or projection, hidden – and affirmed in a radical unknowability – by performance. Dissonant identity has thus by-passed definition in its very projection and the acting out of spectacle. This is, of course, a dangerous act, where the simulation of projection may be taken to be all there is, all that can be said of identity. Yet it is the very danger of projection, the risk taken in such a construction, which suggests that the projection of making a spectacle of oneself may actually allow the other's speech to be heard, and that that speech may constitute a gesture of affirmative resistance. Such a gesture operates riskily along borderlines, those places where projection disappears, and from which it emerges.

To begin then at the title, one of those borderlines which, in the case of *The Yellow Wallpaper* (YW 1990, 39–59), affirms and resists indirectly as the gesture of writing itself. The title, which acts as a frame or boundary, an enclosure or imaginary wall, comes before the story. It shuts you out but, also, closes you in once you have apparently passed it; however, this text very much puts its title ambiguously into place, as the taking place of the event of writing as an act of affirmative defiance, resisting in its way the possibility of the reader being able to pass the title. It thus remains a horizon as well, as the subject of this story. The title, *The Yellow Wallpaper*, is both before and behind its reader. As a title it is enigmatic, ambiguous. The title defines a narrative interest yet resists translation; its limits are absolute or, at least, seem so. The title names both the story and something in the story. Furthermore, it names something which may exist beyond the story itself, something which may well have an extra-narrative material existence. How are we to read such a title, then? Literally? Metaphorically? Metonymically? All of these? Quite possibly, because the title, inasmuch as it can be read in several different ways, is all inclusive. In fact, in being all inclusive, it is excessive as well, because it names something beyond immediate comprehension. The title writes into itself a guarantee of something which either resists absolute understanding or stalls interpretation. The title in this case functions in a manner similar to a signature or aphorism therefore. The title forms a particular shorthand or code that carries in its inscription the promise of other writing, of an excess (projected) beyond naming, the act of naming which a title enacts. There is something named that is not exhausted in being so named. However, that which is not exhausted, which cannot be rendered fully, simply, is, immediately and simultaneously *aphoristic* in the truest sense, being a double writing at least; a writing of inclusion and exclusion, of keeping out and yet keeping imprisoned, of too much being said and of silence. Why should this be so, why should this title, 'The Yellow Wallpaper', be aphoristic? Why am I reading this title as an aphorism? The question is etymological. As Derrida remarks, the aphorism marks separation and dissociation (*apo*) while also terminating or arresting (*horizo*).[3] The title, 'The Yellow Wallpaper', answers to such definitions, as does the story, *The Yellow Wallpaper*. The title projects us towards a certain point, the location of which we are not yet aware. But to turn to the story.

We read the brief – aphoristic – comments of a nameless woman, who commits her thoughts to 'dead paper' (*YW* 41). This dead paper is like wallpaper. It can carry on it the traces of female entrapment. It is a woman who writes 'for a while in spite of them' (*YW* 42) – 'them' meaning her brother and husband, both doctors – in secret. She writes about writing, despite male opposition, about the desire to write, about writing as 'congenial work', (*YW* 42) about the difficulties a woman faces if she wishes to write *as a woman, as a sister, as a wife*. Writing is inimical, it would seem, to masculine performances of femininity. Writing thus constitutes a projection of female identity which is implicitly affirmative of identity, whilst being resistant indirectly to masculine definitions of female identity. The paradox here is that as a sister and wife she must not write; yet as a woman she must write and write that she is forbidden to write according to the 'inappropriate' forms of identity that are projected onto her. This nameless woman – she is unable to name herself but this becomes a strategic, indirect affirmation through the act of writing – writes about the narrative possibilities, not yet written, of romance and spirits, while her husband talks of draughts and self-control. She inscribes the possibilities of being able to project her story, he pro*scribes* them. Placed in the nursery 'at the top of the house' (*YW* 43), the nameless writer writes of the patchy paper with 'one of those sprawling, flamboyant patterns committing every artistic sin' (*YW* 43).

> The paint and paper look as if a boys' school had used it. It is stripped off – the paper – in great patches all around the head of my bed ... I never saw a worse paper in my life ... It is dull enough to confuse the eye in following, pronounced enough constantly to irritate and provoke study (*YW* 43)

The language of this passage resounds with a constant disturbing resonance, which seems to invite an interpretation of the nameless woman's writing as a mocking imitation of the language with which, in another, masculine context, the woman herself might be described and defined. For example what patterns are being written of? female handwriting perhaps, telling forbidden stories. And what do those patterns de*scribe*? Artistic sins possibly, such as a woman daring to write; of her self, her life. Her writing projects a possible future self, a self or identity projected through self-employment, through writing. If a woman who is denied work and denied access to life outside the home writes secretly, because forbidden to do so, her writing might well seem 'dull enough' (*YW* 43). Non-professional writer that she is, denied access to profession as confession, her story might lack whatever is deemed appropriate form or structure, and equally – because of the lack of facility – prone to 'destroy' itself, like the patterns in the wallpaper 'in unheard-of contradictions' (such as writing about the impossibility of writing; another definition provisionally of both catachresis and affirmative resistance) (*YW* 43). Yet the unheard-of contradiction – that speaking, that speech *against* something – is inscribed in the writing of this story of the wallpaper as a figure – like the figures of the wallpaper, a trace to be translated, while also resisting translation – for/of the material existence of women, of 'Woman' who, like the paper, is kept 'dull enough' while also constantly provoking study (*YW* 43; a study involving a necessary male voyeurism in the name of observation) for doctors such as John. The nameless writer thus observes the paper as she herself is observed and turns her writing into a site for sounding the terms of masculine definition in a dissonant fashion. So is the wallpaper, are its patterns, the inscription of the paradoxes of female writing? and is it a writing which is deliberately resistant to exegesis as appropriation and domestication, a writing emphatically aphoristic? Perhaps, but 'There comes John, and I must put this away – he hates to have me write a word' (*YW* 43).

So much does John hate writing apparently, that his wife, after this initial writing, does no more for two weeks. She writes that she can write as much as she pleases, except for weakness (*YW* 43), and so writes in short, enigmatic and discontinuous phrases which, like the patterns on the wallpaper, 'suddenly commit suicide' (*YW* 43). Despite writing about the room, her husband, the maid, the garden, the baby, the writer returns always to the wallpaper, three times on one page (*YW* 44):

> I suppose John was never nervous in his life. He laughs at me so about this wallpaper!

> . . . he said I was letting it [the wallpaper] get the better of me, and that nothing was worse for a nervous patient than to give way to such fancies.

> I'm really getting quite fond of the big room, all but that horrid paper.

The wallpaper and its patterns are woven into her written being, her projection of herself into her writing and her 'nervous' condition (a condition defined by the husband/doctor). The yellow wallpaper, catachresic projection of her identity that it is, although also read in the quotations above as unreadable to the masculine, scientific eye (John laughs at his wife's interpretation of the paper, imagining its inscription as merely part of her neurosis), *is* her story in this projection of female identity; the yellow wallpaper is her story as much as *The Yellow Wallpaper* is her story. We are returned repeatedly to the title, to its aphoristic horizon. We are not allowed to escape.

And she cannot escape it either, no more than she can evade its seemingly sentient patterns (*YW* 45). The traces are everlasting (*YW* 45) and everywhere (*YW* 45), the hieroglyphs of a mute and forgotten tongue. They come to figure the mutations of an untranslatable trace, possibly readable as a projection of 'her' being-silenced, or otherwise forced to write always in other words as a female writer. Twice, the woman refers to the paper's expression (*YW* 45). The immediate meaning is related to that of a countenance and its meanings, yet to ex-press is to give something out, to enunciate or relieve dead paper through the projected communication of writing. But what that communication is, or might be, is unintelligible to the woman, at least initially. She is unable to translate because her husband and brother have shut her off from the world, surrounding her by walls covered in 'the yellow wallpaper'. She has no access to the world, and, therefore, no access to meaning or life. Enclosed by the yellow wallpaper – and by, within *The Yellow Wallpaper* – woman is silent and silenced, her self being dead paper, her meaning placed under erasure by male circum*scription*. Yet – and this brings me back to the title, once again – translation of what is remarked in the paper's patterns, of what the woman can bring meaningfully to such patterns, is what gives the woman a voice, what allows the inscription of a female writing and meaning resistant to male enclosure and erasure; even if that translation is of the untranslatable, unreadable nature of the patterns. So, constantly, interruptedly, the woman writes despite her sister-in-law; writing despite the idea that writing enervates and makes one sick (*YW* 46); writing secretly of being riven by guilt, silence and textuality (the textuality of her own inscriptions, of her own being inscribed within male patterns, and of her guilt inscribed in the acts of forbidden – proscribed – inscription), to paraphrase Francis Barker (1984, 9);[4] always writing, inevitably coming back to the enigma of the text of 'the yellow wallpaper'. She must return, unwillingly, aphoristically, to the 'sub-pattern in a different shade' which can be seen only 'in certain lights, and not clearly then' (*YW* 46).

This sub-text, partially visible, partially hidden – as are all textual traces – bears with it, in it 'a strange, provoking, formless sort of figure' (*YW* 46). The paradox here is clear: if formless, there should be no discernible figure, but, if a figure, then not wholly formless. The writing which we read foregrounds the very problems which the writer encounters, in observing the paper and in writing about it. The affirmation of her voice, and the material difficulties of expression, are announced. Her writing mimes the resistance to comprehension which she apprehends in the patterns; in doing so, her writing resists our attempted apprehension. I wrote above of a poetics of projection without programme, without code, and, in this story, we are witness to an on-going struggle between narrating narrator and narrated narrator to comprehend what is being projected. This struggle comes to be imposed on the reader, who, I would argue, can never be sure exactly, which way the projection will make itself manifest in both the yellow wallpaper and *The Yellow Wallpaper*. We never read more than the narrated narrator does. We can never be ahead of her, and assume the position of husband, brother, doctor or gaoler. It can of course be argued that, as readers, especially professional readers, readers trained to anticipate narrative strategies, we can assume what will happen next. Our position as readers implicated in a knowledge of reading is one of complicity with ideals of order, control, and closure. However, the problem of reading the wallpaper – of reading *The Yellow Wallpaper* – is not that of the writer/narrator's alone. It is ours as well, and it is precisely a mark of the text's affirmative resistance that it shifts constantly between its (mostly) present tense and the past tense, in unexpected ways which catch the reader off guard. The non-professional interiorised inscription of the projection of the other of the narrators (both narrating and narrated) in the form of a private, surreptitiously kept, journal troubles even the most confident, professional reader.[5] This is important in the performance of a resistant female writing because, were, the writer to allow her audience an Olympian, position through the confidence of a meta-narrative, once more would a patriarchal position be constructed, once more would female agency be contained within an oppressive structure as either object of inquiry or narrative subject.

After July the Fourth is over, the narrator writes that she is becoming more involved with the paper, and getting to like the room because of it (*YW* 47). Following the patterns becomes a form of exercise. She writes that she will 'follow that pointless pattern to some sort of conclusion' (*YW* 47). She also writes that she knows 'a little of the principle of design' (*YW* 47) but that the pattern in question is not arranged according to 'anything else that I ever heard of' (*YW* 47). The pattern seems to stand alone, yet is repeated endlessly, suffering it seems from delirium tremens (*YW* 47). Yet despite the alien nature of what she reads, reads as being unreadable, there are certain discernible connections, concatenations and confused relationships, all half-understood. In this page, the writer discerns, then, a poetic sensibility to the paper, readable for its own sake, on its own terms, even though apparently pointless. It is the discernment of this idiomatic quality which determines the woman to find a conclusion to what she reads. What little she does admit to knowing is clearly a little borrowed male knowledge. The patterns however refuse to conform to such knowledge; or perhaps that knowledge is too limited for the more complex semantics of the yellow wallpaper. While the pattern seems isolated, the writer recognises the 'interminable grotesque' as forming a common centre while rushing off into distraction (*YW* 48). We may wish to read this extended metaphor not only as a form of female writing, but also as a figure for women's domestic existence (isolation, distraction, DTs, interminable, grotesque, and so on). Each term remarks a figure of the wallpaper which in turn is a figural remarking available to translation from the perspective of the nameless woman.

To be certain about the pattern is, however, even at this stage, to attempt to fix meaning, to seek a return to our fixation with final meaning. We should also be wary of the pattern as the *Darstellung*[6] of the law which seeks to con*sign* women within its own prohibitions. The unnamed woman understands this and writes now that she does not want to write, that she does not know *why she should write* (*YW* 48), as though she were conscripted to trace and re-mark the patterns endlessly, without questioning, without dismantling: 'I *must* say what I feel and think in some way' (*YW* 48). No female writing, then, that is mere acquiescence or response to the demand to conform or be silent; no female writing without its other which comes to trouble the imposition of structures, codes, models, programmes. No female writing without deconstruction; female writing, *écriture feminine*, is deconstruction. And no deconstruction which does not carry the trace, the double trace, of female affirmation and female resistance.

The woman begins to understand the paper, the meaning of the paper – if not the meanings in the paper – when she writes that there are 'things in that wallpaper that nobody knows about but me . . . the dim shapes get clearer every day' (*YW* 49). Translation becomes more possible, more assured, as the woman gathers knowledge to herself, and for herself only. Connected to this realisation is that earlier recognition of the sub-pattern which works in contradiction to the main pattern. The sub-pattern becomes expressly related to the female, as the figure of the stooping, oppressed woman becomes read – and written – ever more clearly by the writer (*YW* 49). Of this now explicitly female figure, the female writer now writes: 'The faint figure behind seemed to shake the pattern, just as if she wanted to get out' (*YW* 49). *Just as if*: analogy, simile, comparison; translation through reading and re-writing, translation moreover through acts of projection which resist and affirm through a particularly writerly device, whereby the woman who writes a translation of her own, creating rather than merely reproducing. The verb used in the first clause of the sentence is of interest also: to shake. As the story shakes meaning, shakes at certainty in narrative structure, so the female *solicits*[7] male structure, the overlaid, imprisoning pattern. Nothing is held rigidly, and no translation can be held in place absolutely as this solicitation attests.

On the next page, the woman says of the inherent instability in the trace, of its oscillation, that she 'lay there for hours trying to decide whether the front pattern and the back pattern really did move together or separately' (*YW* 50). She then comments, aphoristically, 'On a pattern like this, by daylight, there is a lack of sequence, a defiance of law, that is constant irritant to a normal mind' (*YW* 50). Which clause are we to take first here? This sentence typifies the story, typifies the narrative resistance to closure, and to restrictive, unchanging structure. This sentence, with its five clauses, which can be read in varying ways, in different and differing patterns, is truly aphoristic. It projects its various projections of textual affirmation simultaneously. It both resists and encourages translation; it proliferates and delimits. 'On a pattern like this': which pattern? the story? the wallpaper? that which the writer either reads or writes? And in the sequence of sentences is there a lack of sequence, or a sequence which pushes at the knowable limits of what is traditionally known as sequence? We read also of defiance of law. Whose law? the law

of design, of reading, of male narratives of enclosure and legiti-
mation? of the general economy of patriarchal law? And what,
finally, is a normal mind? If the male mind, if male knowledge,
is the centre, is female agency and female writing to be figured
as sequence beyond sequence, as the destructuring of structure,
as *ex-centric*? As this proliferation of questions suggests, the story,
its structures and patterns, both arrests and separates. There is
much more to be read from this text, exhausting the reader, though
not the writing. The figure of the woman escaping from the yellow wallpaper is other to the nameless woman initially caught
in *The Yellow Wallpaper*. Yet this is not a simple structure. Because, as I have already implied, there is a layering, a weaving,
of resistant yet affirmative identities readable in the text, where
the narrated narrator and the narrating narrator, each figure the
other for the other, and the other of the reader. Every other is
already multiplied. No position is ever simply that: a position *as
such*. For every identity, as the narrative affirms is indelibly remarked by the affirmation of a radical alterity, a female trace
which simultaneously haunts and projects.

Analysis of this would require much longer exegesis of a not
wholly helpful kind, tending as it might to seek something to
pin down, prohibiting projection. The female other doubles the
un-named self; she is the aphoristic writing of that self beyond
the silencing of the woman. To finish with this figure: The woman
who is other speaks for her *self* (*YW* 57). She refuses to be put
back in the paper, to be constrained by the pattern. To borrow
Hélène Cixous' words on feminine writing (from a passage for-
tuitously entitled *Her affirmations*), '[h]er scene of wild writings
forever escapes vigilance, armed reason, force, jealousy, death wish,
Schadenfreude, the traps and bites of life's enemies' (1994, 59).
So the writer finds her voice, voicing and affirming her alterity
through her writings and resists the closure of traditional narrative structure, which desires that representation have its frame.
As the wallpaper is finally peeled away, so there is no yellow
wallpaper, and no more of *The Yellow Wallpaper*. Thus female
writing writes and speaks – projects – beyond the end, beyond
the limits of the title, opening the possibility for other(s) narratives, told differently and differing, deferring, through their telling.

The wallpaper is gone, and with it the enclosing structure has
been ripped away. If all that is left is a blank wall, then this
might come to be seen as the space for projection, a space between

identities too rigidly defined; a space in which, like the idea of *khôra*,[8] has no definition as such, no structure as such, but only comes into being in the act of projection. The aphoristic is that projection of the other, affirming, resisting, otherwise. The title of *The Yellow Wallpaper* is one such possible aphorism, a possible projection, shaping the contours of the narrative without programme and without proscription, in an act of writing. It merely describes, it only names. Yet in doing so, it escapes, projecting as the possibility of the affirmative response to acts of enclosure. In its aphoristic manner, the writing of *The Yellow Wallpaper*, the act of writing *that* title and the event of writing which is gathered in that name, performs so that, in Susan Stewart's words (talking of Kathy Acker's *Don Quixote* but applicable here), '[y]ou begin to see the surface in the metaphor of breakdown. You begin to see the breakdown in the surface of metaphor. You begin to see the metaphor in the breakdown of surface. You can't see what the barricade is' (Stewart 1994, 288). *The Yellow Wallpaper* as hysterical representation? No. The foregrounding of writing begins the erasure of representation's attempts to define identity. Making a spectacle of yourself confounds depth through the affirmative difference of surface, awaiting projection.

Notes

1. It is not my intention to take issue with, or debate these critical points; I have no disagreement with particular readings as such. Rather, my concern is with articulating an indirect resistance to the possibilities by which certain acts of reading are marked, sometimes despite themselves.
2. In his introduction (vii–xxxii), Shulman also looks briefly at the history of criticism concerning the story, while emphasising other contexts of the text, such as the possible relation to the theme of the divided self in American fiction, particularly in the works of Herman Melville and Edgar Allan Poe. Shulman places the tale furthermore within the context of 'female Gothic'. Shulman's introduction does, of course, recover the text into other more obviously aesthetic histories and traditions of reading of which we should be somewhat suspicious, especially as he justifies this in conclusion as locating the story as a precursor to certain post-modern sensibilities.
3. Jacques Derrida, 'L'aphorisme à contretemps', *Psyché: Inventions de l'autre* (Paris: Galilée, 1987), 519–533. I would suggest, following Derrida's argument in this essay, that, given the constantly inter-

rupted style – the immediacy of the present tense, the abbreviated duration of each arrested sentence, each truncated paragraph – that the entire story could be given over to a reading which treats the narrative as a series of aphorisms relating to the material condition of women, to the difficulties of writing under patriarchal scrutiny, and so on.

4. Barker is writing of Samuel Pepys and the act of writing diaries. Barker's teasing essay is singularly appropriate to the Perkins story, because he is writing of acts of writing that try to get around the difficulties of the conditions of guilty textuality. He says of Pepys in the same paragraph already referred to that the diarist is 'forbidden to speak and yet incited to discourse'. This is a possible description of both Gilman's nameless agent and Gilman herself.

5. The story is likely to raise negative responses which dismiss the story on supposedly aesthetic grounds, such as, 'it's not very well written'.

6. I have chosen this now heavily overdetermined term for its relationship to a certain philosophical discourse around the subject, and also around the subject of the subject. *Darstellung* has a significant performative value in relation to my reading of the text, as it doubles, metaphorically speaking, what it describes. *Darstellung* – meaning, amongst other things, representation, performance and, also, in some translations, figuring, figuration – figures the figuration or structuration of the figure, or the economy of the structure; it is the performance of performance, the re-presentation of a certain structural model; it is, in itself, what it speaks of, what it names, what it signs, thereby closing a certain gap. Thus, the yellow wallpaper, *The Yellow Wallpaper*, and the traces read and written, written and read by author, narrator, critic and reader, are inseparably intertwined in a certain disfigurement, a making monstrous, of the 'proper' functions of particular textual 'functions', such as title–function, narrator-function, narrative-function, and so on; each trace, each disfiguring figure, enacts its own and others' skewing, through being projected across the space of the text.

7. I am using 'solicit' here with its Latin etymology in mind, meaning to stir, agitate, shake, set in motion. I also want to suggest a sense of disturbance, of disquiet; of making anxious or filling with concern, as well as implying another use of 'solicit', meaning to entreat, petition, urge. I want to suggest here that a female writing can, in shaking the certainty of patriarchal structures, both cause disturbances, dissonant oscillations, while, simultaneously, petitioning or urging those who position the structures to consider the nature of the structures and the dissonance, the affirmations, which arise as the other of the structure.

8. See Derrida's *Khôra* (1993) for his reading of 'khôra' in Plato's *Timaeus*.

3

'The nervous laughter of writing':[1] *Stephen Hero*, onions, laughter and other lawless affirmations

A work laden with obvious and canonical 'metaphysical' theses can, in the operation of its writing, have more powerful 'deconstructive' effects than a text proclaiming itself radically revolutionary without in any way affecting the norms or modes of traditional writing.

Jacques Derrida

One has to read against so many grains, against at times, the finite here and now of institutional ideologies and political presumptions about scholarship.

Avital Ronell

. . . resisting readers are certainly among the best

James R. Kincaid

Acts of writing can be dissonant, whether they are kept in a locked room at the top of the house (as in the case of the nameless writer's text in *The Yellow Wallpaper*), or whether they occur in colleges and universities. This chapter is concerned not with a nameless author but with an invisible, unread text; it is also concerned with reading acts and the determination of impropriety of certain acts of reading and writing within institutional contexts. The perception of dissonance or affirmative resistance on the part of certain readers in certain quarters may constitute a more powerful effect than the very text itself. Thus this chapter suggests a reading of *Stephen Hero*, James Joyce's prototype

Portrait, as a text which, though obviously 'unfinished' and seemingly less 'experimental' than either *A Portrait* or, obviously, *Ulysses*, nonetheless offers a model of dissonant identity at work in the service of affirmative resistance. This earlier, other novel can be read as demonstrating the beginnings of what Vicki Mahaffey calls Joyce's use of a 'vast repertory of stylistic techniques in order to attack the traditional, univocal model of authority reflected in the organizations of the Church and State' (Mahaffey 1995, 1).

With this in mind *Stephen Hero* may be read as engaging with issues of agency and structure through acts of reading and interpretation, addressing indirectly the limits of agency within structure, and the limitations for oppositional activity as a means of affecting the dead weight of imposed institutional structure. It does so in a seemingly less serious, more insolent, but also more conventional manner than James Joyce's canonical works. At one point, the point which interests me in this chapter, it mocks directly academic structure and authority.

Stephen Hero is a text which we read as directly affirming a resistance to the very idea of the Law, as that Law comes to be masked as knowledge in the guise of conventional scholarship, and what the structure and institution of the academy considers proper to its areas of study. Knowledge, and a certain way of thinking about knowledge, a way of instituting knowledge through the shadowy laws of teaching and other forms of pedagogical practice within the academy (and the protocols attending the limits of academic debate and discussion) are resisted through a dissonant affirmation of the right to read, to write, to think *what* and *as* one wishes. And what both *Stephen Hero* and Stephen Daedalus – as opposed indirectly to the later, more perfectly formed Stephen Dedalus – affirm is what Emer Nolan has termed an 'alternative and heterodox tradition' (Nolan 1995, 37), both within the Joyce canon and with regard to literary aesthetics and canonicity as a whole. This can cause all sorts of embarrassment for the polite or professional critic, or at least the professional academic whom Stephen comes to challenge with his affirmation of textual vitality, and his laughter in the face of the proper.

While Mahaffey's assertion above offers what she calls a 'familiar perspective' on Joyce (Mahaffey 1995, 1), the particular nature of Joyce's affirmative resistance is to be found in the dissonant uses to which Stephen Daedalus puts scholarship, working with conventional models of scholarship to authorise an act of reading which is transgressive and celebratory. It is resistant indirectly to the order within which it is articulated, and affirmative of textuality itself. Stephen's rhetorical gambit is one also played in Joyce's own acts of writing. Affirmative resistance is therefore not merely to be found within the narrative; once again, it is also expressed by the very act of writing, and subsequently readable in the response to *Stephen Hero* in relation to Joyce's oeuvre as a whole, to varying degrees. The relationship between this text and Joyce's other 'finished' works is always ambiguous, and what I want to suggest is that this ambiguity circles around the issue of how one reads the construction of particular identities, the identity, let us say, of 'James Joyce' and his place in the canon, or the identity of Stephen Daedalus in relationship to the reception and construction of the identity of Stephen Dedalus in both *A Portrait* and *Ulysses*. In particular one incident from *Stephen Hero* foregrounds the problematic and ambivalent relationship between identity and institution.

One such ambivalent relationship is that of the subject and the Law, and the subject's position in relation to the Law, explored in the nineteenth section of *Stephen Hero*. The passage (*SH* 88–98) announces joyfully and impertinently what is at stake when one situates oneself in opposition to the Law within the specific context of academic discourse and its formal, hierarchical structures. This narrative presents the problems raised when having to speak in a language against which we may consciously situate ourselves, and the possibility of our own recuperation into the dominant discourse even as we attempt to appropriate the discourse for our own purposes. As such, it seems to suggest the question of the possible position of *Stephen Hero* within Joyce studies today, along with larger issues of the canon and its margins. The passage of which I am speaking is typical of many of the strategies that we can trace across Joyce's writing in general. It is typical because of the knowing and self-conscious resistances to the discipline and judgement of the Law that we can comprehend. Yet it is typical also because the passage is written through with the games of position and opposition which Stephen is set up to criticise. There is thus a simultaneity of movement available which affirms local resistances to mere containment within dialectical structures through what can be defined as self-reflexive pastiche.

In the passage in question Stephen, who is to present a paper on Ibsen, finds himself forestalled. He is confronted by a certain structure: that of academic authority and, implicitly, canonicity – certainly censorship – which has come to place itself before Stephen in the person of the Very Reverend Mr Dillon, in order to silence Stephen's 'illicit' enunciations. Stephen has prepared his paper in order that its delivery will amount to an act of intellectual terrorism, having a 'maximum of explosive force' (*SH* 89). Stephen has thus played into the hands of those whom he wishes to offend and rebel against, by self-consciously situating himself as a figure of opposition. Before the presentation can take place the paper must pass through the auditor's hands, and then be submitted for final judgement to the President of the Literary and Historical Society. As the auditor, McCann, points out to Stephen, the President, Dillon, is the Society's censor also (*SH* 89). Stephen is critical of the procedures and McCann is only able to defend the practices by remarking that the Society provides a training ground for young men who will be called to speak publicly, 'for the bar and the political platform' (*SH* 89). What we recognise here are the parameters of a discourse and the power that is wielded in circumscribing or proscribing the limits of enunciation, and the shape and conditions of knowledge as a medium of cultural exchange.

The Society and its manifestations such as the conference are designed not to allow free interchange of knowledges and thinking, but to promote authorised Knowledge and to sharpen the rhetorical skills of those who will come to constitute a specific juridico-political power bloc; those who will shape and maintain the discursive structures of social and ideological policing. And if the Law and government are anticipated in McCann's comments, then the third figure of the social trinity of non-logical, rhetorical constraint, religion, which will supplement the secular powers already referred to through the language of the metaphysical, is embodied in Dr Dillon. Dillon's is a double function: he stands in for the protocols of a coercive, censorial 'education' along with an equally co-optive religion. The Society within the college performs and mediates the Law out of which the hegemonic state apparatus is built. The scene between Stephen and Dillon is one of those common in Joyce's fiction which, in Cheryl Herr's words, 'call attention to those cultural sites where ideological or semiotic conflict occurs' (Herr 1986, 17).

Stephen receives the news from Whelan, the College Orator and Secretary of the Society, that his paper is 'tabu' (*SH* 89). Whelan, as Orator, is the official and ordained voice for the College. As its most typical representative, he has conferred on him an authorising title, a proper name, whereby he is, in turn, made into a subject of an impersonal, yet all-powerful voice. Furthermore, while being the representative of a particular institution, as a character within the narrative, as a figure who is written and part of the discursive mesh of the text, Dillon's 'voice' is a form of representation, a voice of a given identity larger than merely the college itself. Such a form of representation aims to normalise, to calm down dissonance and reproduce singular identities fashioning them after its own image. Dillon is therefore what Félix Guattari might term the representative of '[t]he normatized agents of production' (Guattari 1996, 143). To take Guattari's point further, Dillon is set in motion by Joyce, his voice activated (much as one would activate a recording repeatedly) apparently in order to transform the individual (in this case Stephen) 'into a speaker-listener capable of adopting a linguistic comportment compatible with the modes of competence that assign to one a particular position in society and in production' (143). At least this is what Joyce allows us to read. Dillon therefore is the representative of both his institution and the idea of the institution, the discourse of the institutional. His official status is as mouthpiece for a range of self-sanctioning discursive structures which operate in society to make figures such as Stephen conform to a pattern in their enunciations and identities. Even as Dillon is a synedochic figure for the college, so in Joyce's text, Dillon's voice is the sound of institutionalisation, of coercion and policing. Should we take Dillon too literally (and figures such as Dillon do exist in what is called the 'real world', to be sure), we would do well to understand Dillon's function as primarily a function of power and that in Joyce's fiction 'all power is discursive', as Cheryl Herr reminds us (Herr 1986, 17).[2]

On the other hand, Stephen is deemed voiceless, without sanction or ordination, and therefore lawless. In a mood of 'politic contempt' (*SH* 90) he decides to confront Dillon over the prohibition of the paper, and the silencing of his voice which has now been judged improper. On meeting Stephen, the President attempts to disarm Stephen with what is described as a '"winning smile"' (*SH* 90). An interesting point is that the description of the smile – the adjective being marked off by quotation marks for our special, ironic attention, suspended so as to encourage a reading of Dillon as constituted merely by a series of unthinking culturally determined discursive gestures – defines Dillon's greeting as being similar to that given by a pretty girl (*SH* 90). Sexual ambiguity surrounds Dillon throughout this passage. Later, he is described as gathering his soutane with a 'slow hermaphroditic gesture' (*SH* 98). This is, I believe, part of a textual strategy for writing Dillon as, in truth, powerless, indecisive and 'improperly' defined. The ironic rewriting of Dillon and those languages he authorises, supposedly being the authority for, reveals a lack of power in that very position which had presumed itself all-powerful. The sexual troubling of Dillon would seem to disenfranchise him, dismantling 'his' thoughts and the ideologies to which they belong. Thus, in the act of conventional narrativisation and the inference of the absolute conservative authority against which Stephen has consciously opposed himself, there is the troubling gesture of the writing itself, which dallies with the figures it maps out. The writing itself partakes of small explosive effects in an effort to undo both Dillon and the rhetorical figures that belong to the discourse of the Law. I would even go so far as to suggest that the ironies of the text make Dillon available to us as being merely one more rhetorical figure himself, only written by the languages he speaks, and mocked in the very act of speaking them. The language in which Dillon is presented has, ahead of and simultaneously with his own enunciations, undone his own position, affirming the impotence of authority, through the positioning of a resistance which, unlike Stephen's own, is not merely an opposition, because it is already in the process of performance as textual *praxis*.

The debate between Stephen and Dillon provides a 'parodic' overturning of the classic Platonic schema, the dialogue (and dialectic) between master and student, even in its observation of the proprieties of the structures that are being mocked; and even as it seemingly observes the narrative proprieties of realist storytelling. The inversion of the structure occurs most obviously because the master is frequently confounded by the student, made to seem stupid, a figure of fun, or left literally speechless on several occasions. Dillon's phrases are often reduced to what the text describes archly as 'expressive incompletions' (*SH* 93). Thus the form can be read as an anticipation of the rebellion of content.

We can translate the text as writing *in other words* Stephen's theories, which Dillon refers to as paradoxical (*SH* 95–6). And there
is a hint in all this of the content of Stephen's paper. Although
we do not see, hear or read the paper, we understand the inci-
sions that it is meant to operate through the textual *praxis* of
Stephen Hero. One of Stephen's first responses to Dillon is 'perhaps I am disturbing . . . ' (*SH* 91). The open-endedness of this
comment and its possible interpretations are humorously mocking. Clearly Stephen or, more precisely, his text, is very disturbing indeed; hence its silencing. Dillon's professional manner and
authoritative position allows him a rhetorical generosity (or con-
descension). Such generosity is expressive of the power of which
he is the agent. This generosity permits the admiration of style
but not the approval of *theories* (*SH* 91). Dillon, on being questioned by Stephen, will comment further: 'I cannot encourage
you to disseminate such *theories* . . . It is certainly not the *theory*
of art which is respected in the college' (*SH* 91; emphases mine).
Theories. Theory. These words are used four times, three times
by Dillon, within a space of nine lines, theory being further poked
at by the use of 'it'. This leads me to wonder: why is it that
language which is perceived as 'theory' or 'theoretical' such a
threat? This is *still* not solely an idle or academic question.

We are led to ask: What are the enduring qualities of what is
identified as 'theory' that the Law should comprehend it as such
a potential problem, feeling the need either to keep it quiet or
else to make fun of it? If the power that Dillon supposedly represents is so assured in its control, why then the need to operate
censorship over something so harmless, powerless, as literary
criticism? Beyond the immediate discourse of the subaltern figure of Stephen Daedalus within the academic structure, we are
all aware that such questions need to be reiterated constantly,
given the still-frequent, and all too often *ad hominem* attacks against
what is identified as 'theory'. Stephen is perceived as a theorist
because he apparently articulates an aesthetic discourse at odds
with the dominant discourse of the college. He comes to speak
as the other and is judged by the college because of his perceived alterity, which is maintained as wholly other by the complete absence of the text in question.

The debate between Stephen and Dillon continues in much
the same vein for the rest of the chapter, with the President seeking
to suppress the public dissemination of Stephen's paper, in or-

der to avoid any association between the College and what Dillon calls, with his usual hesitance, 'very revolutionary – very revolutionary theories' (*SH* 94). The supposedly reasonable Dillon, upholder of logical discourse, makes a staggering leap of illogic, to connect theory and revolution, Stephen being the secret agent of both.

In Dillon's remarks there is positioned against theory the somewhat monolithic and implicitly bullying edifice of 'the college' (I have already written of the college in this way implicitly). What is being offered through this impersonal, aloof structure is an authorised version of aesthetic theory rendered as un- or non-theoretical and made manifest through the architectural–institutional–ideological space and idea of the institution. The theory that is opposed by the President of the college is that of modernity which, in Dillon's view, leads to unrest and free-thinking (*SH* 91).

The connections between the theoretical sphere of unpoliced thought and possible social revolution, or even anarchy, are implicit in Dillon's citation of the threat of the new. Obviously the only safe authors are dead ones; and then not all of them (preferably those out of copyright are a little safer). The question of the threat to power – a threat let us remind ourselves that is constructed by the Law in the first place – revolves around the issue of an apparently aberrant and transgressive textuality which does not acknowledge Absolute Truth. Stephen is not the threat *per se*, despite his desire for explosions. Rather, what we can read in Dillon's responses is that the Law feels threatened by what it comprehends as alien, but which it cannot apprehend in order to domesticate the other in its – the Law's – own terms. The Law fears what it sees as monstrous, what it interprets as a challenge to its hierarchical telos.

Dillon describes Ibsen and Maeterlinck as atheistic and doctrinal, responsible for usurping the 'name of the poet' and producing 'garbage' that is 'not art'. To read backwards for a moment: in these formulations, that which is not art – notice how the definition can only work by what it excludes – is atheistic and garbage. Without a metaphysical superstructure to inform the creation of art, whatever is produced is rubbish, an excretion or remains not proper to the identity of the artistic body (which, by extrapolation of Dillon's thought, exists only to represent the glory of God). Without the deity's breath, the inspiration of spirit that determines the artistic as such, literary writing is 'debased' to the level of doctrine. We find ourselves back, once again, at a variation on the pernicious figure of theory. Such activity, according to Dillon, is a usurpation of an invisible, yet always present, structure, that of Truth, the Truth of Art.

And what is being overthrown, amongst other things, is the *name* of the poet. Dillon requires the name as the signature which asserts the ghostly truth. His concern with naming shows a concern with propriety, property, and the definition of limits; all of which, implies Dillon, are identifiable through an ordained structure. In the President's speech we read a non-logical, culturally justified renunciation of modernity's discourse in terms reminiscent of Michel Foucault's analysis of power.[3] Foucault's well-known argument is that power is essentially proscriptive; it can only function as it does through negation and denial of the activities and voices of others. The power of the Law in its Imaginary, Symbolic and social mediations is limited to control through prohibition. Stephen's response to Dillon is to say that he can see nothing 'unlawful' in the examination of corruption (*SH*, 92). In not recognising the legality – or otherwise – of certain subjects for analysis and critique, Stephen has already avoided the structure of position and opposition. Thus he affirms a critical voice which resists control and containment. However Dillon does not recognise this and replies to Stephen's comment:

Yes, it may be lawful – for the scientist, for the reformer . . .
                                                              (*SH*, 92)

Dillon once more relies on an implicit discursive hierarchy for the valorisation of inquiry (or perhaps voyeurism). Only 'objective' and intrusive discourses have authorisation for their gaze into the corrupt. Science and the moral hygenics of reform have the Law's permission to investigate corruption, while poetry does not and, presumably, should not if it is not to become contaminated, or reduced to garbage (genres are not to be mixed?). If we follow Dillon's thought, poetry and the poet are not merely, not simply above what is considered corrupt and marginal. Instead, the poet and art are maintained within the confines of the metaphysical gaze. They are kept under guard, under the watchful eye of the Law, apparently in order to prevent their contamination, but also to keep them as property. Art is therefore registered as belonging to a cultural matrix, traced along the lines of education, the church, politics and the legal system.

The priest acts as the gatekeeper of poetry and the Law, even as the deaf, stupid porter had tried to guard Dillon from Stephen, earlier in the novel. But Dillon's guardianship is structured not only to keep Stephen's ideas out, but also to keep poetry in, and silent on some matters. Yet Stephen's semi-licit/illicit intrusion and incursion – a kind of incision into the institution, which folds it back for our view – announces indirectly and affirms the already contaminated condition of poetry (a condition explored by Derrida in '*Che cos'è la poesia?*' [Derrida 1995, 288–99]). Stephen puts forward the signatures of particular writers, citing and intruding on behalf of their voices and writings, while Dillon's language is that of generalities, unless he attempts to take back literature from Stephen's 'improper' use. We read that the President, with a 'moral purpose in view' and in response to Stephen's incautious example of Dante, comments that the Italian was a 'great poet' and 'the lofty upholder of beauty, the greatest of Italian poets' (*SH* 92). Dillon's critical powers are not illuminated by these comments. Instead, they reveal him as an acolyte of received commonplaces and critical truisms; his role is to reiterate unthinkingly circular truths, whereby poetry is what is beautiful and the beautiful may be defined as what is poetic.

His critique of Ibsen and Zola shows the fundamental problem with the President's logic or, more accurately, the logic for which the President is the representative, mouthpiece and agent. Dillon objects to an absence of moral polemic or mastery, and concludes fallaciously that such an absence is equivalent to a fault, some discernible lack in the works under debate. However the fault lies not with the text but with the reading. The 'absence' is in fact not one: what Dillon supposedly discerns is an inability on the part of the President's thinking to countenance the possibility that moral argument might be omitted from the text. The presence of moral argument is a crucial determining factor in the aesthetics which Dillon represents. What is at stake for Dillon is not the possibility of corruption or perversity, but that which is unthought in the structures of the Law, and which is in the service of the Law's dominance.

Not to be deterred, Stephen follows up his argument by citing, perhaps ironically, Newman, suggesting an analogy between Newman's thinking and that of Ibsen. The President tries to brush

this off with a chuckle (*SH* 93), seeking to locate Ibsen doctri-
nally by reference to Zola. Stephen informs Dillon that he is
mistaken in this assumption, to which the priest replies, 'this is
the common opinion ... I understood he had some doctrine or
other' (*SH* 93). Arguing yet again against coherent, yet apparently wayward bodies of thought, Dillon's language cloaks itself
in the liberal vagueness of *doxa: I understood; the general opinion;
the public; mixed society; everywhere ... in the papers; such a un-
animity of opinion everywhere; he imagined* (*SH* 93). All of Dillon's
phrasing displays the level to which his thought is informed,
not by rigorous reading or critical thinking but by third-hand
opinion, aesthetic gossip and chatter.[4] Such a mode of 'knowledge'
or 'information' relies on a closure against thinking, a closure
against self-knowledge, a closure in fact to the possibility of thinking the self through internal critique and on-going questioning
as a form on which Being is conditional; it relies on a shared
belief that all can be comprehended. Dillon's 'knowledge' of Ibsen
is founded on non-critical sources. This is the flaw, a deconstructive
moment, in the model of knowledge which Dillon claims to represent: The President has shown himself to be the official voice
of an official body of thought on aesthetic-philosophical-moral
questions, all of which come to be centred on a certain practice
of literary criticism and appreciation, carried out in a prescribed
manner. Yet Dillon has failed to maintain the rigorous requirements of the thought he represents, by not pursuing a proper
and properly rigorous reading of Ibsen, by not admitting that
Ibsen's writing could be subject to such enquiry, and by drawing exclusively on what, from his position, can only be understood as 'unofficial' sources of information. The President's
relationship to thinking and knowledge is an indirect and silencing
mode. It maintains its authority not by authoritative thinking
but, paradoxically by unquestioning allegiance and subservience;
in short, by *faith*, which, as Peter Fenves says, 'is a form of knowledge but [which] does not assume the form of knowledge; it
both provides a criterion for unification [the college, the aesthetic theory of the college; the public] and refuses the principal
criterion of all thought. It, like the paradox – the unknown, the
god, or whatever else one might call difficult – cannot be thought
through; it cannot be made into a matter of knowledge; so every
attempt to predicate it leads to the limit of thought' (Fenves 1993,
133). Faith informed by *doxa* displays the 'limit of thought', the

parameters of non-thinking and knowingness endorsed by Dillon, and this is revealed nowhere more clearly than in his faithful and unquestioning support for what he believes to be thought.

This goes further. The President is even forced to admit to Stephen that he has never read anything by Ibsen. He is also forced to admit that it is not right to *'pass judgement* [a wholly apt, yet ironic, phrase in this context] on a writer a single line of whose writing' he has never read (*SH* 93; emphasis mine). Dillon tries to extract himself from his own admission of guilt by claiming not to have had the opportunity to read Ibsen (*SH* 93). Time, or the lack of it, becomes the guilty party, as the President shifts his ground. Indecisively, incompletely, he offers Stephen the sop, 'Some day perhaps I shall . . .' (*SH* 94). Every word of this expression and its lack of closure betrays Dillon's unease over being proved wrong in a 'debate', his guilt due to a moment of awareness that his argumentative strategies are in some way improper, as are his attempted evasions. The vague moment of 'some day' is rendered even more vague by the tentative 'perhaps'.

We come to understand that important to the shaking of the Law's structure throughout this scene is laughter, which might be defined provisionally as one of the sounds of affirmative resistance. The lawlessness of the laugh now comes into play. Stephen is aware of the power of his discourse, and of its subversive potential, particularly when allied to delegitimating mockery or, as Stephen thinks of it, 'the farcical' (*SH* 94). Later, the President will identify Stephen's 'satirical' relationship to classical aesthetics and an overdetermining morality (*SH* 95). Dillon, who, to his credit, comprehends the subversive power of laughter, enquires whether or not Stephen intends to publish his essay (*SH* 94). Dillon finds such a prospect a threat to both the ideology and the cultural position of the college: 'people would suppose that we inculcated such ideas here' (*SH* 94). *Doxa* – this time given bodily form as 'people' – holds sway over the President's political concerns about the proliferation of a theory read as antagonistic to the function, beliefs, *and identity* of the college. If there is any 'freedom of thought', it is encouraged within the college only within carefully policed limits which serve to reproduce to others the college's official representation of itself to itself, as exemplified by Dillon's words. Stephen's obviously oppositional stance serves Joyce in bringing into the open the carefully obscured institutional structure and knowledge on which

the existence of the college is based. Dillon's real fear then is of
aesthetic emancipation through a well performed act of reading,
which has been taught by the college itself. He understands that
Stephen's 'theory' 'if pushed to its logical conclusion – would
emancipate the poet from all moral laws' (*SH* 95). Once again
the same point for Dillon, a point of return and departure. Obviously what is of concern is that an abandonment of the Law
through the affirmation that theory offers (notice that theory is
not opposed to the Law directly, but resists through ignoring
the Law ahead of its injunctions) is tantamount to an announcement of power's bankruptcy, hence the awful necessity of power's assertion of itself as power, as violence and non-logic
(throughout history, and in the varying contexts of politics and
ethics). Power desires nothing other than the determination of
identity, the control of reading and representation, the damping
down of anything it perceives as dissonance. If, on the other
hand – or, if written *in the hand of the other* – art is emancipated
but does not corrupt as Dillon implies, then the Law would have
no grounds for its continued cultural hegemony.

Such hegemony is brought into question by Stephen's laughter, by his mockery of his masters' logic. Laughter laughs at
hegemonic seriousness, and does so through Stephen's suggestion that Aquinas's aesthetics – a keystone in Dillon's faith –
could apply equally to a 'Dutch painter's representation of a plate
of onions'. Playing the dominant discourse against itself, quoting Latin for the sake of subverting its humanist deployment,
Stephen's figure of the artistic image of the 'low' in the form of
an onion (something, also, without a centre) confronts the aes-
thetic-moral code with its own hierarchical agenda. The citation
of a painting of an onion draws our attention powerfully to various
cultural codes and the ways in which we valorise both form and
content by extra-aesthetic arguments. Even within the representation of fruit and vegetables there are culturally encoded hierarchies of meaning which valorise, say, an apple as a cultural
high point in comparison with the onion's low other. Stephen's
'Aquinian' analogy and analysis offers a lucid example of affirmative resistance: it operates its critique from inside the philosophical structures it resists. It does not directly oppose Dillon's
humanist aesthetics, for such opposition is useless. Instead it resists
by employing the logic of the master against the grain, and
parodically utilising the logic to demonstrate the logic's blind

spots and limitations. Stephen's pastiche traces the unthought of thought, the knowingness at the heart of authorised, institutional forms of knowledge. His imagined representation of an onion strikes terror into the heart of Dillon precisely because the possibility of such a representation (rather than the onion itself) reveals the limits of representation's propriety and what is deemed appropriate to any ideology or teleologically organised discourse on representation and identity.

As Stephen shifts his ground, he draws on Aquinas to support his arguments by emphasising his interpretation of the ironic in Aquinian discourse. Of course, Stephen's rhetorical gesture partakes of appropriation and is, in itself, an ironisation, not only of the Church's text but also of normative and domesticating readings of the text; Stephen's argument militates against authoritative 'versions' by providing an internal dislocation of academic structure, by means of the very elements of that structure. In so doing, he reveals the structuration of the structure, showing it as being open to a degree of play. Dillon recognises what Stephen is doing. He also recognises the danger imminent in Stephen's strategy. As a defence he states that Aquinas 'requires immense interpretation. There are parts of Aquinas which no priest would think of announcing in the pulpit' (*SH* 94). The better part of censorship is self-control, and with that comes the validation of the Law's actions and prohibitions. That validation is not positioned by Joyce's text however. It can be read as moving in such a fashion that Dillon's validity is invalidated by the mimicry of Joyce's writing.

Key to the validity of Stephen's affirmation of the right to read Ibsen at all, or Aquinas as he wishes, at this point is the imitation of Dillon's speech and thought by the narratorial discourse:

> The president far from resenting this hardy statement seemed to bow to its justice: no-one could have a poorer opinion of the half-educated journalism of the present day than he had and he certainly would not allow a newspaper to dictate criticism to him. At the same time there was such a unanimity of opinion everywhere about Ibsen that he imagined . . . (*SH* 93)

The narrative mimics the president's patterns of speech, including even the frequent hiatuses which occur in Dillon's expressions. Joyce has aligned narrative with the president's responses, in order to allow Stephen's voice to be heard more directly. Such a strategy bypasses the positioning of the narrative voice in a location superior to that of the characters or the knowledge which they represent. The narratorial discourse at this moment knows less than Stephen, and only as much as the president; like the authority of the president, who represents the Law, and stands as the gatekeeper to that Law, the authority of narrative convention is undermined. 'Literature', as represented by Dillon's discourse and the apparently objective disinterest of realist narratorial convention, is shown to be limited in its comprehension of the world of the word. The authority of the text is shown by Joyce to be of the order of commonplace statements and *doxa*, partial in their announcements. Stephen, on the other hand, can now be read as addressing Dillon, the reader, and the very conventions and structures of textuality itself. Stephen's voice is already beyond Stephen, other than Stephen's. His voice speaks through the structures and limits, and he is figured by Joyce as the agency for the enunciation of forms of alternative textual practices, practices which, in their enunciation, resist the confining structures of the Law, not by confronting them head on, but by speaking beyond the positions of the dialectic structure on which the Law relies.

Dillon, repeatedly unable to complete any form of argument with Stephen settles on what is, for him at least, a neat rhetorical containment of Stephen, describing him as a 'paradoxist, Mr Daedalus. You wish to upset centuries of literary criticism by a brilliant turn of speech, by a paradox' (*SH* 97). Dillon's position once again is clear; he serves the maintenance of an academic status quo, manifested in conventional and carefully preserved forms of literary scholarship which, for Dillon at least, have a retrospective continuity, stretching back to the Greek dramatists (*SH* 96–7). Stephen's suggestion that the preservation of a literary canon is done only to provide employment (*SH* 97; imagine!) is dismissed haughtily by the President, in favour of knee-jerk utterances concerning competence and culture, the quasi-metaphysical refuges of humanist compromise. From the forced connection between revolution and theory commented on earlier, to the dismissal of ideologically unpalatable argument as merely brilliant turns of speech and so much paradox, Joyce creates in Dillon the foolish figure of the authoritarian academic faced with (farced by) the incomprehensible: which is, in short, the limits of his own knowledge (a knowledge shared, a cultural know-ingness concerning what literature can and cannot be, what it should and should not discuss), and a challenge to the structure which those limits mark out. Not only this but Joyce also antici-pates (once again) Jacques Derrida's discussion of that famous post-card, where teacher and student are reversed, represented forever in a figure which upsets conventional readings, challenges conventional notions of identity, and speaks dissonantly of the exchange of knowledge.

All this talk of theory and paradox, turns of speech, revolution, threat and the opinion of the press on literary matters seems in the 1990s strangely and tiresomely familiar. It may have differ-ent cultural markers, it may be the Dublin newspapers and the Catholic Church instead of *The Times Higher Education Supple-ment*, the *New York Review of Books*, the *LA Times*, or whichever newspaper, periodical or journal with which you happen to be on intimate terms; and it may be Stephen Daedalus and Henrik Ibsen instead of Jacques Derrida, structuralism or, even worse, Paul de Man or Martin Heidegger; but there's something de-pressingly inevitable going on here, shown to us by Joyce. Which is perhaps nothing less than the fact that the keepers of the Law of knowingness have only their own ignorance to protect in the name of liberal culture, great works of literature, and so on. Joyce writes the figure of eternal return, tracing the symptoms of a cultural virus, the virulence of which manifests itself in the robes of authority. But we can read Stephen speaking across this, around it, about it; we can read Stephen's voice affirming an other iden-tity for 'literature'; no, not literature, certainly not Literature with its capital 'L' which it shares with the Law, and which Stephen's discourse resists, but writing, writing without reserve. Stephen is of course recuperated, because he is always before the Law, always in a way subject to its pronouncements. Yet there are his enunciations which escape Dillon, which move beyond Dillon's ability to comprehend We can read Stephen as kept in place. But we can also read in Stephen's articulations, the affirmative resistances of writing, thinking, living, all moving towards a discourse on the way to expression. Unfixity is a possible key to affirmative resistance and while Stephen does not hold the key, his expressions do. His writing – his being written by Joyce and his own writing, his essay on Ibsen, that unread, unreadable essay – are double traces of what Scott Klein calls 'revolution construed as inscription' (Klein 1994, 190). Stephen Daedalus may incorrectly see his writing as a small explosion (it actually takes the Law in the form of Dillon to make Stephen outlawed, to make him an intellectual terrorist, rather than through any action which Stephen might or does take), but, for all that, he is still, quietly, radical, revolutionary, and resisting. He is the other to Stephen Dedalus, the other within Dedalus, even as *Stephen Hero* is the other to the arrogant, authoritative *Portrait*. This otherness is signalled by the almost silent 'a' (perhaps akin to that other silent 'a', in *différance* which has caused so much doxical grumbling in the institution) in Stephen's surname in *Stephen Hero*, but which is erased in *Portrait*. It is another Stephen which Stephen Dedalus of *Ulysses* will remember when he thinks 'other me . . . *lui, c'est moi*' (*U* 3. 183). This other me, the other him that's me, the other is the figure of what Scott Klein has called 'a mimetic echoing which is both a parody and acceptance' (Klein 1994, 196). Parody resists, indirectly; acceptance marks the other's affirmation within identity while resisting, equally indirectly, assimilation within identity.

It is this that is recognised perhaps in *Stephen Hero* when epiphany is defined as 'a sudden spiritual manifestation, whether in the vulgarity of speech or of gesture or in a memorable phase of the mind itself' (*SH* 211). Such affirmative resistance is marked in the novel's often dissonant oscillation between various identificatory states on the part of Stephen, described by John Paul Riquelme as the alternation between 'allegiances to the visionary and to the material, *between* internal fantasy and external reality' (Riquelme 1990, 104; emphasis added). This 'between', it may be suggested, is the space between *Dubliners* and *A Portrait*, a space for which criticism cannot account completely. Colin MacCabe has described *Stephen Hero* as being caught 'within narration and the classic realist text', seeing its narrative act as belonging to a 'constant movement towards the place of knowledge from which narrative can occur' (MacCabe 1983, 52–3). This may well be so, although what MacCabe describes as a constant movement towards the place of knowledge is never a movement which promises to cease, in the realisation of knowledge itself. John Paul Riquelme has suggested that the limit of *Stephen Hero* is marked by Joyce's focus on Stephen's character rather than on style (110). While Joyce may go on to reject epiphanies in *Ulysses* it is the very awkwardness of *Stephen Hero* in its aesthetic struggles which are so fascinating, despite the early privilege of depth over surface which Riquelme acknowledges. This early work may well be caught within certain prescribed acts of narration and the contours of the classic realist text, but it is precisely the focus on character rather than style constrained by narrative and realist limits, the focus on the quite artificial oscillation between states, which makes possible a reading of both affirmation and resistance, located within the issue of the representation of identity itself. As Vicki Mahaffey suggests, moments of revelation in *Stephen Hero*, 'epiphanies', are what will become in *A Portrait* moments of stasis, instances of liberating apprehension of contradiction (69). Lifted out of the narrative, moved beyond a concern with narrative representation, the reader is made to be aware of the movement toward knowledge which always marks identity, but which never marks identity as fully formed, absolutely knowable. It is thus the nature of identity to be always incomplete. This is its affirmation, its resistance within the limits of narrative being the traces, the dissonances, of its movements. Thus identity is recognised in passing, in the act of having passed, while reading fails to apprehend identity as anything other than a series of misrepresentations. Stephen Daedalus cannot make this known to us, of course. Mr Dillon, however, does, albeit inadvertently.

Notes

1. The quotation which serves as the title for this chapter comes from Hélène Cixous' essay, 'Joyce: the (r)use of writing' (1984, 22), in which she talks of the unity of order is broken up through farcical and transgressive acts of writing in *Ulysses* (21–22).
2. Wherever I write in this chapter on Dillon as representative or voice of the institution, I am necessarily thinking of both the immediate institution of the college and the idea of the institution in general, the former implicitly acting as synecdoche for the latter. Following on from Cheryl Herr's point, I take Joyce to be asking us to read all such given instances, as the scene between Stephen and Dillon, as being representative of the cultural and discursive struggle over identity. It is not a question of choosing between lived experience and

discursive formation, as certain 'materialist–poststructuralist' debates might appear to suggest, but of understanding identities as negotiated between the two, and always to be comprehended as being in some manner written. I am grateful to John Nash for raising these issues with me.

3. See, Foucault's discussion of power in 'Le dispositif de sexualité', Part IV of *Histoire de la sexualité* (1976, 107–121).

4. On the nature of chatter and Kierkegaard's negotiations with chatter, see Peter Fenves's '*Chatter*' (1993).

4

Ulysses: memory's identities

... this legitimate–illegitimate collection of excerpts ...
Peggy Kamuf

The Other always knows more about us than we do
Jon Stratton

If the novel has a plot, it is located in the cemetery
Avital Ronell

And each was wrought with his other
James Joyce

The four quotations which serve as the epigraphs to this chapter situate my interests in *Ulysses* here, particularly with regard to the question of fractured and self-fracturing identities in the text which can be read as enacting a poetics of affirmative resistance. How are identities formed, reformed, through acts of memory and citation? how might memory be understood as an already fragmented writing composed of, decomposed by, 'legitimate–illegitimate' excerpts and citations which have little to do with plot or narrative coherence or organic cohesion? How does memory exhume other plots, other narratives, which, in remaining fragmentary and unreconstituted into a narrative whole, announce Joycean affirmative resistance? At a conference in 1996 on Joyce, Lucia Boldrini, in a paper entitled 'Unspeakable Geometries', described *Ulysses* as a 'semi-androgynous fiction'.[1] This phrase admirably addresses one aspect of the problematic of identity within a range of discursive frameworks which Joyce complicates. Of course the notion of androgyny already troubles the stability of identity from a certain perspective, offering us a dissonance within stable heterosexual identity. Boldrini's qualificatory prefix further disturbs what we think we may know of identity and how we believe we read the identities of both ourselves and others. While androgyny is not my concern in this chapter, the phrase I have quoted introduces, for me, quite succinctly the ways in which Joyce's fictions of identity are put to work in response to cultural discourses of marginalisation, enclosure, domestication and fixation.

Identities both affirm the place of otherness while resisting comprehension in Joyce's writing. As written performances, the identities of Joyce's characters resist coherence in favour of affirmation of writing and the textual *within* identity. For example, the enshrinement of Stephen, Bloom and Molly within certain normative and normalising discursive fields (by Mulligan and Deasy, the Citizen or Blazes Boylan) amounts to repeated acts of subjection. Yet the memories of Stephen, Bloom and Molly when mobilised as the narratives of other identities affirm for the reader these figures' dissonant identities. In resisting semiological subjection, they indirectly re-cite – and re-site – their identities otherwise. The rhythms of memory, traced so eloquently by James Joyce, constitute the signs of affirmative resistance. Joyce's textualised use of memory is one more example of the other's writing on the self, a writing which splinters the desired coherence of knowledge, which others attempt to impose from without as a means of keeping the subjects as subjects within a particular culture, adhering to a consensual definition of a given identity in a particular context.

Drawing on Jean Baudrillard, Patrick McGee describes the modernist text as a 'mirror for the production of human consciousness' (McGee 1992, 61). This mirror of production, argues McGee, is cracked by the effects of writing such as Joyce's in both *Ulysses* and *Finnegans Wake* and William Faulkner's in *Absalom, Absalom!* which effects exceed 'the production model' (1992, 61). As a provisional description of the process of affirmative resistance, I would agree with McGee's definition, going further to suggest that the writing of other identities, of the other within identities, is not merely that which produces the cracking, the splintering, the fragmentation, but coming from the other side or the tain of the mirror (to recall Rodolphe Gasché), traces itself in the very cracks which it produces. Terms such as 'interior monologue', 'stream of consciousness', 'style', or the search for allusions to the Homeric parallel (as merely one constant example in Joyce criticism which seeks narrative coherence), while useful and fascinating, are forms of critical glue, which seek to stick together again the cracked looking-glass. Such an act of re-gluing announces a desire for unity, for origin, for the perception of human consciousness as bearing in it the possibility of self-presence. But as Joyce shows us, memory is composed only of shards, of irregular shape and size, which precede and write the self *avant la lettre*. Identities are always other and multiple, composite and heterogeneous, as the self seeks to think itself by peering into the broken mirror.

In the conclusion of the chapter on *Stephen Hero*, I cited John Paul Riquelme's argument concerning that text's limits due to Joyce's concentration on character rather than style. In *Ulysses* matters have changed, obviously. Yet it is through a reading of the fragmentary, *written* nature of characters (rather than, say, attending to style) in the latter work that we come to understand the condition of affirmative resistance, where the identities of Stephen, Bloom and Molly are written out of a dense series of textual, cultural discourses, surfaces and references, which are themselves the excesses of memory. In the writing of characters' memories as being constituted through the traces of the other, and in privileging heterogeneity and multiplicity over and *before* unity and identity, Joyce makes available to us the vitality of affirmative resistance. Understanding the otherness which constitutes Joyce's characters allows us insight into a specific and convincing example of deconstructive chiasmatic inversion, whereby the illusion of unity and self-presence of identity is comprehended as the excessive effect of the projections of the radically multiple other (which projections cannot be reduced or traced back to a single source or origin).

Ulysses is therefore both informed and performed by gestures, movements, and traces of affirmative resistance in its excessive production of 'characters'. The performative nature of the text is registered through its often irreducibly idiomatic language, as is well known. As is also well known, there is always that which remains in excess of any possible translation or dream of such. Therefore language is transformed by Joyce from a merely secondary and parasitic, mimetic function, a function seeking to imitate what may otherwise be termed 'reality', to one that is performative, immediate and living. John Somer states that, '*Ulysses* is ... [a] direct assault on the presumptions of realism by the conventions of self-reflexion' (Somer 1994, 68). This is a plausible enough argument, and certainly one which is accepted today as something of a critical commonplace amongst both Joyce scholars in particular and critics of modernism in general. Indeed the argument can be seen as leading, directly and indirectly, to various discussions concerning the condition of what is called postmodernism and its over-arching debt to modernist aesthetics.

We should perhaps pause, however, at Somer's use of the word 'direct', if only because it situates *Ulysses* as an oppositional text, within a dialectic structure that is employed far too often in the reading of modernist literature; whereby that literature is constructed through criticism as a historical and cultural reaction to nineteenth-century realism. This movement on the part of critical thought necessarily limits the perception of the affirmative nature of modernism. Words such as 'direct' therefore need to be side-stepped. The resistance of the text is itself ethical, political and strategic. It resists the unproblematic containment of critical thinking, resisting not least the neatly ordered and controllable production of meaning; and this is because of what David Farrell Krell calls 'the infinite Babel of Joyce's archive' (Krell 1990, 300). Instead, *Ulysses* offers the possibility of endless communications, along with the possible excess which challenges indirectly notions of interpretive competence, the ability to know a text, and to determine its identity.

By 'meaning' I intend to convey (at least) three ideas for the present, all of which are related and imply the double question concerning knowledge and its limits. These are: first, 'meaning' understood as the accumulation of apparent, selectively chosen 'truths' gathered during the reading process (such as the 'truth' that *Ulysses* provides a 'direct assault' on the 'presumptions of realism'); secondly, the production of 'meaning' pursued through the ability to discern the text's mimetic rendering of the real, or otherwise the pursuit of signs of any detour from the mimetic function. In this case reading has, conventionally, enacted – or, supposedly, merely observed – a normalising aesthetic recuperation of the text, even though that recuperation can apparently position the text as oppositional (whether conventional or oppositional, such meanings can still be situated or approved institutionally, according to certain laws). And thirdly (returning to the first definition), 'meaning' can be read as an ultimate or absolute form of 'truth' being sought: the meaning or truth of a group of dis-

courses, or the assertion of the validity of a particular political–
ideological 'space' in the Imaginary, rethought in the form of
the hegemonic valorisation of representation, such as the English' representation of the Irish, or the Irish' own representation
of themselves according to the dominant fiction (to recall Kaja
Silverman's phrase from the introduction) of an English model
(as might be read in the figure of Gabriel Conroy in 'The Dead').

Ulysses neither allows for, nor admits to, either the conventional reading processes of interpretation or any form of absolute domestication in the guise of that critical work which is
teleologically or hermeneutically governed. *Ulysses* thus resists
even as it tempts the reader with the possibilities of comprehension. It is because of this 'political' resistance – not a direct resistance as such, but a resistance nonetheless, and one which
affirms through parody and other elements of serious laughter –
that the Joycean text has been so troublesome to critics as different in their ideological orientation as D. H. Lawrence, F. R. Leavis
and Georg Lukács. Joyce's writing foregrounds a political-aes-
thetic of 'responsible anarchy' or 'democratic non-identification'.
It shifts identities in its strategic situations with regard to what
Fredric Jameson referred to as the prison-house of language. This
is done not to escape the prison, for no such escape is possible.
However, such strategies do mock the supposed legitimacy of
the Law (a law of culturally assumed and coercive language
convention) and its policing activities, turning the prison into a
playground. The laughter that this playground excites and encourages is predicated on the refusal of, the affirmative resistance to, the fixing of narrative teleology and subject position.
Mimesis is not merely opposed by Joyce in the act of writing;
mimesis becomes *pantomimesis*, echoing, shadowing, implying,
intimating, mocking, punning.

Affirmative resistance in the Joycean text works where one
would least expect it. It works all the more forcefully for that
very same randomness of activity. Language, writing, knowledge
and even narration engage in acts of smiling terrorism and im-
polite, politic laughter through the ploys and plays performed
of a textuality composed by a 'weft of writing that will be all-
embracing and all-consuming', as David Farrell Krell has noted
(1990, 301). Meanings are exploded, and with them, the certainty
of identity, as Joyce conceals the explosive device within the
promise of meaning itself. One recognises an unfixible otherness

in the mockery of such modernist panto-terrorism, and the double play that articulates such possibility. Kate Soper gives a typical example. Writing of Stephen Dedalus, she says that 'one identifies with Stephen (Shakespeare) and his discomfiture in the National Library even as he offers his most phallocentric, patriarchal ruminations' (Soper 1990, 255). In this scene, Joyce partakes of a splendidly vertiginous unravelling. The 'Scylla & Charybdis' episode is full of Stephen's 'eloquence', a drunken giving-out with many Shakespearean echoes that equally mock and celebrate the Bard. As this instance shows, the 'structures' of the text are complex. The more that one attempts to read the rhythms and discourses involved here, the more complicated they become. We find ourselves in the middle of a continuous laughing dissemination. Stephen cannot, *does not*, deliver his theories on Shakespeare until he is at least somewhat drunk. His body pantomimes his theorisation in its own dizzying, unsure and therefore overcompensated positioning and gestures. The body at once enacts and pantomimes parodically the delivery of the lecture. His being-drunk mocks the supposed seriousness of his subject. It is a deconstruction of the hegemonically consolidating, canonising efforts of a specifically English literary criticism that seeks to arrogate to itself those texts which are suitably 'proper' to the constitution of its body. Stephen's body is decidedly improper at this moment, and even more so for the fact that he is narrating in the National Library, an authorised locus for the proper entombment of authors and their works. Stephen's activity, as a deconstructing principle, laughs at, and thereby unsettles, the propriety of the 'proper'. Stephen's locution is also a dislocution, and a dislocation of the literary canon's centre of gravity (Shakespeare).

This brief discussion serves as a useful introduction to the type of reading being proposed. I will now unfold other affirmative resistances to repressive cultural and political positions, structures and discourses in *Ulysses*, focusing on three particularly dissonant yet affirmative 'sites', expressed through the memory of Stephen, the wandering steps and thoughts of Bloom, and the imagination, the fantasy and memory of Molly. All three foreground the textual practice of eliciting alterity through their announcements of their situations. They enunciate the potential for alterity's voices to speak and to be written because, as Toril Moi has remarked, 'the very act of signalling one's place as a speaker establishes an "other"' (Moi 1990, 83). The establishment of other identities involves a series of recognitions: the possibilities and limits on Stephen's part of personal identity within the colonial city, and identifying affirmatively with the other to that city; in Bloom's case, the consideration of the identity one is given as a colonial subject-in-exile; and in the case of Molly, the identities of woman-as-exile, and as colonial and narrative subject.

Stephen's other city

Crucial to the imaginary survival of Stephen Dedalus is the imaginary site – and the imaginary citation – of Paris: as other, as city of doubled activity, of scholarship, artistry and hedonism. For Stephen, Dublin is a classical, colonial city, much as it is for Fredric Jameson in his commentary on *Ulysses* (Jameson 1990, 61–3). Paris on the other hand is not. Its identities offer Stephen the possibility of thinking himself otherwise. Paris is never *in* the text, in the way that Dublin is figured as the place where thought, interior monologue, memory, are placed and take place. Paris is always memory, knowledge, fiction, writing and mythology, distinct from the writing of Dublin which has a presumed reality, and serving Stephen's production of alternative meanings in the quest for artistic authenticity. It is not the real city as such, but understood and written as the trace of symptoms and tropes, figures and splintered memories which do not amount to the mapping of the city as a uniform location. It is in this imaginary space that Stephen can inscribe and perform as a doubled, doubling figure, being both Dionysian and ascetic, the one as the context of and pretext for the other, but neither as wholly determinate. Stephen's memories of Paris and his identities in that other place constitute what Peter de Bolla describes as a 'discursive analytic', which is 'a discourse that attempts to describe and analyse objects that are exterior to it . . . but which constantly phrases its explanations and analyses in terms that can only be understood as indications of internal effects, which is to say internal to itself' (de Bolla 1989, 34). Paris, apparently thought and remembered by Stephen, serves to write Stephen, as the writing of internal effects, written from an other place. Thus Paris, as a text, is always for Stephen a means of resisting and affirming what is to him the oppressive nature of Dublin, in which he recalls his other city, and sees himself as other than

Dublin's Dedalus (merely Simon's son). Paris is the excessive signature of affirmative resistance for Stephen. It is the signature of *de*limitation, *de*structuration; it is that other scene 'outside' or, at least, beyond the confines of the Book and Reality. And it is to the process of thinking the other city as a series of citations that Stephen has constant recourse as his means of affirming his spiritual survival, while resisting the confining structures of Dublin and its deadening culture. Stephen's Paris – which is to suggest not only an other city but also an other proper name for Stephen, one that invokes a figure with two names (Paris was also known as Alexander) from the Homeric tradition – is a *locus* of the imaginary, a constantly discontinuous and liminal non-space. This space is not marked by borderlines, being also an *aporia* that is marked provisionally by, at one end, *A Portrait of the Artist as a Young Man*, and, at the other, *Ulysses*. Paris in a non-place for Stephen, writing a *Stephenspace* between titles, and writing also one of the privileged textual resistances of the Joycean and Dedalean imaginary.

Yet, because of the dates that are so definitely, playfully affixed to Joyce's two texts as part of those texts, Paris exists as an imaginary temporal space that can be intimated at either momentary, supplementary 'end' by the dates April 1903 and June 1904. During this time Stephen, though out of the book, no longer the Stephen of *A Portrait* but not yet the Stephen of *Ulysses*, was apparently *in* the city of Paris, in the year after Joyce's own first residence. 'Joyce's time in Paris, from December 1902 until April 1903, represents his first experiences on the Continent', as we know from Ellmann's biography, and Neil Davison reminds us (Davison 1996, 83); it is out of these first experiences that the other Stephen comes to be written. Residence in Paris informs the identity otherwise. This residence, this *hors-texte*, is affirmed through the memory of this time, though never narrated directly, narration in this case being resisted. More important than the narration is the memory of Paris as other which calls Stephen. As Jean-Michel Rabaté points out in his essay, 'Joyce the Parisian', Paris is a 'call' and a 'calling' for Joyce which assumes in *Ulysses* 'momentous mythical overtones' (Rabaté 1993, 83). The same can also be said for the relationship between Paris and Stephen Dedalus's identity, the city inscribing as it does in Stephen's memory a series of signatures. Paris is itself the signature of the mythical polyvocality of *Ulysses*. Understanding the importance of Paris as an act of writing intimately caught up in the mapping of other identities allows us insight into Joyce's affirmation of the *written* quality of identities. In this light, the text of *Ulysses* should not be read as merely an opposition or successor to the realist text (as Somer's statement implies), but as an affirmative performance of writing which side-steps conventional conditions of reading in its affirmative evocation of the condition of textual surfaces. Stephen's identity is one narrative trace within a continuous/discontinuous textual performance which announces its multiple writings coming from an other place, other places. Such places are, in the case of Stephen, named Paris. Paris is the signature of Stephen's secret, other selves.

Understanding the function of Paris as a performance of non-narrative writing, a writing without closure, allows us to see how Joyce's writing always refers us back to its own practices, practices which are also aesthetic-theoretical propositions on the 'nature' of narrative and the constitution of identity. Paris becomes the figure of an unbounded textuality and writing, not fully readable and not placed as a figure in opposition, yet affirming its writtenness 'Paris' is a trope – perhaps the trope *par excellence* – typical of *Ulysses*'s self-referential practices, a name for the text itself, but always in other words. 'Paris' is typically atypical, a moment of reiterated singularity. It is the emblematic location which announces and affirms Joyce's writing; it is the city, in the words of Jean-Michel Rabaté, in which it was possible for Joyce to 'hear the murmur and prattle of all the languages of man' (100). The city then as other, as babel, and as the projected site of the Dedalian omphalos.

Thus *Ulysses* draws on the condition of Paris in confusing, conflating, eliding and displacing the boundaries of form and content into a seemingly boundless fluidity, undermines once again 'any simple notion of mimesis or iconicity':

> Essential to Joyce's method in *Ulysses* is the way his writing moves in and out of established conventions, thus *resisting* the processes of naturalisation.
>
> (Attridge 1988, 184–5; emphasis added)[2]

Paris is several spaces, any number of coincidental temporal events, all of which challenge indirectly a reading process which seeks to domesticate through the imposition of a particular plan. It is possible, though, to think through that alterity which can be signed as 'Paris' for now; to think 'it' as a theoretical play that signs an excess 'beyond' and within structures. It is that performance which both marks the 'absence of any possible security in the empiri- cal' (Gidal 1986, 231) as Peter Gidal puts it, and the fact that 'if there is always an excess lurking in the spaces of a text,' as William Corlett says, then 'unity is impossible' (Corlett 1989, 161). And, as this performance, Paris articulates silently the cultural differ- ences of Stephen from the Irish, reading him – even as he turns to his memories for both resistance to Ireland and the affirma- tion of his own artistry (which is not to say his identity) – as a figure of resistance to narrative and national enclosure (national enclosure is often narrative in its contours). An other identity is determined indirectly as an affirmation of an otherness not re- ducible simply to a national context. There is for Stephen and the reader a transgression here, in the name of Paris. There is a 'text' that cannot be written down, cannot be given up to a sin- gle meaning. Paris exists radically, beyond mastery for Stephen, beyond the mastery of those contesting narrative voices (Haines and Mulligan, Deasey, Si Dedalus) which seek to master and colonise Stephen, to demand definition (and therefore aesthetic death) of, Stephen Dedalus.

The question that seems to be gathering around Stephen is one, therefore, that situates the issues of artistic creation and textuality alongside the problematic of colonialism. Stephen Dedalus is a writing site, the written citation of a colonial other whose enunciations are acts of desire for a self-becoming-cen- tred; but the centre is displaced because of the self-becoming- aware and thus estranged, made strange and foreign, and thus powerless to write other than through the thinking/writing of the imaginary. Stephen is subject to the voices of those who seek to effect 'strategies of normalisation that play on the difference between an "official" normative language of colonial adminis- tration . . . and an unmarked marginal form' (Bhabha 1986, 156). Stephen as (self-) imagined artist is that marginal form, with Paris being his site (and citation) which signifies for him artistic struggle against normalisation. The texts that write figures such as Deasy operate as a coercive apparatus that seeks the Stephen's oppres- sion through the fixation of Stephen's identity and meaning; which interpretation would offer meaning as prison, as the writing of the prison. Yet Paris remains for Stephen a place outside and before the text. Stephen comes to think of Paris as an act of identity's resistance to being determined through a colonially oriented or produced meaning when Deasy, Irish representative of the English Masters and their Language, talks of the Jewish 'contamination' of England:

> On the steps of the Paris stock exchange the goldskinned men quoting prices on their gemmed fingers. Gabble of geese. They swarmed loud, uncouth, about the temple, their heads thickplotting under maladroit silk hats. Not theirs: these clothes, this speech, these gestures. (*U* 2. 364–7)

Stephen's language, mixing memory with culturally over-determined cliché, might seem at first glance to fall back on racial (or even racist) stereotype. Certainly, his language is ambiguously caught up in particular modes of expression, tending towards anti-semitism. But his thought stops short with the ambiguity of the negation, 'not theirs'. It is not immediately clear just what is 'not theirs'. Nor can we be absolutely sure as to who 'they' are, even though we might be tempted to answer the goldskinned men. Immediately we read that clothes, speech and gestures, do not serve to fix identity, the implication here being that we misread such signs if we assume clothes, speech and gestures as definitive signatures of identity. Stephen produces an image of estrangement that is resistant to the normative stereotypes of the Jew, while at the same time positing a poetic vision of foreignness, an otherness that cannot be defined reductively through the mis-read outer signs. Stephen's performance suggests the fallacy of a merely empirically based form of knowledge, along with an announcement that cultural identity is irreducible to a cursory knowledge of signs. Stephen's reading is a polemical gesture against the ideological fixations of particular narrative forms (the realist, the bourgeois, the xenophobic and the colonial, to translate just a few of the implied structures which might be read to be at work 'in' this passage). It is a gesture also against realist narrative's attempts at the fixing of subject positions through its reduction of identity to the visible signature.

It is crucial, then, to remember the importance of Paris to this scene, to its making possible, through Stephen, the *other* scene, the *other* writing that sympathetically estranges Jewishness in order to proscribe the racist violence of the colonial imperative, as expressed by what Joyce perceives as the hitherto dominant strat-egies of textual hegemony. Joyce is able to write this precisely because he was, himself, a 'product of colonial Ireland', who, as Francis Mulhern suggests, 'wrote out of that formation. His writing is, in this respect, a dramatisation of the "native" as alien [and] the "mother" language as another language' (Mulhern 1990, 255). Stephen's thinking of Paris is also, once again, a writing of that city, the writing of the city that in effect writes Stephen as other. It is a writing of his identity as defined elsewhere through the cultural-historical-aesthetic citation of that other city which serves to preserve Stephen's other self. All of which is, of course, a vital pretext to the introduction of Leopold Bloom into *Ulysses*, as is what Bryan Cheyette describes as 'Stephen's troubled self-identi-fication with Europe's semitic "unconscious"' (Cheyette 1993, 211).[3]

The Paris that we encounter in the Joycean text is constituted between apparently opposed configurations, such as 'the studi-ous silence of the library of Saint Genevieve' and the 'sin of Paris' (*U* 2. 69–70). This invocation of the doubled Paris, a place for text and sex, is in part Stephen's reflex against a late nineteenth-century interpretation of a work such as Milton's *Lycidas*, an interpretation which may well be a contributing factor to Stephen's ambivalence in various places in *Ulysses* concerning the figure and thought of Matthew Arnold (along with the Hellenic and liberalising tendencies associated with this name).[4] Thus 'Paris' is read as a textual figure with which Stephen affirms a trans-gressive textuality against the enterprise of education based on a knowledge of great authors. Stephen employs the fictive sig-nature, announcing the fictive condition through the double read-ing. The binarism mentioned seems an almost inevitable condition of Stephen's thought; both figures of the binary pairing always partake of an already doubled textuality, the one reading in anticipation, and in memory of, the other, the other in the one. Thus they dismiss a naive reading of their gestured hierarchical relationship. Stephen's readings invert and displace canonical hierarchies, even as they apparently depend on, re-instate and seem to support those very hierarchies. This is the very precari-ous possibility of the smiling insolence of affirmative resistance. Stephen's strategic invocation of his Parisian open-ended narra-tives, (non-)narratives of contradiction and paradox, illuminates again the condition of affirmative resistance which Derrida de-scribes in *Dissemination* as the movement of fiction:

But in the first case, fiction is in the service of meaning, truth
is (the truth of) fiction, the fictive arranges itself on a hierarchy, it itself negates and dissipates itself as accessory to the
concept. In the other case, outside of any mimetologism, fiction affirms itself as a simulacrum and, through the work of
this textual feint, disorganizes all the oppositions to which the
teleology of the book ought violently to have subordinated it.
(Derrida 1972, 36)[5]

Paris in Stephen's memory illustrates the deconstructive double-
principle through its initial production of meaning and its subsequent dissolution of oppositions and hierarchies. The condition
of 'Paris' is clearly potentially narrative, referring always to its
own explicitly textual status. And it equally clearly refuses to be
organised through reading as a simple opposite within a series
of oppositions which we might wish to read, whilst it also plays,
as a 'textual feint', a pair of apparent opposites – sin and the
library – which themselves invoke a pseudo-Aristotelian metaphysical pairing only to disorganise all such oppositions.

The double figures of Paris are also subject in part to Stephen's
own memorialisation and re-reading of the Aristotelian text
(amongst others) that drifts across *Ulysses*, along the margins of
Stephen's conscious thoughts, around the thinking of Stephen
as a textual figure, and in the play of some of the text's broader
currents. Stephen's rethinking of the Aristotelian suggests the
necessity of the other non-oppositional economy in the text, the
economics of the *parage* (that all-important figure of 'between'),
the symbolic importance of which is remarked in Stephen's walk
along the beach, his abstracted inner discourse given metaphorical figure in the dissolving boundary between land and sea. The
parage is the boundless waterway that is written into the deferring, differing 'structures' of those Aristotelian phrases such as
'actuality of the possible as possible,' 'thought is the thought of
thought', and 'the soul is the form of forms' (*U* 2. 75). Thought,
soul and textuality are all *parages*: formless forms and boundless
articulations of a radical otherness beyond the thought of structure (of books, for example, or canonicity and colonisation).

Another name for all of which is, in this context, Paris. Paris
drifts in and out of Stephen as Stephen drifts in and out of the
labyrinth of the city, the labyrinths of his citations of the city.
These labyrinths will cause him to remember any number of French

texts in (then) current circulation throughout the waterways of
the metropolitan citation, along with the shadows of exiled Irish
nationalists such as Kevin Egan 'of Paris', whose exile is also
marked by the other city (*U* 3. 164, 250; 164–264),[6] and with whom
Stephen, as another native in exile, associated. This difference
that is Paris has its most forceful articulations in French, but
also doubled, also English, when Stephen thinks, remembers
thinking, 'Other fellow did it: other me ... *Lui, c'est moi*' (*U* 3.
182–3). There are several Stephens in at least two tongues, the
doubled-one who remembers (as both third and first person),
and the one(s) remembered, all of these becoming multiplied in
the processes of thought and narrative, Being becoming opened
to affirmative translation, rather than meaningful fixture and
closure. Stephen thinks through himself, his selves, narrating his
own creative, narrative possibility, and Paris writes him as such.
It is because of the ability to think through the otherness of the
Parisian scene – to think of the self as figured through the trope
of Paris, to be figured by that protean trope, and to think the
otherness of the trope – that Stephen can deconstruct any moment of readerly gathering. Stephen writes his own multiple
existences beyond the closure of the unity of identity, thereby
effecting a provisional escape from both conventional reading's
assurance of a 'subject-position' and its opposite, the simple, single
position of exile or absence within the teleology of binary logic.
And it is with such potential moments that we can hear and
(not) read the unwritten radical text by 'Stephen Dedalus'; which
'book' would have as its possible title a letter, *P*. The idea of
books 'with letters for titles' (*U* 3. 139–40) suggests such a future
text, a post- or hypertext of almost infinite narrative chances and
inscriptions for the fragmented and, therefore, free agent. Paris
is that post-text, directing its missives through memory, and
Stephen remembers and thereby writes his other self as its
Hero(es).

'L'étranger, l'étrangeté du chez soi': Bloom's doubling/ Dublin

The first part of the title of this section, taken from Jacques
Derrida's *Schibboleth*, offers an oblique but appropriate comment
on the subject of Leopold Bloom (Derrida 1986, 58). It is also
appropriate to the subject *in* Bloom's writing/walking of the city

of Dublin, his doubling of Dublin, so to speak. Dublin in *Ulysses* is mapped out for Bloom, and by him, as the city of the other, as Paris is Stephen's other labyrinthine articulation, the geo*graphic*al city or labyrinth of the double. This includes perhaps even the man in the Macintosh whose shadowy presence haunts both Bloom's steps and the reader's progress.[7] Derrida's remark concerning the stranger who is strangeness itself, refers to the marks of the subject as stranger, being at once both strange and estranged. In the figure of Bloom, and in his aleatory weaving, the strange and the estranged are traced in the Joycean text. In this phrase Derrida is writing of, as well as reading, the difficulties surrounding the inscription of Being in the texts of Paul Celan. He writes of being un/familiar, because of Celan's being both Romanian and Jew, talking and writing in a language not his own, a master tongue, that of German. This indicates a fragmenting simultaneity that allows the subject neither unity nor identity other than that which is already at threat, both outside and inside but also neither. The same is true of Leopold Bloom: he is both outside and inside Irish culture, never wholly belonging. His father, Virag, was of middle-European 'origin', if we can use this word for the moment. Bloom is both self and other, doubling each figure. His otherness is that which his self keeps handy, to paraphrase Hélène Cixous, 'in case the self should perish, which in literature becomes "the double", a stranger to the self' (Cixous 1984, 19).

And, more immediately in the case of Bloom, there is in the line concerning Celan a strikingly apposite pun in the play on the phrase *chez soi*. This play is one of translation, and I want to suggest that Bloom is, in many ways, a translator; his thought and memory translate for the reader, sifting and interpreting the experiential, the sensual, and all that is immediate both in the present of the Dublin through which he wanders, and in the past of his memories (once again the question is that of narrative possibilities, and of narrative as the metaphor for all experience). Bloom also translates for us an almost endless, random discourse of speculation; he keeps textuality in play through his affirmative questioning. But to return to the phrase *chez soi*. It can be translated as either 'himself' or 'his home'. Yet Bloom is locked out of his home; he has no key, no access and becomes a stranger to himself, becoming *unheimlich*, quite literally.

This phrase – *chez soi* – can then point to a condition of Being that is materially affected by the question of national identity, whereby one's country is also one's home; one is, supposedly, not foreign. In 'Cyclops', Bloom remarks that a nation is the same people in the same place. Or in different places (*U* 12. 1422–3, 1428). This statement and its supplementary revision is not as facile as it may seem, because it narrates the truth of the Jewish (dissemi)Nation, of Diaspora. But personally Bloom is never at home, not even in his own home, the place where he can say 'me' (as the horse's neigh in 'Circe' reminds him). Nor is he ever wholly at home in Dublin, in Ireland, even though he says his nation is Ireland, and that he was born there (*U* 12. 1431). Bloom is cast out, unable to return to Eccles Street because he has no shibboleth, no key, to either his door or the questions that he posits. Yet his search is resonant of a greater wandering, that of the Jews in search of home. As the French phrase above resists recuperation, leaving something untranslatable beyond the frontier of definable meaning (and therefore beyond the possibility of colonisation), so the issue of identity, of being at home with oneself, with the political contingency of identity, is being commented on through the figure of Bloom. Identity is not domesticated, not rewritten by Joyce in a familiar and comforting form. Instead it is empowered with a potential for political efficacy through being left at large to trouble those readers – such as the Cyclopean nationalist, the Citizen – with whom it comes in contact. Bloom is written in order to remark a strangeness and an estrangement that inhabit identity, foregrounding the foreigner as that other without which there cannot be articulated any conception of 'self'.

The estrangement of the individual from naturalising, metaphysical philosophies that produce the subject as necessary but surplus to the dominant culture enacts the materialisation of the hidden forces of coercion and containment that are otherwise written as natural and essential to a culture's – and therefore a subject's – construction. 'Slippery' Bloom (as Bryan Cheyette calls him; 1993, 220), the Middle European-Irish Jew estranged from 'his' country (which is also not his) estranges our familiarity with the idea of the fictional subject and the topography that the same subject performs through his narrative trajectory. This is so for, no matter how Bloom's actions are comprehended, his every encounter or action can only be understood as being of a chance nature. His actions, movements, thoughts are all in passing. As

Bryan Cheyette suggests, Bloom even escapes being merely real: '[a]s a "Jewgreek", who displaces the Homeric myth onto a Judaic double, Bloom is always more than his "reality" at any one moment in the novel' (Cheyette 1993, 219). Any attempts to fix Bloom's identity in *Ulysses* are invariably on the part of those who desire to pin Bloom down as part of an anti-semitism and general unease about racial alterity. Yet, quoting Cheyette again, 'Bloom always elides . . . narrative resolution . . . threaten[ing] the certainties of nation and religion' (1993, 220).

Nothing written of Bloom gives the idea of the inevitable, of foreshadowing, *of a particular narrative plotting*. Bloom is the rewriting of the discourse of the foreign in a given culture, which Stephen's revisions of Paris anticipate; which rewriting uses the inquisitive, questioning, questing mode as a method for making strange the reader's familiarity: with the word, the world, Dublin, Irishness, narrative form, or whatever confirmations of knowledge the protocols of our readings search out; a possible narratorial voice for example, a voice that can be fixed, or which could provide a response to criticism's activity, thereby producing the meaning that criticism had believed was there all along. Bloom, being a stranger, is also an estranged – which is to say denaturalised and therefore demystified in terms of traditional linear narrative forms and reading methodologies – reading of the material conditions of the 'individual', and of the material production and control of that subject's labour. To move beyond Bloom, this also the project of the Irish stranger, James Joyce, whose exile encourages his writing of the story of Bloom, the Jewish stranger at home, a stranger in his own homes.

So there seems to be a gesture here that is, provisionally, a positive refusal, an affirmation of resistance, not only of the recuperation of Bloom. What Bloom acknowledges throughout his wanderings, and in his speeches in 'Cyclops' and 'Circe', is an nervous optimism to be found in comprehending the 'impossibility of fully comprehending the world, of reducing it to a single rational order of communication . . . [this] is not a methodological or cultural defect, for it leaves us *free to acknowledge an irreducible heterogeneity*' (Chambers 1990, 10; emphasis mine). Bloom's name is a translation, a domestication that may only finally reinforce his marginality. His is a distanced signature and foreign language. This effect of translation does open up a gap, pushing away the desire for unity. And, even though, within the text,

Bloom is resisted as foreign, he also remains resistant. At the moment that Bloom remarks 'I was happier then. Or was that I? Or am I now I?' (*U* 8. 608) it can be understood that he is refusing his location as a subject of others' languages, others' mastery. By multiplying his 'self' through an awareness of the radical contingency of self (through the repeated I), and then leaving those subject positions up for grabs through his interrogative mode, a mode that does not effect closure, Bloom produces what Philippe Lacoue-Labarthe has termed a 'destabilizing division of the figural'. There is the enunciation, again to quote Lacoue-Labarthe, that 'the subject "desists" because it must always confront *at least* two figures (or one figure that is *at least* two figures)' (Lacoue-Labarthe 1989, 174–5). Bloom can never be at home with himself, because he recognises the alterity that insists in him. But this is not recuperable as some tragedy that is Bloom's. His reading of his self foregrounds the lived strangeness of all Being. Bloom's resistance is a resistance to being pinned down, defined by some form of master discourse. Bloom is not a figure of opposition, for his perception does not admit of such fixed locations. His wandering figure and questioning thought affirms Being as the constant articulation of otherness and the need to comprehend the destabilising, doubling condition of Being-strangeness-itself-estranged. As Bloom says

– Everyone according to his needs or everyone according to his deeds.

(*U* 16. 247)

Bloom's doubling requires that as readers we rethink reading and alterity. His Being affirms itselves by not becoming subsumed by what Terry Eagleton has called, with reference to Ireland, 'virulently metaphysical forms of identity' (Eagleton 1990, 24). Such forms reduce identity either to submission or opposition, but always singularity. On the contrary, as Bloom shows us, the figure is never one.

Molliloquy: 'this that and the other'

Molly, wrote Joyce, is a textual figure for '*der* [sic] *Fleisch der stets bejaht*' [the flesh that always affirms] (Joyce 1966, 170).[8] If she is a flesh that always *affirms* then 'she' is also a text of affirmation, composed of a dizzying simultaneity. Enda Duffy argues for a post-colonial reading of Molly as the 'last in a line of women ... who are the text's most abject subaltern subjects' in 'a male-dominated colonial system' (Duffy 1994, 184). Duffy goes on to suggest that Molly is 'markedly apolitical in any conventional sense' (185–6). There may be some obvious truth in such statements, but such suggestions are far too negative and limiting in their reading of Molly, Molly's 'purpose' in the narrative, or what we might want to call the 'Molly-function'. Duffy's argument misses much of Molly's affirmative resistance through her language-play, through her fragmentation of narrative, through her subordination of men to their limit as phallic functionaries. Furthermore, Duffy also misses Molly's rendering of literature into a series of codes, signals, fragments, notes and postcards, all of which are transmitted, distributed, posted, to an ever open address which has no hint of either a location or an addressee. And it is precisely because Molly is 'markedly apolitical', because she does not oppose directly, that she is able to affirm the voices, the transmissions, the weavings and writings acknowledged by Jean-Michel Rabaté (1991 64–5) and the non-site, the non-locatable site from which the endless citations of the other resound, in gestures of a most radically political kind. Molly is only '*markedly* apolitical' to the extent that her voices are *marked* by the aporia in politics in the conventional sense. Politics emerges 'conventionally' from a place which cannot speak or write sexually, conventional politics being the concatenation of the simulacra of power without any traces of pleasure. Molly opens (onto) the aporia affirmatively.

Joyce does not spell out what Molly's affirmation is, the reader is left to infer that the affirmation is a radical form, one that is not to be pinned down to any finite meaning. Not even Joyce can say what Molly 'is', his seminal creativity being frustrated in the very act that he supposedly 'engenders'. Emer Nolan has suggested that Molly's voice amounts to 'an affirmation of femininity and the refusal of conflict' (Nolan 1995, 163) and that 'Joyce is seen to adopt the voice and position of the marginalised woman' (164). This seems a pertinent and convincing commentary which announces a sense of political engagement and taking responsibility in what might be considered a scandalous fashion, inasmuch as Molly's resistance is to any programme or pre-conceived structure, code or model (Derrida 1996).[9] Molly awaits the coming of responsibility, awaits the chance occurrence which cannot be predicted ahead of arrival; hence the improvisatory, performative, affirmative nature of her utterance and writing, which, as Rabaté informs us, is always a double-writing where 'every statement occurs at least twice' (1991, 65), a constant multiplication of identity's traces. Molly's marks are always re-marks, Molly writing herself as other than herself. Thus, yet again, though in a different fashion, affirmation resists. What I have just referred to as the 'performative' element in Molly's discourse is described by Joseph Boone as 'theatricality'. Boone is right to suggest that this 'theatricality' or 'performativity' 'constitutes one path whereby Molly's representation evades authorial and readerly mastery' (Boone 1993, 215). Boone is clearly aware of both the affirmative and the resistant qualities of the text, and this resistance has a specifically materialist purpose, being grounded in and working against a contingently 'historically' comprehensible textuality, identifiable as belonging to the restricted economy of Victorian/Edwardian fictive constructs of female sexuality displaced through the literature of sentiment or enclosed within the pornographic. This is important to an understanding of the radicality of the Penelope section, if this text is not to slip unnoticed into the universalising (and implicitly patriarchal) discourse of academic humanism. I do not propose a sustained materialist analysis at this juncture but wish, instead, to point to an important trace, read by Suzette Henke in her work on the issue of sexual politics in the Joycean canon.

In her reading of 'Penelope', Henke suggests that Joyce attempts 'to simulate the mysterious and polymorphous iterations of a woman's psyche' (Henke 1990, 127) an attempt which, like Molly, has 'been excluded from male discursivity' (127). At the same instance, Molly's 'hysterical' discourse has the material traces of a particular scene of writing that is historically, culturally identifiable. This scene, suggests Henke, is the mediation of voices 'inherited from nineteenth-century sexual/textual metadiscursive conventions . . . through the language of pornographic fantasy . . . [Unfolding as] a curious rehearsal of erotic desire encoded in a frame of Victorian sentimental fiction . . . [and] Edwardian sex-role stereotypes' (Henke 1990, 127). Molly's explicit textuality transgresses the boundaries that are at stake (Henke 1990, 127). Molly performs as literary critic, effecting the deconstruction of modes of female representation and exploitation to be found in the literature that Henke identifies. The connection between literary representation of a supposedly realistic kind and the reality of the everyday is foregrounded by Molly, with regard to the phallogocentric discursive and specifically textual oppression of women. In her recitation of Boylan's adventures, Molly's critique of male narrative reduced to issues of colonisation and penetration turns Boylan into everyman in her proto-feminist reading: 'because thats all they want out of you with that determined vicious look in his eye.' (*U* 18. 152–3) Throughout this passage, Molly shifts between personal pronouns almost endlessly in an erasure of the phallic selfhood of the male individual through the registration of the concomitance of masculine desire. As Henke acknowledges, 'she acknowledges the impersonality and sadism of . . . sexual attentions' (1990, 136).

Yet Molly is being much more than merely negatively critical, seeking a rejection of all men in her discourse. Were she only this, then she would be, herself, merely the negative half of the phallocentric structure that her text finally militates against. It should be borne in mind that Molly is a performer and entertainer, a singer of particularly sentimental songs, popular during the late Victorian and Edwardian periods. Such songs, their lyrics, abounded with typical representations of women (Michael Furey and 'The Lass of Aughrim' spring immediately to mind).[10] Her relationship with Boylan is a double one, and his 'enjoyment' of Molly is of the same order as his presentation of her as object for public consumption on the stage. He thus procures her both publicly and privately. Yet her remembering is another kind of performance beyond the limits of Boyle's control; she dismembers Boylan through re-membering her own subjectivity in a performative fashion which shows an awareness of the strategies of Boylan's exploitation. Molly thus demystifies Boylan's roles, as entrepreneur and lover. This militation against fixed roles is equally both sexual and textual, and we should bear this in mind if we are to comprehend the extent to which Joyce attempts to recognise the extent to which conceptual, discursive (un)thought models of identity dominate our intersubjective world. This can be pursued further with a reading of the end of 'Penelope' in order to read how, through an internal critique of the textual overdetermination of sexuality, Molly seeks to write a re-vision of that space that is not just a new binary structure of dominance and oppression, but is, importantly, an opening up of the site of heterosexual, heterotextual relationships.

Molly gives way in the final 'pages' of her speech and thought to the language of flowers, to the iconography of female sexuality *as flower*.[11] She unfolds and reveals the ecstasy of *jouissance*, utterable only in the excess that is promised by the reiteration of the doubled yes, a doubling which promises and affirms more to come. She blooms, she is blooming, and the pages open like a flower, like a new bloom for the reader. This free-play between textuality, the enticement that the text offers up to the reader, and sexuality, which tempts and has tempted more than Bloom, is a form of a remarkable foreplay also, foreplay with the promise of an always deferred climax-to-come, a climax the 'Penelope' chapter leaves us on the edge of in those multiple yesses. For what blooms is not the same old story of a dead flower (Virag) and a withering Bloom, tracing a by-now redundant Homeric trail. What is in bloom, what is 'in Bloom', is the life that Molly puts into him, that which she gives birth to: Bloom as the living memory of the possibility of the moment of passionate affirmation, an affirmation beyond the stallion-like attentions of Boylan and those like him who reduce all intimate relationships either to a forced textual encounter or to some otherwise violently dialectical struggle.

There is in Molly's memory a bloom/ing of other stories, of stories-to-come which are not dead myths. There is her bloom, her 'Bloom'. Molly blooms herself; her blossoming, her return to her sexuality as the figuring of a flower attests to her being a bloom, her being Molly Bloom, Bloom's Molly. Bloom's Molly (she does) because she is Molly Bloom, due to the living trace of memory. Molly doubly affirms the spiritual-sexual connectedness with Bloom, through her re-marking of her self as a Bloom, and also as a bloom. She refigures herself in the foreplay without climax or conclusion that traces the repeated folds of an unfixed identity and an unfinished narrative. Molly offers the potential for another story that will not attain closure. She offers her self as an other, as other of the other, erasing her self, while leaving the supplementary echoes of her voice (yes, yes, yes) in the reiterated affirmation of the dissolution of the boundaries between text and sex. And in the moment and movement of that dissolution she traces the space where 'ex' – as in sex, as in text, as in that X which draws attention to the place under erasure – marks the spot. Yet it does not. Because the ex re-marks that which is beyond, thereby placing under erasure the fixable moment through the gesture of affirmation.

In having said that Molly says Yes, in saying that she is Bloom's, I would not want to say that she admits to her being his in any trite sense of marital possession. I am not saying that she is merely a married woman who accepts her position and thereby recuperates herself into an oppressed position. In saying that she is Bloom's, I read her as also saying that she offers us through her affirmative dissonance an other Bloom, a new way of telling the story of the man, a way which breaks with the old phallocentric imperative in conventional narrative, from Homer onwards. Molly *is* a narrativisation, as well as an act of self-becoming-writing, telling a story that is her own. Furthermore, her voice is multiple: it affirms its own expression and resistance to definition through its multiplicity. Molly is also, as Colin MacCabe argues 'the destroyer of phallic pretensions of . . . suitors' (MacCabe 1979, 132). This brings us to a line of Molly's, where she has rejected all those fictional Mollys that have been brought to her by a man. Molly says:

I dont like books with a Molly in them like that one he brought me.

(*U* 18. 657–8)

Molly does not like those male textual representations of the female that are brought – and bought – by 'he'. Although we can assign a proper name to this 'he' it is also important to keep it up in the air, to see it as indicative of men, of Man, as, earlier, Boylan had become dissolved into all men, 'he' becoming 'they' as a general indictment and commentary on Molly's part (*U* 18. 152–3). Man is the one who buys and brings. But Molly rejects the deliveries that she neither desires nor believes, those representations of her self as something other than what she is, which cannot be defined anyway, certainly not by 'he'. Molly defies definition and thereby the limits of the representation of her body within a restricted and restrictive mode of production. And it is fascinating to note that, following this critical dismissal of books with a 'Molly' in them – which also will have included *Ulysses* up to the Molliloquy – Molly cites a specific example of a 'Molly' in literature, Moll Flanders, who is a whore, that most typically debased figure of female sexuality in male narrative, and the one most explicitly connected with male-dominated forms of economic exchange and commercial enterprise:[12]

> I dont like books with a Molly in them like that one he brought
> me about the one from Flanders a whore always shoplifting
> anything she could cloth and stuff yards of it
>
> (*U* 18. 657–9)

It is this debasement and recuperation of 'Mollys' into male
textuality that the Molliloquy disrupts and abandons in fragments,
while not simplistically giving up Bloom, only giving up, instead, a particular (per)version of the male.[13]

Which brings me to a possible 'final' point, a full stop that does
not effect closure but raises instead a question. Between 'Ithaca'
and 'Penelope' there appears the following:

●[14]

There is an apparent separation here which makes me want to
ask what are we witnessing? Is this the full stop as the end of
'his' story? Is this the declaration by Joyce of a margin or bor-
derline over which those having only the correct passport can
cross? And, if so, does the Molliloquy belong to the text, properly speaking? If not – and this not is big, an important resistance – where does it belong? Is it inside or outside the text? or
neither? or both?

The questions could proliferate endlessly and I do not pretend to have any answers; unlike the 'Ithaca' chapter which, in
examination fashion (are we back in Clongowes?) proposes perfectly exemplary answers, yet does not really answer anything
except the questions of the examination. Joyce proposes the end
of reading and the end of certifiable location in 'Ithaca', while
also demonstrating both the ends to which reading is put of-
ficially and the limits of types of knowledge. He demonstrates
through 'Ithaca' the purpose of a type of reading which, in the
wake of *Ulysses*, has no relevance. Hence – perhaps – the large
full stop, which could always be interpreted as an ink blot, the
random gesture of the pen refusing or defying translation. 'Ithaca'
ends with the mark, and also with a question: Where? This is
unanswerable. The question being asked is a multiple one, to do
with location, reference, citationality, topography. It leaves us

all at sea with no landmark, save the full stop which, in itself doesn't answer the question. The blot does not serve the same function as 'X'. Here is the spot – where? – and it is not marked by an 'X'. Location unknown, nothing that is mappable. Furthermore, the full stop marks off Molly, placing her in a relationship to the property of the text as being something improper. Her voices worry at boundaries, cutting into what we might want to define as the edges, ends, or endgames that are conventionally re-marked through the positioning of titles, and words such as 'book'. Her voices give access, as does her sexuality, to a space that is neither to be confined, nor defined in terms of lines, edges, borders that can be drawn around it. Like her playful textuality, her sexuality is a text-ile weaving, a weaving which both unravels and rewrites. It might be argued that the figure of Molly in bed is just one more figure of oppression, a denial of possibility; but this reading is still a male reading of Molly, a reduction of Molly to a Molly in a book, a Molly of the male pen. For Molly's bed is not only the place of sexuality. It is also the place of imagining, of flowering and Blooming-into-being of all possibilities of narrative, where endless stories bloom. Thus Molly resists; and, in breaking with the literary conventions of female oppression, desists also from the ideological imperatives of the realist textual frame. Molly's languages comprehend, make complex, and thus open up moments of blindness in the cultural logic of relationships, while simultaneously saying yes (yes, yes). This is not a sign of acquiescence to patriarchal mastery; rather it is, as David Farrell Krell has suggested, an appeal: 'the yes appeals to an other yes, the yes of an other' (1990, 303). In Molly, through Molly, and because of her doubly affirmative deconstructions, it is possible for to read the affirmation of the possibility for a community of discourse, and an ethical communication of that space-to-come where the voice of the other will speak.

Avital Ronell has suggested that 'it is Joyce who excites the hope that an explicit link might be forged between the call to the beyond and a maternal connection' (Ronell 1989, 21). With her image of Joyce as a telephone operator, Ronell's language transmits an ineluctable optimism; and why should this not be so, given the infectious enthusiasm that marks every Joycean sentence, and which comes to remark those who get caught up in that telephonic exchange that is engaged every time Joyce is read? *Ulysses* resists as many Homeric parallels as it invites, not least because it delegitimates the phallocentric epic mode of narrative production, by turning the focus of that mode onto all that is distinctly un-epic, the details of ordinary lives in a single day, otherwise unreported. In Joyce's text we encounter a thinking-otherwise as a non-structured form of agency. We experience, in Jacques Derrida's words, 'the experience of thought itself, its most essential and risky passage, in those places where the experience of thought is also poetic experience' (Lacoue-Labarthe 1989, 6). As *Ulysses* shows us, we can never, with absolute certainty, say to whom the thought belongs, who or what dictates the writing, or from where that writing is dictated. Stephen is no more finitely identifiable than are either Bloom or Molly.

I would suggest that, in relation to the question of identity, we read the affirmative and affirming optimism of *Ulysses* in all its questioning and open-endedness. It can best be read as a text that resists; but its resistance is neither a negation nor an opposition. It provides not merely a critique of oppressive structures from an oppositional situation, for the reasons already stated. To halt then, for the moment, with a reiteration, as a way not of ending but of opening up, and being opened up to other readings of Joycean affirmation, suggesting that we must always remind ourselves of a certain spirit, in Joyce, which is that of 'une tout autre écriture, une autre langue'

L'autre signe

(Derrida 1987: 137, 143)

This wholly other writing, this other language, this other signature or a signature of the other, is the Joycean trait, the trace of a poetics which cannot be codified. It surfaces through memory, across the surface of writing, and as the affirmative resistance to absolutely knowable identity.

Notes

1. The conference was 'Re: Joyce', held by the Department of English, at the University of Dundee (18–21 July 1996). A volume of essays from the conference is due to be published in 1997, under the title *Re: Joyce – Text • Culture • Politics*, ed. John Brannigan, Geoff Ward and Julian Wolfreys (Macmillan). Lucia Boldrini's article is not

included in this collection, as it is appearing in two other places in different forms. At the time of writing, I was unable to consult the printed versions, but would like to thank Lucia Boldrini for allowing me to quote her conference presentation.

2. This 'moving in and out' of which Attridge writes is similar in effect to that of the anamorph of Holbein's *The Ambassadors*, discussed in the introduction, above.

3. Cheyette offers a fascinating reading of Stephen's resistant thought processes which serve to challenge the myopic anti-semitism of men like Deasy (209–12). Paris is clearly connected to the question of Jewish identity in Stephen's thought as a place of cultural otherness, rather than racial otherness.

4. On this, see Cheyette (206–9).

5. It might be suggested that if fiction affirms itself as simulacrum and, in so doing, disorganises all oppositions and any subsequent teleology, then the fictive and its narrative qualities can never be said to reside 'in' the book; or, indeed, anywhere that could be termed 'in', 'inside', and so on. Fiction, the fictive, in its affirmation affirms itself to itself, and sidesteps *en passant* any locatable referent to 'inside' or 'outside'. Hence the importance of the figure of Paris, in this reading of Joycean textuality.

6. Memories of Egan in Paris, 'of Paris' as the first phrase has it, construct for Stephen yet another narrative of an other Irishman, Egan being, for Stephen, the other of the other, which complicates Stephen's identification of his other self.

7. The man in the macintosh is, perhaps, the figure of affirmative resistance *par excellence*. His identity is so multiply overdetermined, so highly indeterminate, yet so open to misunderstanding, misapprehension and misrepresentation, that nothing can ever be assumed about his identity with any certainy. The descriptions, thoughts and representations surrounding this figure are heavily inscribed with clichéd fictional traces. He is considered as a possible terrorist, an enigmatic flâneur, subject to the discursive remarks of mystery stories and cowboy fiction; his garment assumes the status of a proper name, which is misspelt; he is traced by the shadowy figures of bomb-makers, while his garment itself holds a teasing clue to identity in its name relevant to *Ulysses* as a whole. The action of *Ulysses* takes place mostly on 16 June, although, arguably, the last hours occur in the early morning of 17 June. This latter date is, coincidentally, the date on which the patent was obtained for the macintosh as a garment, made up of layers of cloth coated with india-rubber. Are we to make anything of this?

8. Making connections between textuality and sexuality through parapraxis, Jean-Michel Rabaté points out in that Joyce in this letter makes a gender slip by making 'Fleisch' masculine (it is a neuter word) (1991, 51).

9. On the subject of this 'scandalous' form of responsibility, I am drawing on an interview between Jacques Derrida, Ruth Robbins and myself in *Applying: to Derrida* (1996).

10. On the subject of popular songs in Joyce, and popular culture in general, see Cheryl Herr's comprehensive *Joyce's Anatomy of Culture* (1986).

11. On the subject of the flower, and flower-imagery, see, for example, Ewa Ziarek's, 'The Female Body, Technology, and Memory in "Penelope"' (1994, 264–87). Ziarek's essay reads in 'Penelope' a dialectic between organicism and technology, which, she argues, deploys another binary, that of private and public. She further argues that, out of this 'bifurcation' of desire, there emerges a 'certain nostalgia for "natural" sexual identity but also a promise that the organic female body might be a site of resistance to the mechanisation of public life' (265). The flowers which Molly remembers are located as being on the side of the organic, as is female language and the body. However, Ziarek does not read the organic without irony, seeing, after Cixous, Kristeva, Henke and others, subversive possibilities for Molly's sexuality, as a writing which disturbs 'the mastery of male authorship' (274).

12. One of Molly's many interesting references is the one to the 'jersey lily' (*U* 18. 1148), which connects flowers to another entertainer, Lily Langtry, the mistress of Edward VII.

13. The pun here is Lacan's, who is playing on the French echo of the Father's name (père) in the first syllable of the French/English 'perversion' (1987, 45).

14. The full stop or period has recently been omitted from Declan Kiberd's Penguin edition of *Ulysses* (1992), although, in the annotated version of this edition, Kiberd is generous enough to provide the dot in the notes following the text (*U* student's edn, 1180). Despite taking it out of the text, Kiberd does offer an interpretation of the mark as possible conclusion to 'mathematical demonstration', the 'extinction of the literary tradition . . . or the end proper of the book's narrative'. Kiberd goes on to note that '[t]he final question of *Ithaca* 'Where?' was answered by a large full-stop' (*U* student's edn, 1180). Kiberd fails to explain this editorial decision, and it seems to remain open to interpretation as to whether or not the dot is to be included.

5

Meshes of the Afternoon: the dissonant identities of avant-garde film and problems of interpretation

The gaze sees itself –
. . . .
The gaze I encounter . . . is, not a seen gaze, but a gaze imagined by me in the field of the Other.

Jacques Lacan

Cinema, Jacques Derrida suggests in semi-improvised manner (in Ken McMullen's film *Ghost Dance*), is the art of letting ghosts come back. Following this proposition, we can expand the definition of the art of cinema, describing projection in all its possible senses, its possible meanings and identities, as the art of letting ghosts come back. Projection lets ghosts speak and write to us, on us, through us. In order to understand this, let's return briefly to Chapter 2: what Charlotte Perkins Gilman's writing suggests is an apparent unravelling and unfolding of a possible site of articulation which resists recuperation. *The Yellow Wallpaper* is perhaps a map, certainly a topography of paradoxically unmappable dimensions, of experience, onto which is projected the affirmation beyond experience of an otherness which is not to be reduced through definition.

Thus there are readable certain areas of engagement, figures which tempt a certain desire for definition, yet which affirm their irreducible condition. As much as we are tempted to interpret, we must learn to resist such gestures. Projection in *The Yellow Wallpaper* defies the dialectic structures of reasonable/unreasonable, sanity/madness, normality/hysteria which conventionally

133

frame interpretation of the text. The figures in the wallpaper and the narrator of *The Yellow Wallpaper* are projections-otherwise which engage the dialectic possibilities, tempting us into interpretation according to the limits of such paradigms, while voicing projected identities which do not acknowledge such limits, yet all the time speaking otherwise of material experience. And what our reading might bring is either the confirmation of that experience, in which case we reproduce the experience by determining – reading – behaviour as reasonable/unreasonable, logical or hysterical; or else we read with the projection as an affirmative resistance to the imposed determination of experience. We respond in the act of reading to the event of dissonant identities which are always in process of becoming.

Projection, then, is a ghostly writing, a possible affirmation of an other, haunting voice, of other voices and other ghosts which suggestively communicate. They affirm in by-passing closure, suggesting projection as an act of becoming as part of a series of gestures, all of which are readable as belonging to a heterodox community of resistances. Such voices, such projections and such spectres, offer the reader interested in hearing them, viewing them and reading them, weaves, traces, filaments, meshes; they project a range of identities never quite at home, never at one with themselves or with the assumed identity of the viewer. Projection offers a 'becoming-spectral' which is nothing other than the dissonance within the idea of a single, unified identity.

And if the voice which speaks in silence through the ghostly image is one other possible projection, what can we say of the places of memory and image? Can we not suggest that these are also projections of affirmative resistance, the affirmative projections of resistant, dissonant identities? Can these also be said to be projections, projections of the constant becoming of identity, identity always other than itself in the process of becoming, and therefore dissonant? What can we project onto, through, the gaps which open up and out as the necessity of projection? What can we witness being projected? If projection opens out, do we not then begin to read resistance, once again, as an indirect refusal of either absolute meaning or stable identity? Projection, we might say, is the *en passant* gesture.

In a different manner, we will see similar possibilities in Maya Deren's first film, *Meshes of the Afternoon* (1943, 14 mins; in collaboration with Alexander Hamid). The film resists interpretive closure while affirming dissonance as key to the becoming of radical identity. If we comprehend this we can see how the film can be engaged in at least two distinct, yet interrelated (meshing) areas. The first area is that of interpretation and the problems encountered – the ensnaring difficulties – by traditional reading activities in their engagement with the text. In foregrounding what has been a relatively unexplored area of *Meshes* that is its problematic modes of signification, I shall be arguing against delimiting readings which treat the film merely as a 'puzzle' (both Deren's own word, in her 'Letter to James Card' [Deren 1977, 230], and the Oedipal nature of reading practices which aim for textual closure through the solving of what are identified as textual riddles, paradoxes, contradictions and inconsistencies). At the same time, I shall be arguing against statements found in Deren's own theoretical writings in order to provide a *caveat* against readings which are seemingly structured around another form of exegetical totalisation, that of authorial intentionality. As I shall show, there are irreconcilable contradictions and tensions between theory and practice. These create a tension or strain forcing open lacunae – meshes of the mesh – into which the anti-interpretive analyst can insert him/herself, and through which the film may be read affirmatively as projecting itself in the event of affirmative resistance.

I also look, throughout the chapter, at the problem of interpretation by looking at possible context's for the film's narrative identities. Here I will be introducing the relationship between *Meshes* and its discursive, cultural and, possibly, historical contexts and looking at how the text intersects culturally through certain pro-filmic signifiers and technical aspects with the Hollywood system. I will be arguing that the construction of the text is entangled with codes and signifying systems which are recognisable as belonging to dominant cinematic practices, such as *film-noir* and B-movie thrillers. Certainly, Deren's term 'puzzle' invites us to place *Meshes* in an oblique relationship to the construction of *noir* narratives, a suggestion borne out by the codes referred to above. By their appropriation and insertion into the avant-garde, these recognisable codes are used to establish what is apparently a dialectical process in the diegesis of the film-text, a quasi-dialectic between Hollywood mainstream and the avant-garde, and between text and viewer, which the film ultimately is readable as side-stepping. The quasi-dialectic is embraced as a means of moving beyond the oppositional tension, whereby 'elements', momentarily and provisionally recognisable as serving a pastiche-function, affirm their own irreducibly textual status through a wayward rewriting of the clichéd elements of typical narrative-oriented techniques. As will become clear, the dialectic is not a dialectic at all, but a form of semantic erasure through an excess of non-significant signifiers, codes, images. Hence the term 'quasi-dialectic'. The dialectic is never simply that, but a self-conscious and self-reflexive, oblique deployment of apparently concatenated and overlapping images which affirm nothing other than projection itself, projection into the *mise-en-abyme*.

The (apparent) quasi-dialectic of *Meshes* can be approached if the text is engaged with, and understood as having, formal elements in common with aspects of modernist literary poetics. My reason for such a frame of reference is not merely to appropriate a particular discourse from literary studies in order to recuperate *Meshes* into certain aesthetic traditions. Rather, this strategy is a necessary ploy which serves to avoid a restatement of positions from within a merely dialectical paradigm. And, as Colin MacCabe makes clear in *James Joyce and the Revolution of the Word*, the strategies of modernism are not merely aesthetic but have political and ideological importance for all forms of discourse on a revolutionary scale (MacCabe 1979).[1] Certainly, Deren's writings on film (however much we may be critical of them in relation to Deren's film practice) are informed by politicising gestures similar to those of modernists on the political left. Furthermore, the relationship between *Meshes* and mainstream Hollywood cinema of the 1940s and 1950s is somewhat analogous to the relationship between the texts of Joyce, Eliot *et al.* and the Classic Realist Text of the Nineteenth Century, as described by MacCabe. Even as Eliot and Joyce draw on a dominant tradition in ironic modes and modes which utilise pastiche for the purpose of providing new textual forms, so the discourses and structures of Deren's film seemingly refer to or are drawn from a dominant tradition that the film-text is readable as breaking away from (the modernists' texts being the product of another historical avant-garde which moves beyond the dialectic through affirmative reinvention which, initially and ultimately, refuses direct recognition of its hitherto dominant sources).

Deren situates the problem of the film as 'puzzle' or enigma to be solved as an ironic gesture toward the viewer. In doing so, she develops the avant-garde film *through* the appropriation of the filmic enigma so popular in *film noir*. However, in film noir, the enigma can be and often is established quickly, even though it takes the rest of the film to solve it (as in the question of who kills who and why at the beginning of *Mildred Pierce*, or why a woman is running barefoot down a road in the middle of night in the opening of *Kiss Me Deadly*). Deren's film is the enigma, an enigma without solution. Avant-garde film constructs a different identity, performing the difference of and within identity, an identity constantly reformed through an excess of differences, whereby the rhythm and temporality of enigma assumes the entire space of the film, without the suggestion that there might be a solution (its only possible suggestion being that the solution to the enigma is that there is no solution). *Meshes* never promises this.

Instead, *Meshes of the Afternoon* can be read as affirming Derrida's proposition concerning the ghostly art of cinema. It is nothing if it is not a haunted and haunting text. *Meshes* is haunted most affirmatively by its very own self-referential traces and the constant movement of difference. Its movement is composed of a series of events and scenarios which are played over and over again: an arm drops a poppy, and disappears. Someone walks along a path. This figure, seen initially as a series of shadows and a pair of feet, turns up some stairs, to enter a house. Objects are observed, apparently from the point of view of the figure's gaze. The figure moves around the house, eventually coming to rest, to watch a scene apparently similar to the one we have already seen, and subsequently played out a number of times. Each time the scene occurs again there are slight changes, changes of detail, differences of observation and camera angle. As these reiterations occur, the previous scenes are folded into the current narrative rhythm. Each figure from every event, whether shadow or body, part or whole, comes to occupy a position in all the succeeding variations and scenes, whether as agent and viewer, both simultaneously. It would be a misreading of the film to see the figures in question as *either* viewer *or* agent. This reading would be to impose a structure against which the film ceaselessly mediates. It erases the opposition and, in so doing, is available to a reading which understands a concomitant erasure between the diegetic figure or event, and the extra-diegetic event of watching the film or being a viewer.

The differential play keeps occurring until the point where three of the four figures are seated around a table, the fourth apparently asleep in a chair. Each figure appears to resemble the others exactly (all are played by Maya Deren). However, whether or not these figures are *really* the same figure is kept absolutely open. Each figure is given equal importance, or lack thereof, within the filmic events, as *both* participant and audience, object of the gaze and would-be analyst from whom the gaze appears to emanate; which perspective is nearly always shared (with the constant suggestion of a somewhat dissonant parallax) with the audience beyond the events within the film. None of these figure-positions are kept separate. None are privileged as a source or origin, a generator of narrative. Similarly, each scene in its iterable condition (always already becoming the other to itself and to its other productions) reinforces the impression that no scene is separable; no scene has a discrete identity, to which it is true. They recall one another endlessly, without there being the suggestion that temporally one event or scene is prior to any other, or that one scene may taken as the original source from which the other scenes spring as variations despite the arbitrary order imposed by the film sequence. The constantly iterable *mise-en-scène* suggests and affirms that the viewer has entered into the middle of something, the dissonant multiplicity of which cannot be damped down into a meaningful whole. The folding and weaving of events resist stable identities and meanings, as narrative limits are transgressed and repeatedly erased in acts which affirm multiplicity. The events project onto, through, and beyond the other narrative events. And these other events are always the other of events which are already other. Projection projects projection. The voices or writings of projection multiply, disseminate and complicate dissonant identities, thereby affirming them.

The film is thus is nothing other than a series of continual disturbances throughout and across the field of identity, even as it appears to invoke dream logic, for example. The dissonance of the film is composed out of a resistance to interpretive depth as the variations without a theme come to seem a series of endlessly folded surfaces which mesh with one another. Even within a single moment of the film temporal movement is different for different objects or figures, so that one figure, hooded and cloaked, appears to move slowly, while another figure runs at full speed after the mysterious hooded character, a series of jump cuts between figures showing that the running figure merely covers the same ground a number of times. At other moments a key falls in slow motion down steps, while feet chase hastily after it. Film space and film time create dissonance through the free play and interweaving of a seemingly endless temporal and spatial movement of moments of becoming – for the figures and for the viewer equally. There is no present in *Meshes of the Afternoon*. There is only the always reciprocal pull and push of past becoming future and future returning to the past, past and future as events of cross-projection, projecting incidentally, *en passant*. Surfaces fold across one another, collapsing the illusions of depth and the present as the condition of affirmative projection.

Deren's *Meshes* plays, then, with the possibilities of projection in all senses of that word, encompassing the aesthetic and the technical, and yet also toying with interpretation and experience in relation to potential constructions and interpretations of identity.

In this sense, *Meshes of the Afternoon* shares its foregrounding of dissonant articulations through the forcing or skewing of recognisable figures with Tsukamoto's film *Tetsuo* (discussed in the introduction to this book). The apparently dialectic structure is always problematised, therefore; its mock-use confounds interpretation and makes difficult clear-cut decisions, either about the identities of figures within the film or about the possible identity and meaning of the film-text. This problematised and self-problematising structure, and the troubling of that structure, opens up the space for the projection of the other. *Meshes* plays such an affirmative opening through the constant reduplication and over-projection between figures in the confused roles of agent and observer, participating in and simultaneously watching unexplained, apparently recurring actions (the collapse of depth is also temporal collapse). Thus the multiple figures can be seen not as real, but as traces, projections, inscriptions in, through and on the filmic text, figures which write (on) the (surface of the) film as the affirmation of dissonant identities. The figures serve the projective function of inscribing identity's otherness. No successive scene amounts to a reading of previous scenes. There is no greater knowledge, no further revelation or resolution of any perceived enigma, provided by reiteration. No depth of narrative is produced, other than the depthless depth of the abyss. Instead, interpretation, meaning and identity are inhibited because the film plays itself out in a series of projective, project-ing surfaces, each being the event that is the film's dissonant writing of difference. The figures of narrated narrator and nar-rating narrator multiplied four-fold in the image of the same 'character' inhibit interpretation.

Clearly then, the question with which *Meshes* toys is always one which acknowledges culturally comprehensible referents concerning possible identities (as *The Yellow Wallpaper* had toyed with the discourse on cultural, narrative and textual construc-tions of madness), albeit temporarily, whilst citing those disson-antly, in order to foreground a textual methodology which partakes of devices of (non-)reading, and citation otherwise. Meaning is thus deferred as the referent is shown dissonantly, always al-ready in a condition of being destabilised. The film constantly articulates the possibility of having interpretive depth, only to defer such depth in its play of reiterations and the excessive folding of surfaces, as in the film's use of mirrors in the place of faces. The enigmatic hooded, cloaked figure has a mirror for a face which only reflects light. The male figure who enters towards the end of the film, is seen reflected in mirrors twice, the second time his image shattered and replaced with the image of the beach. Identity is thus a plane or surface determined by the gaze of an other.

Despite *Meshes'* overt display of potentially interpretable im-ages, such as numerous 'Freudian icons' (Sitney 1970, 6) – the constantly reappearing knife and its interchangeable double, the key, or even the poppy, which at one point is (apparently) sugges-tively placed over the genital area of one of the female figures – there exists for the viewer a transgressive semiosis and unfixity of apparently conventional signification (which images or types of images are still comprehensible seemingly as signifiers be-longing to a conventional practice), which mark the film-text as a product of an avant-garde. There are images which appear and disappear for no narrative reason: the arm at the beginning of the film which drops the poppy onto the sidewalk. The series of individual footsteps, each of which falls on a different landscape, the beach, a gravel pile, long grass, paving stone, and then car-pet. We may construct a narrative of continuous walking, a joined-up movement through a single space at a single time, but this is to ignore the differing contexts of each step. Suggesting the se-ries of disparate acts as a single act is, however one way of making what we see 'make sense', unless of course we try to describe what we have just seen in another fashion. Given that there appear to be (at least) four figures, all of whom look the same, then one footstep may well belong to each of these figures.

The film may be recuperated, of course, if one is tempted (by the film?) to limit one's reading of the text to an interpretation of certain of the images and 'visual metaphors' which seem to suggest or invite a psychoanalytic reading (see the discussion of the mouth and sausage scene from *Tetsuo* in the book's introduction). We may take the footsteps described above as indicative of the fragmentation or split of the identity of a single character, and this may well be supported by seeing the four identical figures as versions of the same identity. Such an exegetical activity would, however, attempt to impose reason, unity and order, from a supposedly stable or ideal location, such as the viewer's identity or 'the gaze' (the film's affirmative dissonance troubles the viewer's identity equally, albeit in a more indirect manner). It would seek to hierarchise the filmic discourses into a binary order of importance and non-importance or relevance within a particular reading practice which can only search for those elements which its programme recognises and acknowledges. Such a reading constantly redefines its own manoeuvres in terms of already established reading processes, which it either follows in the wake of, or against which it establishes itself in opposition. The film resists all such hierarchical ordering of its images.

However as we have previously suggested, *Meshes* is so constructed that either everything in the film is of equal significance or of no significance whatsoever. Do we choose certain scenes and not others? Because something seems to be repeated a number of times do we accord this greater or lesser significance? The problems of a limited and limiting interpretive activity are double fold: not only would such a reading process obviously be working still within a predetermined structure, predetermined that is as the *a priori* reason for the reading practice; also, any such reading practice would necessarily tend to ignore those referents and other 'non-relevant' traces. Any rigorous reading must, of necessity, ignore the boundaries of particular professional disciplines, if it is to begin any form of critical activity which allows for all forms of dissonance to be sounded or cited, as part of a more general act of affirmative resistance, one which mobilises whatever traces might be to hand in a manner which both respects the play of those traces whilst ignoring the knowing competence which goes with domesticated forms of academic and theoretical practice. Maya Deren's film is an important text for opening up the possibilities of such readings, because it challenges competent reading processes which seek to assert stable identities through calming dissonance as a knowable and limitable quality through its play, its resistances, its affirmations, and its dissonant citational iterability, in relation to dominant film and narrative practices. And it does this precisely through the projection of the already problematised image of the female.

Another self-problematising area of this text with regard to reading practices is its ending. The last scenes of the film break with the reiterated patterns, even though they assume similar rhythms. The hooded, mirror-faced figure already mentioned is replaced by a man who, unlike Leopold Bloom, holds a key (we could be forgiven for misunderstanding his intrusion, seeing him as holding *the* key). His is an apparently solid figure, his shadows minimised. He enters the house to find the woman in the chair, seemingly dead, covered in shards of glass and strings of kelp. The woman had just been seen breaking a mirror with the previously mentioned knife, in which mirror had been reflected the man's face (the man having appeared to have been in the room, where there is only the mirror; does the mirror then reveal the woman's face as the man's, hence the reason for its being broken?). The mirror having been broken, the face dispersed and displaced, the beach and waves are revealed through the broken looking-glass. This had occurred in the bedroom; now the woman is in the chair, head back, eyes open, gazing at nothing apparently. Why are the shards of glass scattered around the armchair in the lounge, when the mirror – or at least a mirror – had been broken on the bed upstairs? And why the seaweed, unless the breaking of the mirror as the attempted destruction of the suddenly revealed male identity had caused some kind of drowning for female identity?

In the face of all this, even the most rigorous anti-interpretive critic might be swayed by Maya Deren's pronouncement of that closure in the 'Letter to James Card', where she states that *Meshes* is a film concerned with suicide (Deren 1977, 226). The problem which interpretation faces is that a narrative solution cannot be formed which convinces. As P. Adams Sitney pertinently points out, even such a meaning as one suggested by Deren is suspended; the reality of the suicide remains ambiguous (Sitney 1970, 6). As the use of mirrors – and the knife blade which also acts as a mirror – in the film suggests, and the broken mirror seems to back up, identity is only ever a refracted surface, a somewhat distorted projection, subject to the gaze of the other, an identity only when read by another whose identity cannot be known; identity awaits interpretation and yet is always open to misinterpretation. Breaking the surface to discover depth only banishes the plane of identity, on which on possible identity is projected in the act of reading or viewing. There is nothing beyond the looking glass. The point here is that, given the contradictions between the written word and the filmic text, and given the affirmative resistances across the filmic text, which become so clearly mapped as discursive lacunae, critics should be wary of statements – especially those of the author and their own – which attempt to fill the gaps.

The presence of gaps, or rather the presence of absence – 'mesh' can mean both the network or the holes between the string – points to the play, the give and take, of difference.[2] It is this articulating torque of deferral and differentiation, in which *Meshes* partakes; and it is this possibly infinite, excessive dissemination of the sign beyond polysemy that refuses the construction of a filmic meta-language; the critic should therefore be wary of exactly that kind of analysis which leads to closure (given the Freudian framework with which I am indirectly playing in this chapter, the reading gesture being described here might resemble significantly what Freud himself termed countertransference). The reader who reads for both affirmation and resistance need not be wary of the lack of a meta-language, because although the film-text might not seem to address women in any apparently positive manner, reading ambiguity and equivocation can be a more positive interpretive gesture than focusing, seeking, desiring a specific (implicitly monolithic) discourse.

The example of the multiple imaging of several Maya Derens in *Meshes of the Afternoon* is interesting for the ambiguity it provides when discussed under the *aegis* of the debate about the filmic exploitation of the specular female and the discursive desocialisation of women concomitant with such an objectifying strategy. The multiplicity of Mayas simultaneously projected on the screen appears comprehensible as the performance of a quasi-modernist fragmentation and pluralisation of subjectivity and identity. Also there is performed, projected, the denial of unitary consciousness or subjectivity which, historically, it has been the dominant project of both filmic and literary realism to promote. Thus the multiple projection is not merely an aesthetic and technical device, but also serves to project the female image as a projective and affirmative image beyond the limits of definition, and also, importantly, beyond a recuperative critical gesture which *is* recuperative precisely because to reads multiplicity as meaningful, through the trope of polysemy. This affirmation of multiple female signification, inferring an equally multiple presence always elsewhere but never merely *there*, resists interpretive closure, though not through the direct opposition of a deliberately constructed oppositional female character; Deren's multiple images pass by oppositional locations and locutions, resisting recuperation simply by ignoring the possibility of the oppositional space.

Furthermore, the female figures are not endowed with personalities in the conventional sense. These are not 'characters' enacted or endowed with apparent verisimilitude, whether psychological, cultural or social, except for the outward signs of clothing and so on. There is nothing about these figures which is anything other than a surface of signs. There are no psychological features which act either as mimetic markers of the 'reality' of the figure or as a means of promoting narrative coherence. They are not given emotional depth. They are characters, inscriptions, traces, without 'character'. Furthermore, the multiplicity of Mayas – those behind, as well as in front of, the camera, are also implied, *projected*, as editor, author, camera-person, and so on – project the implicit sounding and citing of the affirmative possibility of female identities and agencies, as figures and events of a writing which inscribes the erasure of a programmed female identity imposed from an external source. There is the potential for reading a world of women moving in independent, unpredictable, *unprogrammable* ways, engaging and meshing with social, cultural and narrative structures in a dissonant fashion which cannot be anticipated ahead of the movement. In *Meshes* the multiple female figure is not yet one more recitation of the women's conventional objectification within realist narrative structures, but belongs instead to what is potentially a feminist poetics – and politics – of refusal, a projective poetics without programme, a poetics which is absolutely idiomatic, singular and yet iterable. And this refusal or resistance is bound up with the refusal to present the illusion of presence (presence for some-one, presence as the guarantee of the viewer's subjectivity) or to construct, in the words of Jonathan Dollimore (albeit in another context), a 'telos of harmonic integration' (Dollimore 1984, 63).

It may be asked, of course, in what sense, then, does it matter that the figure is female? It matters because the female projec-tion of affirmative resistance can be understood as a projection of the other which does not await the coming of some subject or master discourse – the male gaze – which can make the projec-tion, the image, the 'character', supposedly meaningful. To reiter-ate: 'Character' here suggests, as elsewhere in this chapter, the inscriptive trace, rather than 'personality'; it suggests the writ-ing of the other on the surface of identity which the other comes to inscribe or project on and across me, the person who I name as 'I' for example. The female projection affirms its irreducibility to a single personality by being unpredictable, while leaving its mark, as the mark of the other, on identity in a dissonant and troubling fashion.

There is another shot in *Meshes* that marks the intersection between the manipulations of the female image by an avant-garde modality, and the question of the (im)possibility of interpreta-tion (these meshes – of the film-text and my own analytic dis-course – can be seen to be growing into an ever more entangled web of discourses; such is the refusal of the film to accede to any particular set of 'truths'). The image in question is that of Deren's shadow,[3] early in the film. Shadows are absolutely cru-cial to *Meshes*. Understanding their importance as projections, ghosts, writing-events or writing-effects is vital in acknowledg-ing how the text affirms and resists. The shadows write and haunt the condition of the film itself, unfolding for us the film as a projective text composed entirely of surfaces. *Meshes of the After-noon* plays with a textile of shadows – hands stretching, torsos halting, legs running, shadow-fingers apparently grasping for a fallen poppy – as gestures which tempt interpretive activity, yet which show both the nature of film projection in its production of the illusion of a 'reality'. The shadow fingers will never be able to grasp the flower. Thus the shadows as projections, as possible and seemingly plausible signifiers appear to be inviting us to create meanings for them, to produce a sense of depth out of the surface effect. But is this not how all narrative traces work? for example, isn't this precisely the structural gambit of the classic realist text or film noir, where the reader/viewer is invited to respond by seeing the world behind the word, or to perform and construct hidden meanings and hidden identities out of puzzles?

The shadow, anatomically clearly that of a woman, is projected onto a wall. It might be argued that such an image defines women exclusively by sexual or biological difference. However, the shadow posits a dubious specularity offering an ambiguous double writing – and therefore a doubled, dissonant reading – of the female image. Difference comes into play once again in the comprehension of the signifying process. The shadow is itself a signifier of the female and not the woman (nor her image) at all. That which is signified is deferred by the signifying practice of cinema. The image of the shadow self-consciously foregrounds the nature of filmic projection, whereby an image on celluloid – filmic inscription – is presented as the phenomenological other that is absent, and signified as already absent by the presence of the trace. Thus the shadow's shadow takes on the status of the 'structure of the placement in abyss/[l]a structure de la mise en abyme' (Derrida 1984, 50/51), where the process of textuality is represented *within* the text as the affirmation of a purely textual signifier (how could it be anything else? certainly not a stable referent giving access to an even more stable 'reality'), announcing textuality and the repetition of the scene. Yet all the same, it is a repetition with a difference, being, as it is, a singular reiteration. The image of the shadow is presented as projection in the projected text, with the wall being the screen within the screen. In the act of displacement as a metonymic trace of filmic signification there occurs a jarring trope for all that we watch but which we cannot read with any clarity. In the words of Jacques Derrida, 'Il y va d'un débordement de la signature/It has to do with an overflowing of signature' (Derrida 1984, 80/81). The self-reflexivity of signification precludes translation/interpretation through its own ineluctable plenitude. The shadow signs the play with identity, signing affirmative resistance itself, otherwise. The shadow sign is the signature of an absolutely impersonal signature, a signifier in a realm of potentially infinite semiosis placing final semantic value in suspension. The overflow empties all possible value. The shadow is only the shadow of a woman by virtue of the fact that the viewing subject is constructed by the Hollywood context of other filmic and pictorial codes to recognise a certain absent specularity (how can specularity be constituted in absence, when it is specifically a signifying system for the promotion of the illusion of presence?). What the projection should remind us of is *its own construct as projection*. Beyond and before the illusion of reality, an objectified fetishised female 'reality' constructed for the God-like eye/I of the male subject through the tricks of perspective, the image of the shadow in *Meshes* plays with the meaning it refuses to assign. Spatial and temporal referents are closed down as the *mise-en-abyme* forestalls *mise-en-scène*; shadow – or the image of a shadow – on a wall inside light and shadow on the screen. 'Inside' cannot exist, neither can 'outside', merely pure filmic projection, endless textuality which itself places *sous rature* the codes of the reference it employs, *at the very moment that it employs them*. Thus we have a moment of overflowing dissemination that is, quite literally, inconceivable from the point of view of any conventional exegetical process. Such an excessive inscription might be mistaken, Derrida wryly hints, for 'style', the arch-referent of *authorial trace* (Derrida 1984, 50). Deren's writings show that such a trace is clearly not intentional, nor should it be mistaken as such.

In her article, 'The Point of Self-Expression in Avant-Garde Film', Pam Cook suggests that avant-garde film making is essentially a vehicle for individual self-expression (Cook 1978, 275). She qualifies her initial idealist statement by historically locating this 'romantic' vision of personal film production as part of 'New American Cinema after the Second World War' (1978, 275). Although made in 1943 (before the period cited by Cook), *Meshes of the Afternoon* is a text available to us as belonging to the mode of 'individual expression'. Deren's first film was *Meshes*, and she continued to produce films throughout the period described by Cook. Concomitant with this is Deren's output of theoretical writings. I mention this in relation to Cook's article because there are moments in Deren's writings which prefigure Cook's own analysis. From what I have stated it may be inferred that there is a certain similarity and unity between the written and filmic texts of Maya Deren. This however is not the case. Rather, there is a marked dissimilarity – a gap, or dissonance between identities – between texts, and this is rendered visible by Deren's attempts in writing to project her somewhat self-conscious image of the individual artist while at the same time prohibiting the possible plurality of meanings that the film-texts appear to keep in play.

In the opening pages of 'Cinema as an Art Form', Deren develops what might be considered a polemic against the Hollywood factory. In quasi-Marxist terms, she writes of the 'monstrous division of labour' and the making of an 'assembly line product' (Deren 1978, 255). Her own position is far less radical than might be first thought:

> Intrinsic integrity is possible only when the individual who conceives the work remains its prime mover until the end.
>
> (Deren 1978, 255)

What appears at first to be a materialist argument is quickly mediated by this presentation of the romantic artist in isolation, in control of the art form. Many other criticisms can be levelled at Deren's writings, not least the deification of the artist pointed to above, and the esoteric vagueness of discourse made apparent by the choice of words and terms such as 'creative' and 'experience' (Deren 1978, 255) 'necessary pulse' and 'meaningfully' (Deren 1978, 69). Although there is not enough space here to discuss all of the problems in depth, I will point to major sites of trouble in the texts.

There are two fundamental problems with the written texts, and these problems certainly arise in any attempt to recuperate 'Maya Deren' for specific, narrow ideological purposes. Firstly, Deren writes of the camera's 'indiscriminate' or 'absolute fidelity', and the presentation by the camera of the 'innocent arrogance of an objective fact' (Deren 1978, 60, 63, 65). In what appears, somewhat paradoxically, to be an almost Barthesian 'Death-of-the-Author' gesture – 'this exclusion of the artist' – there is inscribed in the text itself a counter-argument to the notion of the Romantic author/artist based on the apparent objectivity of filmic representation, the image being caught 'as it is'. What this, of course, does not take into account is the obvious and, therefore, overlooked 'fact' that *the camera is always positioned by someone*. A point of view, controlled by the operator of the camera, is what the viewing subject is being presented with. Given the degree to which artifice is demystified and subsequently foregrounded in *Meshes* – the shots of the four footsteps, each footfall occurring on a different, unidentified terrain, or the multiple Mayas provide obvious examples – the viewing subject cannot but help be archly aware of directorial/editorial intervention. Secondly, along with the individualist tendencies that are expressed elsewhere, there is inscribed a longing for the enunciation of 'truth' through the medium of film; Deren refers to film as though it were a picture puzzle, 'where, if you draw a continuous line . . . you end up with a picture' (Deren 1977, 230). Here is an argument for closure in film practice which is impossible to reconcile with the experience of watching or reading *Meshes*, as has been shown. The film affirms its own textuality and resists certain conventional interpretations as if by chance, despite the author's desires.

Thus Deren's film practice is seen to be at odds with her theorising. Using her own title against her, I turn again to the term(s) 'mesh/es'. Deren's writing attempts to bring together certain gears or cogs in an effort to close up, to mesh, the inscriptions of the pen with those of the camera. Such a tension of wheel against wheel soon forces them to move apart (as with any gear system, always based on *differential*), exposing the gaps in the network. Clearly, it is this engaging system which entangles the interpretive viewer. Yet at the same time, textual force arrests meaningful flow while foregrounding an intertextual/semiotic/ideological flow. Given that this is the case, it would be a more valuable task to examine *Meshes* with regard to the codes from which it is constructed, some of which have already been considered, in passing. I will turn now to an explanation of the text in relation to certain cultural and historical operations.

As already mentioned, there are particular codes in *Meshes of the Afternoon* that bear striking resemblances to codes belonging to dominant cinematic practices. Everything we see projected on the screen suggests possible *other* identities, or a play with identity: from the suggestion of the film as a puzzle, to the incidentals of location and clothing, the soundtrack, to the camera work, lighting, cutting and editing, every element of *Meshes* teases at the possibility of a knowable identity, or several knowable identities in the context of contemporary mainstream film narrative and production. Similarly, there are also noticeable signifying systems apparently belonging to an avant-garde modality. Yet neither practice or system is given any hierarchical precedence or valorisation, and it is this cultural intersection that is fruitful for analytical intervention. The film involves itself in an act of pre-emptive inversion, suggesting hybridity prior to the narrative of origins. Projecting itself across the surfaces of its own textual, cultural and technical references, it affirms its own textuality by projecting itself as being *between* filmic identities, becoming both and yet neither. It always already affirms its otherness as avant-garde *noir*.

Like *noir*, *Meshes* employs extreme lighting contrasts and chiaroscuro effects, oblique camera angles, repetition and enigma, maintained through technical intervention with temporality, and the synecdochic dispersal of the female body, already alluded to above in another context. There would again appear to be moments, therefore, of simultaneous collusion with and a departure from (a departure discernible as such due to the apparent textual privileging of a 'phantasy' paradigm rather than one that is realist) specific signifying systems. This noir-effect is achieved not only through the more obvious technical means but, once again, through the projection of shadows. We believe the shadow-torso to be female because of the hair and the breast; we see hands and feet, the nails of which are painted. Noir becomes rewritten by *Meshes* as a micro-text, its mysteries reduced to seemingly insignificant enigmas, almost instantaneously solvable. Apparently. Significance is reduced to a matter of observation, even though in the bigger picture observation will not lead us to a meaning or identity which brings with it resolution. The small details all project across and filter through consciousness as a play of and on surfaces, implying identities as a game of masquerades or charades. *Meshes* thus engages in and projects a ceaseless historically, culturally and discursively aware activity which determines that the text be encountered, not as a finished, hermetic product, but as on-going process of iterable, dissonant projection already described. The topography of the film is understandable as both terrain and aporia, a map on which locations are constantly erased and reinvented, as gaps are opened between ideological overdetermination (Hollywood) and radical textuality (the avant-garde). Textuality seeks constantly to arrest and displace the dominant modes of cinematic signification. To turn back to an earlier discussion as an illustration of the arresting process, the image of the shadow demonstrates how misleading is the 'philosophy of presence' (Eagleton 1978, 149) which articulates mainstream cinematic practice in the 1940s. The avant-

garde textual mode wrests an anatomical signifier – the ephem-
era of the signifier constructed from difference in light and dark
– from dominant codes. It is in this appropriation of codes that
Meshes reveals, to quote Terry Eagleton, a particular 'ideological
conjuncture . . . the complex interplay of determinants in any
historical context' (1978, 150).

Meshes foregrounds process and so upsets certain stabilities –
for example, a unified subject position – such as those traditionally produced by the either the Classic Realist Text or the conventional narrative film. In doing so, the avant-garde text assumes
qualities and strategies of structuralist/materialist avant-garde
film defined by Stephen Heath in his essay 'Repetition Time'
(1981).[4] Process and construction are reflexively foregrounded
throughout the text; the four footsteps and other repeated actions provide direct examples. Such foregrounding frequently has
a specific relationship with temporality. Temporal movement is
displayed as a method of film signification, rather than being
merely clear, all film works with time: 'narrative cinema classi-
cally depends upon the systematic exploitation of a multiplicity
of times' (Heath 1981, 166–7). This is certainly the case with both
film noir and *Meshes*. However, a noticeable difference between
the two types of text is the degree to which temporality is either
overtly manipulated and exposed as a structuring device, or else
is effaced as a transparent, 'natural' quality. *Meshes* exploits temporality as does dominant cinema. Yet, in *Meshes*, temporal exploitation is employed to disrupt unity, to affirm the projection
of dissemination, as moments are re-worked and repeated with
variations, implicitly as variations of themselves, all of which
serve to unfix the idea of the unified subject or the promise of a
stable identity.

The film introduces dissonance into the very idea of identity.
Dissonance is affirmed as identity's non-locatable heart, a centre
which is not one, dispersed throughout. And this projects, writing itself onto the viewer. In Stephen Heath's words, 'The dis-
unity . . . is, exactly, the spectator' (1981, 167). Reiteration and
fragmentation refuse the viewing, reading subject's potential
mastery over the film while, in the process of alienation, creating the possibility for the projection of the *jouissance*, the ecstatic
movement of the pleasure of the other through the lack of a
fixed perspective. 'The spectator', writes Heath, 'is produced by
the film as subject in process . . . with repetition an intensification

of that process, the production of a certain freedom or random-ness of energy, of no one memory' (1981, 170). The uses of rep-etition in *Meshes* are then potentially liberating, affirmative of the freedom of dissonant identity. We can read the film as offer-ing to undo the conceptual knots which imprison our identities as viewers. Here it can be seen how the avant-garde text ex-ploits a code – that of repetition – against its mainstream use. Heath states that repetition is used in narrative cinema to main-tain or produce subject unity. *Meshes* cannot be understood as working towards this. Indeed it affirms its difference by resist-ing indirectly the conventional use of repetition.

The use of repetition can be examined further. Its use posits a refusal to reach closure, as already suggested. Whereas in *noir*, the repetitive mode – often in the form of the crucial flashback (the revelation of the murderer's identity in *Mildred Pierce*; we see from the murder victim's perspective, rather than from that of the murderer) – is used to establish 'truth', to reveal through a variation of repeated shots a certain hitherto undisclosed 're-ality', in *Meshes* reiteration affirms only the variability of unpre-dictable event. As we have previously conjectured, no truth is made available. Certainly, the initial appearance of Deren's rep-etitions and reiterations seem to be closely related to, or com-pared with, the 'flashback' technique of noir. The reiterated events of *Meshes* are somewhat more accurately described as apparent 'flashforwards'. The temporal movement toward closure through the gradual revelation of truths – new, previously unseen clues, pieces of information – effected by flashback in *noir* is reversed, so that the temporal rhythm of the flashforward opens and un-folds, displacing a possible meaning or identity. We are given new information, new details, changes of perspective, but these never amount to anything, they only erase the possibility of meaning. Once the process is set in motion, we are tempted in-itially to predict a possible outcome. As viewers whose identi-ties are constructed by responding to *Meshes of the Afternoon*, we still read the signs in a manner appropriate to *film noir*. Caught in the rhythmic reiteration, we predict the possibility of yet an-other similar outcome, which expectation is frustrated. Each re-iterated sequence appears to offer, if not a reading of previous scenes, then, possibly a reading of scenes yet to come. Yet even this is frustrated.

Through its constant re-working of temporal and spatial situations, the inverted mode of Deren's film manages to resist the imposition of discernible codification. As we stated earlier in this chapter, each variant is a variation without original; each is a projection with shared contexts but without a recognisable common key or code which either binds the reiterated scenes together or allows access to a shared meaning. Deren's film-text utilises reiteration without suggesting an original narrative or scenario from which reiteration is generated; once again, this seems a direct inversion of *film noir* narrative structuring. It might even be possible to suggest that the entire film seems to run back to front, except that the reversal (if it is one) is never simply linear or one-way, but of a multiple, rhizomic nature. Furthermore, the reiteration is a highly self-reflexive gesture which foregrounds the practice of projection.

Meshes adopts then 'ready made positions' (Heath 1981, 173). The text engages in an effective reconstruction – a reconstruction which is also a deconstruction – of the 'available ideas of film' (Heath 1981, 173) through a process of appropriation. Just how politically effective this process might be for a politically engaged film-making such as that desired by Deren in her writings is open to debate. There is a sense in which the codes that are reconstructed in the text are so ideologically overdetermined by dominant film practices that no appropriation can wholly 'subvert, attack or deny . . . meaning', as Stephen Heath puts it (1981, 174). That we can recognise certain forms of signification as historically specific points to their ideological enclosure. However, *Meshes* is a valuable text. Through the tensions and spaces it creates between narrative and process, between transparency and reflexivity, the text does reveal, to quote Heath once more, 'the historical problem of meaning as subject position' (1981, 174). It does this, most importantly, by refusing to accede to that position for the most part, while working with the codes that historically are so vital to the structuring of stable identities in realist cinema. *Meshes of the Afternoon* thus says yes, but as a sign of affirmative projection, rather than acceptance of, and acquiescence to, the dominant hegemony of narrative realism. In so doing, it troubles repeatedly and insistently anything we might be able to believe to be true about our own identities. And its gestures of affirmative resistance are mapped, coyly, in its very title. The term 'meshes' implies weaving, along with other possible meanings mentioned elsewhere in this chapter. Vicki Mahaffey reminds us that weaving 'is a complex intermeshing of opposites to form a web, or network, that figures both interconnection and entrapment' (Mahaffey 1995, 145). The text seems to offer us a web composed of a 'complex intermeshing' of any number of strands. However, the problem with interpretation is that it only serves to weave the web ever tighter; in looking for interconnections, we find ourselves entrapped, not by the text, but by our own desire for certainty of meaning and identity. Deren's film can be read as opening our own practices to resistances which are projected onto the very act of reading, by which the other is always affirmed ahead of identity; identity is only an effect which, without affirmative alterity, is nothing.

Notes

1. See especially the first two chapters, 'Theoretical Preliminaries' and 'The End of a Meta-Language: From George Eliot to *Dubliners*', 1–39.
2. See the discussion of Deleuze's concept of difference in the introduction of this book.
3. Although I am referring to 'Deren's shadow' because Maya Deren is the only female actor in the film, the point is that, while we might identify the shadow as that of Maya Deren, there is a sense in which I at least cannot be sure of this. Nor is it that important, because the shadow exists as shadow primarily, as a signifier or projection of the female which is, in turn, not the signified, but another form of projection.
4. Heath is writing of an avant-garde film-making, that of Brakhage and Gidal, which is historically later than the period in which *Meshes* was produced. It should not be thought that I am confusing historically marked modalities in drawing on Heath. There is a distinct overlap between the films of Deren and those of Brakhage, in that both work with the 'aesthetic of personal vision', as pointed out by Pam Cook (275). Furthermore, Heath's theorising is valuable in that it can be used to point to material processes common to both mainstream and avant-garde texts which find a possible, uneasy meeting place in *Meshes of the Afternoon*.

6

Affirmative memories, resistant projections: Sylvie Germain's *La Pleurante des rues de Prague*

Otherness can survive in different ways in identity forming memories...

Gabriel Motzkin

La pleurante: how are we to translate such a term? Perhaps as 'the mourning woman', 'the female mourner', 'the weeping woman'. This would make a certain sense, in English at least, but there is clearly something in the singularity of the French, something in the French idiom, which troubles the translation, an excess or overflow, a certain 'other' quality which the English is troubled by, and for which it cannot account in its own tongue. Clearly, the French names an unknown mourner, who is identified in writing as female. This much is given in that untranslatable, resistant, yet affirmative definite article. The definite article projects the other of the identity, the other which is not to be recuperated comfortably in any apparent or obvious English term. There is no equivalent. This gendered definite article projects itself in writing, in a manner always strange to the anglophone world. We know what the definite article is, how it should supposedly function; yet, explain it as we might, we are at a loss to recuperate or domesticate it. Yet, in French, in the French I have written above, there seems so much at stake; as I have said, something other is affirmed, while, simultaneously, something other resists, though clearly not directly.

Un/e pleurant/e: A mourner, two mourners, one male, one female, both being defined partly by the act of weeping, crying,

155

and how we are made to distinguish between them is by acknowledging, responding to, the trace in writing of the split in
identity projected by gender. Projection is a trace, not wholly
comprehensible, always projected ahead, always marked, marking itself, with a certain overflow, which we cannot translate
but by which we find ourselves obligated to respond. You might
be forgiven for thinking that I am making too much of this when,
in fact, I cannot make enough. This is the nature of affirmative
resistance: We can never make enough of a text such as Germain's,
and this is because of the questions it appears to raise concerning interpretation, reading and representation. Projection affirms.
Projection resists.

But to ask a question which is always behind this study: how
can a text make possible both affirmation and resistance? Through
the very figures and medium of projection, that act of becoming
which resonates within a poetic space before and beyond the
limitations of analysis. Projection is of the order of what the Greeks
termed *aletheia*: unconcealment. Projection reveals the nature of
that which it projects to us, throwing Being, as it were, Being-
becoming projected onto the space between – between the reading and the read, the expression and the expressed. This space
of 'the' between,[1] where Being finds itself projected and where
the voice of the other is articulated, is the space which Maya
Deren and Charlotte Perkins Gilman (as read in Chapters 5 and 2)
seek to initiate. In these texts the connection between women
and projection, women as projection, makes available the affirmative resistance of Being-female as a non-essential condition of
material contexts and circumstances. 'Femininity'[2] is an other,
non-essential yet, perhaps, primordial trace, obligating the reader
to an ethical response in the name of the other. We cannot yet
name 'femininity' because the concept itself does not name, define or translate the feminine element of 'femininity'. Thus the
place from where this femininity might call us to witness, this
non-place, is the non-place of projection, or where projection takes
place. The projection then is a saying, a speaking, an articulation of a certain kind, (which I would be over-hasty in attempting to define at this moment). This does not mean, however,
that 'femininity', the 'female', or any other related term is an
enigma or fetish. For the moment it can be said that the female
projection is that which reveals to us in its projectedness the
truth of a certain state of Being-in-the-World; which projection

we mistake as essential. What I think is beginning to unfold here, as a necessary gesture of unconcealment, is brought about by allowing in our reading the taking place of dissonance. Dissonance allows us to know, and thereby affirms, if not what might in other circumstances be called 'the between-ness' of projection, then, instead, projection's condition of being-between.

Sylvie Germain's *La Pleurante des rues de Prague*[3] (1992) traces the taking place of such dissonances, with all the attendant sightings, sitings, citings and soundings. The text embodies a project of unconcealment through a writing always concerned with the fraught nature of reading, representation, and identity. It is a novel concerned with memory, mourning, affirmation, love, and ethical responsibility or care. *La Pleurante* is haunted by a seemingly spectral, weeping female who, projected throughout the pages and the streets of Prague, brings to bear upon the reader a sense of the necessity of shared responsibility, for past-presents, the here-and-now, and the future present to come, but never a present as such. Projection in this case moves through and beyond temporal frames, as it speaks, writes, and projects the affirmation of a constant return and a singular series of interruptions to the narrative. Through the prologue, epilogue, and twelve appearances or apparitions,[4] the weeping woman traces fragments of narratives, and, in these, signs of an ethical writing, a textuality committed to an ethical expression. The appearances of this spirit, this *geist*,[5] generates a command, a demand, certainly a call, to responsibility, a responsibility to remember and represent other identities obscured in the narrative of history, amongst many other things. Indeed, it seems that she has always done so.

This projection, with its demands, comes from beyond conventional notions of ethical responsibility. It points not in any particular direction, but traces its way in an aleatory fashion, calling to mind, projecting, so many 'European' scenes, which were projected in the names of spirit, and of identity. But with a difference.

Germain's text involves an affirmation of an other spirit which resists interpretation through its poetic, and double, reading of a certain project/projection of Being which is readable as distinctly Heideggerian[6] in its traces and possibilities. The narrative bears witness to this weeping woman who, herself, bears witness to the memory of personal and political fates. In disclosing this, the text can be read as requiring us, its readers, to bear witness also. The weeping woman bears witness because she is the bearer – though not the memorial – of, amongst other things, very private loves and very public losses; losses which, like the rents in the woman's garments, speak and trace certain aporia of identity, of history: the aporia, for example, that we try to name the Holocaust. This name however can never identify what took place; hence the aporia, from which comes projection. This text, it can be said, places us, as we place our (reading) selves, in relation to its projectedness; inasmuch as we are called by the other, by this weeping woman to bear witness, we come to be, in our reading of the text, that on which Being is thrown or projected. Thus this text projects an affirmation on the way to becoming, even as it resists resonantly our attempts at comprehension. For even if we can come to believe that what we know about this text is that it appears to represent something apparently 'enigmatic', something 'strange', something *unheimlich* even, all we will have realised, to paraphrase Maurice Blanchot, is the familiar, 'we never think anything but the familiar' (1993, 44). Thus this text resists even the most banal of readings, and for the simple reason that its structures (of which I shall say more further on), refuse to acknowledge even the most obvious of limits, such as 'outside' and 'inside'. This is already hinted at, or stated quite plainly, in and by the title itself, for all the reasons discussed by Jacques Derrida in his reading of Kafka's parable, 'Before the Law' (Derrida 1992a, 181–221).[7] More importantly, for the moment, the weeping woman on the streets of Prague will always have been in the future, on the way to the future; and as any attempt at reading will show, she will always have been in a past that is wholly other. And, moreover, *once again*, her movements are never predictable.

This weeping woman wanders in an aleatory manner throughout both the streets of Prague and the pages of the book, onto, and through, which she projects herself, and is projected. This split must be announced out of necessity and out of a sense of attempting to do justice to the narratorial 'voice'; which is, itself, not itself as such, but, rather, a thrown or projected trace of Being, even as it appears to project the weeping woman, even as it mimes and traces its own deferred Being-projected; even, *also*, as it remarks its own project of projection, a project attempting to affirm, as project, as sketch, blueprint and design, the thrown project, the sketch, which the weeping woman/*The Weeping Woman* maps out, again, on/*on* both the pages of the book and the streets of Prague/*the Streets of Prague*. But if this woman who weeps (weeping tears of ink as the traces of her project) and this narratorial 'voice' speak the possibilities of thrown Being, of *Dasein* no less – or a certain reading, a certain *projection* of *Dasein* – then they also bear amongst themselves, in and on themselves, the projections of memory. The weeping woman and the narratorial 'voice' bear witness to, and are being-projected for, the projection of others, those others which we, as readers and writers, must also bear witness to, acknowledging our responsibility as the places onto which the memory of others, the memory of the other – both that which we remember of the other and the other's memory projected onto us in the place of translation – are, once again, projected, thrown, sketched.

It will have been noticed, no doubt, that I seem to have re-peated certain ideas, certain sketched readings; I appear to have reiterated, more or less insistently, particular traces or projec-tions in a certain manner. This scenario of reiteration, which is a doubling of Germain's textual reiterations, occurs inevitably, and out of a sense of necessity involved with trying to express that which is inexpressible. And it is shown in the multiple functions of the weeping woman, multiple functions which are also, already, the multiple affirmations which projection makes possible. Figuration as the event of identity in writing acknowledges in the text, and in the trope of the text's title, that there are a series of apparently stable identities to be read, or which are represented. Projection disturbs stability through its dissonant oscillations. Inasmuch as the weeping woman is a projection of certain traces, as has al-ready been suggested, then, equally, she is also that non-fixable place onto which the other, Being, and the memory of Being-there, are projected onto her non-fleshly body, into and amongst her tattered garments which serve as both the mesh of traces and one more projection screen, the blueprint and the blank page.

This weeping woman illustrates and illuminates how care is constitutive of Being, as Heidegger is at pains to show in *Being and Time*. Her non-essential 'nature' or state of Being is one of both Being-there, Being-in-the-world and Being-in-the-text; and, furthermore, in Being-there, of disclosedness. In her Being-there she demonstrates, projects, discloses (the project of) the disclosedness of Being, both her own and that of others, of the other, the other as other. In this she appears to project a mode of existence which allows the reader to understand and so care for the world of beings. This is immediately and always disclosed, projected by the narratorial 'voice' (a voice acknowledging its own being-written), which, in itself Being-there-disclosing, affirms *Dasein*. In so doing, it marks the very limits of the representation of identity in what it can say and not say about the weeping woman on the streets of Prague. This occurs even as its disclosedness attempts to close the gap *between* the act of representation and what resists representation.

The same can be said to be true, albeit in a different manner, of the weeping woman who, in projecting herself, in being projected and as Being-projected, onto the pages and the streets of Prague, bears witness and seeks to represent as narrative traces, ink traces, the projections of others, of the other. Identity, precarious in its traces, is always written, always spaced and different from itself. All at once, in the reader-narrative-mourner-other(s) configuration, representation simultaneously reaches its own limits, closing itself, and opening onto the abyss. The abyss is figured by the absence of a proper name for the weeping woman on the streets of Prague. Although this name – la pleurante – also names the text, it names, as name of the text, the unnameable. It names that which cannot be named, and which is always, radically other. The name of the unnameable woman is of the order of aporia. In various texts, Derrida names the absence of a proper name as trace or cinder, themselves merely provisional names 'when considered', as Ned Lukacher puts it in his introduction to Derrida's *Cinders*, 'in relation to the still withheld truth of Being' (Derrida 1991b, 1). The weeping woman or, to translate *la pleurante* another way, the female weeping, is the name of no one; it names, and thus, affirms that which is withheld, bearing witness to the unrepresentable. In resisting naming indirectly *la pleurante* suggests the possibility of returning. In recognising this, while we cannot apprehend the other, in the sense of both understanding and arrest, we can comprehend the disclosure of the other-to-come.[8]

There occurs, endlessly, the disclosedness of disclosure, the projection of the project of projection. Our reading discloses, making us aware of, the project of *Dasein*, which, as Jacques Taminaux puts it, 'makes itself manifest to its own seeing, acquir[ing] a self-understanding' (Taminaux 1991, 92). Thus projection, its constant temporal unfolding as revealed in this particular instance of the act of reading: you read my reading of the narrative, reading the readings of the weeping woman who reads the streets and who, in doing so, in Being-there, makes possible for us the acquisition of the sight/site of (self) understanding from the impossible place of the other. What we shall see and hear, what we shall locate, in this reading of *La Pleurante des rues de Prague* is an understanding of the dissonant affirmation, a violent trembling, a solicitation, of what Heidegger terms the 'fundamental *existentiale* which constitute the *Being* of the "there", the disclosedness of Being-in-the-world, [which] are states of mind and understanding' (¶34, H161, 203). The 'existential constitution of *Dasein's* disclosedness' is, as Heidegger affirms, confirmed by language or discourse, which are *'equiprimordial with state-of-mind and understanding'* (¶34, H161, 203). Sylvie Germain's project(ion) is closely bound up with the Heideggerian assertion that 'discourse, as the articulation of the intelligibility of the "there", is a primordial *existentiale* of disclosedness ... disclosedness is primarily constituted by Being-in-the-world ... discourse too must have essentially a kind of Being which is specifically *worldly*. The intelligibility of Being-in-the-world ... *expresses itself as discourse'* (¶34, H161, 204). However, while Heidegger seems implicitly to privilege speech and all voiced, verbal communications, Germain is at pains to demonstrate, through the tracing she attempts to effect between world and text (world-as-text and text-as-world), that disclosedness is textual or written, and inscribed in (as, by) its projections. If Heidegger's apparent logocentrism may also be read as an implicit phallogocentrism, then Germain's textual trace (a trace which takes us back to the title and to the very moment of engendering in the untranslatable definite article with which I began, above) offers an affirmative, resistant counter-trace, the trace of the female, remarked everywhere without centre, without origin.

To rewrite Heidegger's expression then, writing is a primordial *existentiale* of disclosedness; the intelligibility of Being-in-the-world *expresses itself as a writing, a textuality*; and a textuality, moreover, haunted by the traces (projections) of alterity.

We can witness this in the prologue, in the opening of the narrative:

Elle est entrée dans le livre. Elle est entrée dans les pages du livre comme un vagabond pénètre dans une maison vide, dans un jardin à l'abandon.
Elle est entrée, soudain. Mais cela faisait des années déjà

qu'elle rôdait autour du livre. Elle frôlait le livre qui cependant n'existait pas encore, elle en feuilletait les pages non écrites et certains jours, même, elle a fait bruire imperceptiblement ces pages blanches en attente de mots.

. . . .

Elle s'est glissée dans le livre. Elle s'est faufilée dans les pages comme un songe s'en vient visiter un dormeur, se déploie dans son sommeil, y trame des images et mêle à son sang, à son souffle, de fins échos de voix.

(*P* 13)

She entered the book. She entered the pages of the book as a tramp breaks into an empty house, or an abandoned garden.

She entered, suddenly. But for years she had been prowling around the book. She would brush past the book which however did not yet exist, she would leaf through the unwritten pages, and some days, she even made its blank pages, awaiting words, rustle imperceptibly.

. . . .

She slipped into the book. She threaded herself into the pages as a dream visits a sleeper, spreading itself out in his sleep, weaving images and mingling, with his blood, with his breath, the slender echoes of voices.

(*W* 27)

She entered. The Book. Suddenly. All 'characters' enter their books at some point; to make one's entrance is a standard, conventionally understood, performative metaphor. However, because the text's being is understood to come into being by the entrance of the weeping woman, an entrance which is already past, she having left already, we are given to understand a fundamental condition of being, which we ourselves perform on opening the book: Being finds itself projected, thrown into the world, the world of the text, the world of the word, as a possibility of understanding. We have an understanding of the weeping woman because she is projected as a possibility of the world and the text, a possibility of Being-in-the-world as an event of writing. In understanding this incipit, we also understand the nature of our own Being-in-the-world, our own narrativity, the very temporal/spatial difference of identity already being recited and projected by the other. The book does not exist unless the weeping woman is projected as one of its possible traces, unless she is *between* as the other trace, in fact – trace of the other – which traces identity as being marked by otherness. Neither does it exist unless we understand, that is to say, interpret it *as such* by the act of 'reading', which itself is constitutive of both understanding and Being-in-the-world. Our very own thrownness, our own Being-projected is revealed, disclosed, to us in our comprehension of what occurs in the opening paragraphs. The weeper's Being is, thus, both a singularity and a Being-in-common, as is our own Being. In attempting to understand the weeping woman we comprehend, in Heidegger's words, that 'the character of understanding as projection is constitutive for Being-in-the-world with regard to its existentially constitutive state-of-Being . . . And as thrown, Dasein is thrown into that kind of Being which we call "projecting"' (¶31, H145, 185). Projection, Heidegger informs us, 'always pertains to the full disclosedness of Being-in-the-world' (¶31, H146, 186). As we shall see, this woman's projectedness partakes of a constant temporal disclosure concerning Being-in-the-world, and contributing to our own states of mind and understanding. And, furthermore, as we can already begin to understand, there is no understanding without projection. If this weeping woman, without a name, with a body of tears not her own, might be seen as *Dasein* – albeit momentarily – we might also see how 'any Dasein has, as Dasein, already projected itself; and as it is, it is projecting' (¶31, H145, 185),

The weeping woman is always already there and yet, paradoxically, also not simply there in the present of reading, having already departed, leaving only her trace, or writing. Without her Being, without the trace which allows us to comprehend her alterity, we could, as readers, as witnesses, not be; this moment would be impossible. She is already projected ahead of us, never in the place where her trace, her overflow, is said to remain as 'the taste of ink . . .' (W 27):

La couleur de l'encre, mille fois séchée et ravivée, luit depuis toujours dans les traces de ses pas.

(P 14)

The colour of ink, endlessly dried and revived, has always glistened in the traces of her steps.

(W 28)

Le vent, le vent de l'encre se lève à son passage et souffle
dans ses pas.

(*P* 15)

The wind, the ink-wind, rises at her passing and blows beneath her steps.

(*W* 28)

Le vent, le vent de l'encre qui souffle dans ses pas fait se courber,
se balancer les mots, déracine des images qui demeuraient
enfouies dans la mémoire à la limite de l'oubli, et par avance
effeuille les pages du livre qui ne peut être que fragmentaire,
inachevé.

(*P* 16)

The wind, the ink-wind which blows in her footsteps, makes
the words bend and sway, uprooting images which had re-
mained buried in memory at the very limits of forgetfulness,
and in anticipation leafing through the pages of a book which
cannot but be fragmentary and unfinished.

(*W* 29)

Projection escapes ahead of its traces; projection is what allows
the traces to be the marks of that which is never present as such.
The traces are themselves partial inscriptions reinscribed, transcribed by the witness of the narrated narrator as wind-ink, ink-
taste, ink-colour. The wind of ink blows throughout the pages
and the city; reader and narrator alike – both narrator narrating
and narrator narrated – follow these traces, always in the wake
of an already vanished projection, always following in the footsteps of where she is not.[9] We can never hope to be in the presence of projection because of its very 'nature', for want of a better
word. What we see already mentioned is the limit of representation, traced in the limit of citation and recitation, being described
in ink, an ink trace recording the absences, marking the aporia,
which thus tremble dissonantly under the trace of the trace, which
solicits our comprehension of the unremarkable space in an attempt to represent the unrepresentable.

Thus the pages tremble even in our act of reading. And projection – this woman – always already having been ahead of the
traces which she will have left and to which we bear witness,

moves in no predictable manner, responding – as we must do – to the call of the other:

Il lui arrive de s'immobiliser au milieu d'une rue déserte, ou d'oubliquer sans raison apparente. C'est qu'elle a perçu alors un bruit inaudible à tout autre. Le battement de cœur oppressé par un excès de solitude, ou de peine, ou de peur. . . . Il n'est pas rare que le battement de cœur humain qui l'ainsi mise en éveil et mouvement soit celui d'un cœur éteint depuis longtemps.

(*P* 14)

She may come to a standstill in the middle of an deserted street, or move obliquely without apparent reason, having perceived a sound inaudible to all others. The beating of a heart oppressed by too much loneliness, or pain, or fear. . . . Not infrequently it is a human heart long dead that has aroused and diverted her.

(*W* 27)

The woman's movements are dictated unexpectedly, always ahead of the narrator but, equally, always in response to an imperceptible, unexpected call; there is no programme to her movements, she alters direction according to the involuntary, barely audible, sign of otherness. Her Being is thus, once again, it must be said, a Being-there-for-others, and manifests in its projections the affirmation of care at every turn, whether that turn be the turn of a street, a turning as we say in English, for any side street off a main route. A turning then, which, in turn, turns the weeping woman, directing her towards an other heading, or, to paraphrase Derrida, the heading of the other[10] (for she is, as are we in relation to her, the other of the other, or the other for the other); or the turn of the page, which as it occurs in our reading, as our reading 'seems' or 'appears' to dictate its happening – the event of the turn is marked by ambiguity; for the narrating voice implicitly 'dictates' our turning of the page, even as the woman's movements do, and even as those very same movements are dictated by the inaudible, and dictate the passage of the narrator narrated/narrating narrator – in fact turns us, into an other direction, in the direction of the other once again, that other who this woman both is and is not.

For she is not some other simply defined by some fixed, reading self (for example); the traces multiply, as do the aporia, and between the fibres of the text and the rents opened more and more, the space between vibrates, resounds, with the solicitation of chance. And these chances, which, clearly enough, undo the certainty of where we think we are ('where are you in the story?' is a common enough question) are reinforced at every turn:

> Elle surgit sans crier gare, en un lieu et un instant où on ne l'attend pas, où on ne pense nullement à elle.
>
> (*P* 14)

> She looms up without warning, at places and times where she is least expected, where one would never think of her.
>
> (*W* 28)

> Mais nul ne saurait dire où mène son chemin, ce qui rythme sa marche, ce qui la pousse ainsi.
>
> (*P* 15)

> But no-one could ever say where that path leads, what rhythm she walks to, what pushes her so.
>
> (*W* 28)

Clearly then, we have no control, no more control certainly than the narrator. We have no more control, it would seem, than even the narrator over her narrated, other, self. And, to come back to this point once again, all that remains in her wake, in her footsteps, her being-not-present, is ink, and the spaces within which the trace traces the alterity of projection. The weeping woman's Being (Being-other) dictates and traces the project(ion) of the text, she having been always projected ahead of that text which her absence remarks. Which, perhaps, serves to explain why the text is 'fragmentary', 'unfinished', and why:

> Et le livre qui suit, n'étant composé que des traces de ses pas, s'en va lui aussi au hasard.
>
> (*P* 15)

> And the book which follows, being composed purely of the traces of her steps, proceeds also by chance.
>
> (*W* 28)

Germain's writing recognises in its acts of inscription, the very limits to which it can go, being dictated to, as it is, by chance, by the responses of the other which is – supposedly – its 'subject'; which gives it its title, its name, its purpose, its supposedly unifying signature, of which there is an overflow. And these responses of the other, these also are to the other, the other of the other, which will have obligated writer, narrator, and reader, albeit obligation in different registers. Germain's textual representation is forced to acknowledge the limits of representation, as I have already suggested; but I reiterate this, at this juncture, in order to acknowledge how this 'limit' is never singular, never simply an 'only once', but a constant series of 'only onces', always trembling (at) the edges of writing and reading, disturbing the presumed stability of identity. And this reiteration – a reiteration of reiteration installed in Germain's text, which this writing is, in turn, obliged to acknowledge – alerts us to the problem of comprehending the limit's limit. For how can that which is only intermittently and randomly visible be represented in writing, a mark or trace of a trace which, at the very most, only and always comes after that which it both seeks and fails to represent (acknowledging both search and failure simultaneously), and which is already projected away from those places where it is not? Indeed, the acknowledgement of the limit of the representable is clearly reflected upon:

> En fait c'est l'écriture seule de ce texte qui avance à tâtons, qui louvoie à l'aventure, par défaut de vue d'ensemble et absence de repères précis.
>
> *(P 16)*

> Indeed, it is only the writing of this text which feels its way along, which tacks aimlessly for lack of any sense of a whole or the absence of any precise marker.
>
> *(W 29)*

All at sea, the writing admits to a possible misreading of the movements of the weeping woman, already installed as the possible condition of reading. She moves as she does, and, in so doing, affirms her Being-in-the-world as a Being-for-others. Yet, in moving as she does, she resists indirectly – certainly not through any discernible, deliberate opposition – and in passing (both literally

and figuratively; how can we even use such terms, given that
the two appear to be collapsing in upon each other, into the
aporia of the weeping woman?), the fixed definition. Writing is
subjected to the limits of the representable and, in this subjection, is forced to find its way without a compass.

There is the suggestion here that this mourner knows or in
some manner understands her own Being. She is, or seems,
reminiscent of what Heidegger calls 'thrown projective Being-
in-the-world' (¶31, H148, 188). She appears to project for us an
understanding of her most fundamental nature as Being-a-project,
Being-towards-possibilities, although neither we nor the text can
say 'who' the subject is, even in the most facile sense of giving
a name.[11] We can understand this much precisely because of the
thrownness of her Being into the 'there', to borrow once again
from *Being and Time* (¶31, H 148, 188). She is, it can be suggested, a projected 'thereness', a being-witness, to which, *by which*,
we are obligated to bear witness. Her projection is an affirmation of this, oscillating as she does between alterity and the read.
Her Being-projected is of the order described by Heidegger in
the following manner:

> An entity whose kind of being is the essential projection of
> Being-in-the-world . . .

Such an entity, such an *essential projection*:

> . . . has understanding of Being, and has this as constitutive of
> Being.

> (¶31, H147, 187–8)

Thus, what is being introduced by Germain in the prologue,
despite – or, perhaps, because of – a lack of awareness on the
part of the narratorial voice, is readable as the affirmative nature of *Dasein* as an indirect introduction to a seemingly ontological narrative constructed out of a double temporality: that of
its own narrative moment and movement, spacing and time, and
the time, the multiple, unspecified time of the others' narratives,
gathered together, yet still – as we will have come to see – marked
by a radical heterogeneity, as the narrative of the other in the
name of the city of Prague, and in the face of the nameless weeping
woman. As possible figure for *Dasein* the weeping woman is

projected/projects herself as understanding's possibilities; she has the possibility of developing her own ability to affirm the narrative of the other and, out of this, comes another possibility: that of the development in ourselves of 'the understanding we call "interpretation"' (¶32, H148, 188).

With this in mind, and given that Heidegger interprets interpretation as the 'possibilities projected in understanding' (¶32, H148, 189), what may be possible is that the weeping woman on the streets of Prague may project – may have as part of her project – the possibility that we will arrive at an understanding of the kind which is a fundamental *existentiale* of *Dasein*. We may therefore, in tracing the traces of her steps, arrive at a fundamental understanding of our Being-in-the-world and the responsibility to others which such understanding entails.

But this is still to find ourselves no further along than the prologue; we have not as yet come to the apparitions or appearances. All of which, and in a certain way, still remains to be projected, even as projective traces are re-cited otherwise in Germain's prologue. For now, what we have come to understand, and what will become clearer as we proceed, is the nature of the affirmation which writing, the text, 'art', can make, and this is best expressed by Jean-François Lyotard:

> What art can do is bear witness not to the sublime, but to this aporia of art and to its pain. It does not say the unsayable, but says that it cannot say it.
>
> (1990, 47)

Responding to Lyotard's remark, we might recall, in passing, Heidegger's definition of art as a 'letting happen' of the truth of being. Art affirms this, though not through attempting to say the unsayable. Heidegger seems to understand the impossibility of such a saying. He seems to comprehend also that art can bear witness to the aporia in art while saying that it cannot say it. He does so through the gesture of the 'letting happen', itself an *en passant* affirmation which side-steps, without necessarily avoiding, the modernist dilemma to which Lyotard alerts us, a dilemma which, coincidentally, what we call the modernist text had already installed as the trace of the other within itself, as other to its identity.[12] But art, and more importantly for Heidegger, poetry or the poetic – let us say the untranslatable *in* language, *lets happen* the possibility of the wholly otherwise, the wholly unsayable in its very acts of projection:

> Truth, as the clearing and concealing of beings, happens in being composed. *All art*, as the letting happen of the advent of the truth of beings, is as such, *in essence, poetry.* The essence of art . . . is the setting-itself-to-work of truth. . . . What poetry, as clearing projection, unfolds as unconcealment and projects ahead into the rift-design of the figure, is the open region which poetry lets happen . . . it becomes questionable whether the nature of poetry, and this means at the same time the nature of projection, can be adequately thought of in terms of the power of the imagination.
>
> (1993, 197)

Poetry, the poetic, projection, and the question of the event in the text of 'letting happen' (another possible projection of singular reiteration) are connected for Heidegger. There is, implicitly drawn between these traces, the question of the unsayable and the untranslatable. Untranslatability and the absolutely, singular idiomatic are at the heart – a heart which is also an aporia – of Heidegger's writing. As Krysztof Ziarek elaborates in the first chapter of *Inflected Language*, Heidegger's use of the term *Dichtung* (in close proximity to *Denken*) is not simply translatable, in the Heideggerian context, either as 'poetry' or poesy (K. Ziarek 1994, 21–42). That which is marked by the poetic is the place in language where the poetic, having been projected, is not; although it has left its mark, has left a gap or rift. This mark or gap, this aporia spoken of above by Lyotard, is not simply an absence but a highly ambiguous opening out, a projection, through which the saying of the other can be understood as having always already articulated, albeit without the possibility of being fully translated. We may note the traces, and we may thus believe we are in the neighbourhood of the other, but it is only the vibrant sight/site where the other is not, to which we can attest as a sign of the 'poetic' series of traces (in this instance the apparitions of the weeping woman), whilst disclosing the paucity of language in the act of failed representation. Germain's writing admits that it cannot say the unsayable, to use Lyotard's words again. In so doing, constantly, we arrive at an understanding of the poetic as that projective allergy which opens and unfolds the truth of being in the face of the ineffable other. The weeping woman as projection of the other reveals indirectly what Heidegger above calls 'the setting-itself-to-work' of truth.

As Heidegger points out, the imagination is barely adequate for thinking the nature of poetry, which is also the nature of projection. What is therefore at stake and in question in *La Pleurante* is precisely the question of the adequation of language which acknowledges that it can hardly keep up with the other. The gap, opened by the other in the weave of language, is both a gap in comprehension and a gap which the woman discloses by her appearances through the spacing spoken of by the narrator, in narrating her own spacing between her selves.

Elle marchait devant moi, à quelques mètres de distance. Je la suivais sans accélérer le pas.

(P 22)

She was walking in front of me, some metres ahead. I followed her at a steady pace.

(W 35)

The apparition is not, clearly, a projection of the narratorial voice, nor of the narrator's narrated, other, self. The weeping woman is not some phenomenal figure of the imagination. The narrator's other self is called to testify to the appearance and does so with surprise and astonishment, becoming her own projection, as memory and other to the trace of, and in, the act of narration. 'I' is an other identity who, in being narrated and as being-narrated, is at a distance between the self who narrates and the other who is projected. 'I', as other 'I' to the 'I' who narrates, is called on by the apparition to trace her footsteps, her appearances, a trace subsequently doubled in the act of narrating, an act which further opens up the rift in language, between saying and said being. 'I' already acknowledges the spacing of writing. With this very first appearance, the other has obligated narrative art to bear witness to, and affirm, the trembling dissonances of the poetic, of alterity, in discourse.

What we therefore read in this opening up and unfolding of the narrative, which installs the difference of the subject, difference as a primordial condition of Being-in-the-world, is what Ziarek calls the ' . . . twofoldness of the trace . . . its marking itself within language and at the same time erasing itself from it. Thus the trace is possible only as the trace of the trace. It is the trace as the erasure of the trace' (K. Ziarek 1994, 93). The narrator in narrating her self as other to the other of the apparition, erases her self in marking her self as tracing the trace of the weeping woman. Her being, her doubled being, traces a proximal relationship (within its selves) which is also the dissonance of *Dasein* as it is manifested in language. And this occurs while the otherness of the weeping woman is in no way affected or touched, she having gone on ahead. The projective antigen of the weeping woman effects an allergic response in the narrating/narrated subject which establishes the doubling oscillation of the subject's being disclosed through the spatio-temporality of narration, of being-narrated. The writer thus becomes a reader, remarked as one by the trace of the other.

Meanwhile, this weeping woman comes and goes, leaving in her wake the traces of 'serial interruptions' (K. Ziarek 1994, 95), which interruptions allow us to understand the nature of our Being, as a being-there-for-others, and as a bearing-witness-to-the-other. The apparent absence of any determinable destination on the part of the weeping woman only serves to remark her radical alterity. Yet, as I have said, her otherness and the trace of her trace obligates the self ahead of any demand or call on the part of the other to the subject (K. Ziarek 1994, 97). All we can observe is, as Krysztof Ziarek puts it in his discussion of Paul Celan's poetry of the Holocaust, 'an encounter with the other . . . both *in* and *despite of* or *against* language' (K. Ziarek 1994, 133). I raise this at this juncture, precisely because, as we shall see, Germain's writing, like that of Celan, is marked by a 'preoccupation with acknowledging the unrepresentable alterity of the other of his/her suffering, pain and death' (K. Ziarek 1994, 133).[13]

What unfolds across the apparitions is an attempt on the part of Germain, on the part of the narrating narrator and the narrated narrator, *the narrator being narrated by the other within narration*, to be faithful to the alterity of the weeping woman, despite the problem of language. We quickly come to realise that this mourning woman, whose trace troubles the very limits of what we name language in general and 'metaphor' in particular, describes with her steps a project. Part of this project is traced in the projection of the trace across the text, where projection-as-trace through its overflow in language deconstructs the possibility of presence except as a possibility already transcribed and translated, as an *a posteriori* sketch. Writing the other becomes an attempt to project onto the reader an outline of the other's trace cited in the place where the other was not. Presence is merely the inscribed acknowledgement of an already deferred projection. The narratorial voice admits as much at the beginning of the second appearance:

Elle s'en allait.[14]
    Elle a toujours cette allure de quelqu'un qui s'en va, de quelqu'un qui s'éloigne pour ne plus revenir, et cependant, chaque fois qu'elle paraît, elle arrive en plein cœur du témoin de son apparition. Elle avance à rebours dans le regard et la mémoire.
    Le temps de l'apercevoir et de la reconnaître, elle avait disparu.

(P 26)

She was going away.
    She always has the air/appearance of someone on their way, someone who is moving away, never to return; yet each time she appears, she arrives right before the witness to her appearance/apparition. She moves in reverse through sight and memory.
    By the time I had seen and recognised her, she was gone.

(W 39)

Both proximity and deferral are enacted, spacing and temporality working with projection to affirm the unspeakable otherness. A recognition of nearness, the nearness of the other to the subject, of the subject to the narratorial voice, is essential to an understanding of the other's affirmative resistance. The 'in-between' of beings in their *Dasein* is crucial to the effectivity of the other on the one. This closeness which is not spoken of directly, but which is traced in the untranslatable 'en plein cœur', allows for the projection of the other onto the place of the subject to occur. The proximity between apparition and narrated subject is further traced in the proximal relationship between narrated other and narrating self (a self which is other to ourselves as reading subjects, as I have already suggested), a proximity announced in the mention of serial iterations and interruptions effected by the projection-as-affirmation on the part of the other, as traced in the language of the text's movement; yet such traceries are fleeting, because in the time it takes between paragraphs, in the passage between paragraphs, marked by the introduction of the narrated 'I', the other is already gone, already unrepresentable except by those marks of testimony recorded by the narratorial voice. By the time we reach this point of understanding, the other has already gone, on her way to other appearances; in following this trace, we are avoided.

Yet it is not only ink that is left; there is another resonance of affirmation, a resonance which happens also at the end of the first apparition:

Cet étonnement était un confus remuement du cœur.

(*P* 23)

That astonishment was the vaguest stirring of the heart.

(*W* 36; first apparition)

Mais l'étonnement de la revoir avait déjà l'élan troublant d'une émotion, et provoqua la même sourd remuement du cœur que la première fois.

(*P* 27)

But the astonishment o   f seeing her again was already gathering disconcerting momentum, and provoked the same faint stirring of the heart as it had done the first time.

(*W* 40)

The other has the ability through its projections to arrive at the very heart of something or someone, and to stir that heart by its appearances. The subject bears witness and the heart responds. At a time and place where there occurs 'the foundering of the visible', (39) only the obligation that the other invokes and the heart's response have any force. What we come to comprehend is 'the relationship between poetic language and the ethical meaning of otherness' (K. Ziarek 1994, 134) which is the text's putting-to-work of truth. The subject and the other of the text come to define each other reciprocally; but between them is projected the possibility for the reader of an understanding of the nature of being. In order to understand this possibility it is necessary to turn to some of the possible conditions of reading, of being a reader.

Conventionally, when, as readers, we approach a text, our habitual reading practice may be to question or demand of the text particular meanings or values; the act of translation becomes mistaken as the truth, and this occurs through a misunderstanding of translation, not simply as the truth, but, instead, as representation, as the particular representation of the truth. We do not question the text on its own terms but, rather, according to our knowledge, according to the limits of that knowledge, and through an implicit understanding of the text, not in terms of its condition, but according to our comprehension of a text as an object. Yet the text's 'textness', its thingly quality, is self-concealing in its being; thus it resists our attempts to 'know' it. This occurs even as there is affirmed the 'letting-happen' which Germain's strategies or projects faithfully acknowledge and project.

What I have just described amounts to an understanding of what it means to read and the violence we do to the other in our efforts to come to terms with it through a certain desire for a control over the other-effect or other-work, the allergy, of language and within identity. Reading as outlined above involves a much sought-after 'damping down' of alterity's affirmations and dissonances. This understanding comes about through a recognition of the relationships between the idea of the subject and other in *La Pleurante des rues de Prague*. We arrive at this understanding, furthermore, in the wake of a narration revealing to us the limits of its own comprehension when faced with that allergic-projective project of the other. The subject's response to the other is, in the in-between of its doubled selves, an allergic reaction marked initially by this faint trembling of the heart, over which the subject has no control, and barely comprehends. What the narratorial-voice-as-reader reveals, discloses, through the act of reading/writing itself in the face of the other, brings about – as the tell-tale heart murmur makes manifest – is what Heidegger terms a projective saying. Projective saying:

is poetry ... Poetry is the saying of the unconcealment of beings ... Projective saying is saying which, in preparing the sayable, simultaneously brings the unsayable as such into a world ... language is the happening in which beings first disclose themselves to man each time as beings

(1993, 198–9)

What the weeping woman brings about, what her projectedness unfolds despite her apparently mute condition, is a double affirmation of Being in the trembling of the heart and the narrative of the subject thrown into a world.

Projection is, then, the manifestation of allergy; as with apparitions and self-projected fantasies or what we might call projective consciousness in the gothic novel, the projection is readable, quite literally, as the other effect, the other-work to the I in language. It sets discourse and the reading subject to a reactive, contemplative trembling, which, in its seemingly involuntary condition, offers, equally involuntarily, a bearing witness to the coming of the other. What this coming-to-me on the part of the other signals is what Levinas calls the 'initial event of meeting' with the 'absolutely other'; in this coming, a coming which is a series of single reiterations (already noted): ' . . . the other "regards" me, not in order to "perceive" me, but in "concerning me", in "mattering to me as someone for whom I am answerable"' (Levinas 1993, 124). And what this meeting, this always singular event, calls to mind is, again in Levinas' words, 'the affirmation, as a manifestation of freedom, of the rights of the obligated person . . . One's duty regarding the other who makes appeal to one's responsibility is an investing of one's own freedom . . . An inexhaustible responsibility: for with the other our accounts are never settled' (Levinas 1993, 125).

What we read, then, in *La Pleurante*, is nothing other than this inexhaustible responsibility, for which we are called to account, insistently, repeatedly, as though every apparition were the first – which is why one has to speak of each event as though it were the first – by the project(ion) of the other. This allergic project(ion) which causes us to shiver in uncontrollable response, as a mark of the other's work within the marks of language, is a constant weave of tensions between the ineffability installed as the condition of representation's inadequacies in representing projection (projection affirms its being in resisting, unravelling the limits of representation) and the apparently concrete naming of locality and topography, topography as banal taxonomy in the face of the unrepresentable. Such naming seeks, in the act of providing seemingly locatable referents such as the Žižkov district and the Olšany cemeteries (*W* 43), to pin down, at the very least, a context in which the subject encounters the weeping woman. Is this not the very same paradox which is being played out in the title, which seeks to suggest that the weeping woman is contained within the streets of Prague, and is also containable, representable, in a text, named after those same streets, named as *les rues de Prague/in the Streets of Prague*? The name, the title, attempts to limit the movements of projection within this border-title, this border-guard which sets out a possible map and area to patrol.

The locations already named begin the recitation of the third apparition, as though this device could somehow, once again, fix the projection. Instead, the naming of the locale merely serves as the backdrop on which the weeping woman is found projected, and on – and through – which she projects herself, her self as other, her other, selfless, self. We notice that her entire movement and projective 'presence' is marked by the absence of the mark. She limps 'in silence', she does not 'disturb anything', her 'lame feet' make 'no sound' (*W* 43). She 'was even more delicate than a cat, for she:

Elle était même plus discrète encore qu'un chat car ses pas ne laissaient nulle empreinte sur la neige boueuse qui souillait le trottoir.

Ni bruit ni traces; cependant, si l'on prêtait attention, on percevait dans son sillage un très léger bruissment qui provenait, peut-être, du frou-frou de sa robe trop longue, de sa cap flotante, ou d'un chuchotement qu'elle aurait ressassé sous son voile.[15]

Mais presque aussitôt on s'apercevait que ce n'était pas cela, qu'il ne s'agissait pas d'un froissement d'étoffes ni d'un confus marmonnement.

C'était comme un bruit d'eau – mais si ténu, infime. Ainsi susurrent les sources souterraines, les eaux encloses au fond des gouffres, dans la pénombre, le froid. Eaux invisible qui suintent au creux des roches millénaires et qui déploient d'étranges résonances dans l'immensité du silence et du vide.

C'était un pleurement très bas, un sanglot retenu d'une infinie douceur.

Quelle douleur pleurait ainsi en elle?

Car il semblait que quelque chose pleurât en elle, et non pas qu'elle-meme versât des larmes. Peut-être bien d'ailleurs n'en versait-elle aucune. L'humide chuchotis sourdait du dedans de son corps, comme si l'inaudible rumeur[16] du sang qui coule dans la chair se fût faite perceptible. Était-ce le frémissement interne de sa chair, ou le tremblement de sa peau? Mais sous l'effet de quelle peine?

(P 30–31)

... left no imprint on the muddy snow which dirtied[soiled] the pavement.

Neither noise nor trace; yet if you paid attention, you perceived in her wake a very slight rustling, which originated, perhaps, from the swishing of her overly long dress, of her drifting cape, or of a whispering which appeared to have been constant under her veil.

But almost immediately one could make out that it was not that, that it was not a question of a rustling of fabric, nor any confused muttering.

It was like the sound of water – but so faint, so minute. It was like the murmur of subterranean sources, of water enclosed at the bottom of chasms, in the half-light, the cold: invisible waters trickling in the recesses of ancient rocks, which set up strange echoes in the immensity of that silence and emptiness.

It was a low weeping, a restrained sob of infinite softness.

What grief was weeping within her?

For it was as though something were crying within her, and not as though she herself were shedding tears. Perhaps indeed she was not crying at all. The moist whispering welled up from within her body, as though the inaudible murmur of the blood which flows in the flesh had been made perceptible. Was it the internal tremor of her flesh, or the trembling of her skin? But under the effect of what sorrow?

(W 43–4)

This passage traces the paradoxical absence of the trace. Also here, we read of the almost immediate confusion of understanding that occurs for the reader/interpreter in efforts to comprehend the identity of the woman and the possible source of barely audible traces. The abyssal source of watery sounds mocks the search for knowable location as a possible origin, such sounds being projections without knowable source, locatable identity. The weeping woman projects from her being, a being as we now know, marked indelibly by the historicity and temporality of Being-there, Being-for-others, a low keening, an almost imperceptible

sobbing projected from the margins of the in/audible. Such projective audible trembling causes the narrator's language to strain
after metaphors and similes, literary marks which can mark the
projective trace in other words. The narrator, narrating her other's
efforts to recall the event, multiplies the iterable and idiomatic,
precisely in the act of not capturing, except in other words, what
she hears, and what she remembers hearing.

Also being multiplied are questions, questions in search of an
effect of speech, of writing, which might adequately in*corpo*rate,
literally give body to, the resonances set in motion by the weeping woman. This is the allergic response. The woman does not
exactly embody all suffering; rather, she projects a projection –
which is not simply the same as a representation; projection is
beyond all mimesis – of the suffering of others, the suffering of
the other as her project, her work, if you will, work-as-project of
the other; a suffering which cannot be represented to any adequate degree, the intimation of which language reveals –
unconceals, even as it offers understanding – as both the excessive dissemination of the other and the paucity of language's
own abilities, the limits of its power, the power to represent, the
power to make narrative.

Not only are the woman's movement's unpredictable; so too
are her 'rare and ephemeral' appearances, although, apparently,
this is of little importance because she is always in the city, though
invisible (*W* 49). Her projective being can even by-pass the senses,
taking ' . . . [the form of] a certain *je-ne-sais-quoi* which slips lightly
across the surface of your awareness/conscience[17] . . . a vague,
very vague agitation of thought . . .]' (*W* 49). This stirring recognition, the barest of phenomenal traces projected as the other,
the other within, onto one's identity and memory, causes memories
to appear, further projections of the other-effect, the allergy already spoken of, which, coming with the echo of voices long
since silent, (*W* 49) bring tears, along with the memory of ashes,
(*W* 50). What we read here, in a certain, poignant way, affirmed
as being so close to us all, through the relentless interiority of
the other which Germain projects, is what Derrida has called,
with reference to ashes, to cinders, '*ce thème poussiéreux de
l'humanité*/this dusty theme of humanity' (Derrida 1991b, 31).
And there is a certain similarity, perhaps an homology, even,
between the weeping woman in her constantly reiterated projectedness and the incorporeality Germain assigns to her projection,

and the provisional definition of the 'nothing of being' of the cinder, the ash, provided by Derrida in *Cinders*:

> – *je comprends que la cendre n'est rien qui soit au monde, rien qui reste comme un étant. Elle est l'être, plutôt, qu'il y a là mais qui, se donnant* (es gibt ashes), *n'est rien, reste au-delà de tout ce qui est* (konis epekeina tes ousias), *reste imprononçable pour rendre possible le dire alors qu'il n'est rien.*

> – I understand that the cinder is nothing that can be in the world, nothing that remains as an entity [*étant*]. It is the being [*l'être*], rather, that there is – this is a name of the being that there is there but which, giving itself (*es gibt ashes*), is nothing, remains beyond everything that is (*konis epekeina tes ousias*), remains unpronounceable in order to make saying possible although it is nothing.

> (1991b, 73)

Although, literally, she is nothing, nothing other than this constantly, often barely perceived phenomenal trace or projection of alterity, the weeping woman, like the cinder, being nothing, like the cinder, traces in the text, the ashes, the unpronounceable traces of an otherness which inhabits, and is projected onto, being; this being-there that there is there, which is both nothing and beyond everything that is. Beyond all entities she projects herself, she is projection herself, unpredictable, unremarkable. And it is this projectedness, this projection of the nothing which is being-projected, which causes tears.

These tears come about, arrive, are the projective traces of certain states of mind, the trace of the other on the self, and not the property of the subject who remembers. The tears are the trace of the other, as a trace projected by the murmuring in 'the great immaterial body of the weeping female of the streets of Prague' (*W* 50), tears which recall us to obligation, as we, like the narrator, like her other self narrated, await projection as the coming of responsibility, and as the injunction from the other not to forget. And as if to re-mark this coming, this injunction, and as a mark of the erasure – an erasure which is also a weaving of the trace of being, the cinder which remains beyond all enunciation – between the positions of narrating narrator, narrated narrator, the memory of the one in the other, the projection of these others by the reader and onto the reader (so that the reader, in turn, is made aware of being marked by the other of being), there is woven into this sentence the trace of the title; which is also the projection of the other, as a weaving and tracing of the ineluctable interconnectedness which projection – projection of the other, by the other – projects onto, throughout, *beyond* identity. As we read we are made aware that we must concede to the other. Our ethical responsibility is projected onto us by a giving-up of idealised subjectivity. The weeping woman is always before us, before the reader, the writer, the narrator and the narrated. This is what is being announced, *projected*, in the title, as it was, in other words, in another manner, in the title of *The Yellow Wallpaper*. What *La pleurante* has us recognise (about ourselves) is that, in the words of Emmanuel Levinas, '[t]he other haunts our ontological existence and keeps the psyche awake' (Levinas 1984, 63).

This haunting projection keeps the psyche awake to the very possibility of responsibility, the possibility that we respond to the summons of the other, even if that response is with our death. Such a response, and a responsibility, is affirmed as the necessity of understanding the affirmative projection of the weeping woman who, on the final page says '«Me voici!» Les mots du seuil et du pas au-delà. Les mots de la comparution[18]/ "Here I am!" The words of the threshold and the step [not] beyond. The words of appearance' (*P* 126/*W* 127).[19] As Derrida puts it, the condition which makes responsibility possible is the condition that there is no longer a transcendental objective which one allows to dictate one's responsibility, but that there is a movement related to both 'the relation to the other, [and] a response to the other' (Derrida 1995a, 50). And it is this of which we become aware, this which we affirm in our reading, and our acknowledgement of the summons projected from the other.

Yet notice this phrase 'Here I am'. In the time it takes to say it, much less than the time it takes to respond, here is never simply *here*, nor is 'I' ever simply 'I' except as – and this is very much in relation to the function of the 'here' which is not one – what Maurice Blanchot describes as the 'solidification into a fictional or functional identity, in order that the game of writing may be played . . . [in which the] principal player . . . displaces itself and takes the place of the change itself, displacement that lacks placing and that is missing from any placing' (Blanchot 1992, 4). Here names the impossible place of presence, presence always deferred and this deferral, this differentiation, being marked also in the 'I' of this paradoxical exclamatory fiction 'Here I am'. 'Here I am' names where 'I' is not except as other, as the other's trace of an identity partially erased by this re-citing, re-sited elsewhere, re-sounding otherwise, traced in the steps. The constant difference of the trace is, then, both spatial and, also, indelibly, temporal, so that being, being-there, is also a being-not-there; not a being-beyond but, instead, a being-not-beyond, which is yet, because of difference, the difference in identity affirmed by the resistant 'Here I am!', a being-ahead-of-itself, other-than-itself. This is not to imply the totality of *Dasein*'s projection read in Heidegger by Charles Guignon (Guignon 1993, 225). Rather, this is to understand how *Dasein* and any project of totalised identity perhaps envisioned by Heidegger is always undone from within by the very temporal spacing of *Dasein*.

This is witnessed in the Sixth Apparition of the weeping woman (*W* 63–9). She appears silhouetted against a stormy sky. She moves but the movement is not discernible (*W* 63). However, it appears, disturbingly, that the woman is capable of pursuing in silence two different directions (*W* 64). Time gives way beneath and is caught up in her steps. Not only do her steps map out the text and the spaces of the streets; they also trace time. Time is thus incorporated into projection. It might even be possible to suggest that time *is* projection. Projection projects the past onto the future, the present having given way in the affirmation of the projected trace. Indeed, the simultaneity of projections is such that the past, in being projected at the utmost speed is 'also the future' (*W* 64).

It is then pointed out that:

Il n'y a pas de temps abstrait; le temps est toujours celui d'un corps qui le porte et l'éprouve, celui de l'histoire d'un vivant.

(*P* 53)

There is no abstract time; time is always that of a body which feels and bears it, the time of the history of a living person.

(*W* 64)

Projection becomes specific through its event within time and across time. If time is always the time of a body and that body's ordeals, then projection is the affirmation of the other's being-

in-time. All projection is the projection of the specific, the singular, the material, even though that projection as other to the experience is immaterial. We are confronted by this, and respond
by affirming the nature of projection, across the time of reading,
and, especially, in a number of places where the other of the
other is projected through the woman, as the projection of the
historical as material experience:

Elle est le mystérieux frisson . . .

(*P* 58)

She is the mysterious *frisson* . . .[20]

(*W* 69)

Elle est la peau du temps, du temps des hommes. La tendre et
vulnérable peau du visage et du corps des humains.

(*P* 58)

She is the skin of time, of human time. The tender and vul-
nerable skin of the faces and bodies of humans.

(*W* 69)

. . . tous ces Très-Bas anonymes qui ont enduré, pâti l'Histoire,
et en sont morts . . .

(*P* 69)

. . . all those anonymous Outcastes who have endured, who
have suffered as a result of History, and who are dead . . .[21]

(*W* 78)

Comment pourrait-elle avoir un visage qui lui soit propre,
et même un corps de chair et d'os, quand sa face n'est faite
que l'effacement de milliards de visages et que son corps n'est
fait que des sueurs et des larmes des morts et de tous les vivants.

(*P* 69–70)

How could she have a face which was properly hers,[22] or indeed a body of flesh and bone, when her face is made up
only of the erasure of millions of faces and her body only of
the sweat and tears of the dead and all the living?

(*W* 79)

The woman projects herself as the other of experience, and as the projected affirmation of the material experience of all others whose being is indelibly traced and erased within what we name history. These statements of death – surely death is the horizon, the limit or border, which each of these citations acknowledges, and from which the overflow of the other is projected – affirm, through the projection of the other, what Derrida has called the characterisation of death as '*Dasein*'s most proper possibility' (Derrida 1993, 64). And this is despite *Dasein*'s inability to testify to death, as Derrida would have us believe (1993, 51). Thus it is the affirmation of the proper possibility which the other comes to project through the unconcealment of *Dasein* within its properly historical unfolding. The other affirms the death of the other – an improper death – as part of the structure of our acknowledgement of the properly-improper in being. We bear witness to the other in la pleurante which cannot be translated except improperly and otherwise as the trace of the history of being, which is to suggest history as a history of death.

Near the beginning of this chapter (and then, elsewhere, in other ways) Heidegger was invoked as a possible means by which to approach Germain's writing. In this event, it will be remembered that Germain's text came to be seen as bringing itself indirectly to bear on the Heiddeggerian concept of *Dasein*. Out of this engagement, an engagement in passing and from which there emerged various dissonances, it was possible to witness a certain folding back, an opening up, an *unconcealing*, which was also the making of a rent or tear. Through this projection emerged as both an affirmation and a resistance. What we might read as Germain's radical break with a Heideggerian *Dasein*, in which her writing is caught up, is made clear in her attempts to bear witness to the weeping woman's own bearing witness to the death of others, and to the memory of those who have died, to which we are obligated as a necessary ethical moment. Indeed, this is something 'in Heidegger' which Derrida has discussed in *Aporias*, and which Levinas discusses as early as 1932 in the article translated for the first time in 1996, 'Martin Heidegger and Ontology' (Levinas 1996, 11–32). The instauration of the ethical being pro-

jected through Heidegger involves the affirmation of the otherness
that articulates the difference of identity and between identities,
and which announces a resistance to any illusory notion of a
subjectivity which is either ideally unified in an imagined present,
or which can be imagined as having been an originary unified
position, out of which the narrating, narrated, reading subjectivities
have emerged as the facets of the split or divided self or psyche
(which is a possibility of reading toyed with by *La pleurante* and
la pleurante).

This has already been discussed with regard to the text; but,
as is wholly necessary, the question of ethics returns again in
the epilogue of the text. Projection of the other for Germain is
that which differentiates what can be read as her quasi-Levinasian
ethical notion of otherness and being from a purely Heideggerian
notion of Being which insists on the self-possession of Being by
myself, and marked in the articulation, the inscription of I. To
suggest this, however, is to acknowledge that this reading of
Heidegger is already being articulated from within a Levinasian
critique of Heidegger's concept of *Dasein*. In reading Germain
through the Heideggerian lens, and bearing in mind both the
trace of the Holocaust in Germain's text and Levinas's readings
of Heidegger, in relation to the former's articulations of the ethics
of the other, I have tried to read Heidegger somewhat against
the grain, as it were. I have sought, in passing, then, to re-read
the Heideggerian concept of *Dasein* from an ethical place afforded
by the projection of the aleatory narrative construct in *La pleurante
des rues de Prague*.

We can begin to understand *Dasein* in an other manner, from
an other place, with an other, ethical project in mind as the projection of the ethical. This is the act of understanding which is
also an act of caring, as Levinas reminds us in his appreciation
and critique of Heidegger (1996, 18–19). We cannot programme
such a project, we cannot anticipate projection, as Germain shows
us. Projection is one possible figure for what Levinas describes
as *Dasein*'s anguished 'mode of understanding' (1996, 29). Anguish, we read as constitutive of the weeping woman's affect, in
which we must share as readers. We must await projection's un-
looked for, unpredictable coming, from which event we come to
understand. Even if we believe ourselves to speak first, in truth
our enunciation is always already a response, a yes to the call of
the other, as Germain affirms: 'Our call, which we believe comes

first, is in truth always second' (W 125). *La pleurante* suggests, then, the possibility of an incessant projection, to which we are obliged to respond, and to which we are obligated to remain open. In its infinite and ethical dimensions projection, we may have come to understand, resists subjectivity, resists closure, not least the closure of the idea of a self-possessed and self-sufficient identity. And projection affirms in its openness the necessity of love as what Levinas has called the incessant watching over of the other (Levinas 1984, 66). Certainly, the weeping woman bears the mark, the wound of love, 'the deepest, most patient and generous love' (W 112) and, also, we are told that '[t]he word lovers . . . demanded giving, sharing and exchange' (W 124). The word 'lovers' (and also the lovers of writing) demand that which gives up stable identity in favour of the space of between, as the words 'don', 'partage', and 'échange' suggest in the original (P 122). 'Partage' also meaning 'dividing', there is the mark here of the division of identity brought about by acts of writing and loving. There is in this love, these lovers, in the words, and the implication of the incessant watching over of which Levinas speaks. For what else can we say that the weeping woman does, except watches over the other in loving anguish and care, watches over the dead, watches over this double trace, demanding that we understand our obligation to do the same. Her writing demands that we give (give ourselves, our identities over to giving); that we share, and thus divide our selves, our identities, and that we exchange with the other. Our Being-there is marked by a demand that we give up our dream of a separable, stable identity.

However, even as Germain breaks with Heidegger (and, in doing so, affirms her connectedness), so it is necessary to break (thereby re-establishing the connection), albeit partially, with Levinas at those places where his thinking encounters God. Indeed, this is what Germain appears to do around the double question of God and the other as questions having to do with the female trace. This is what projection, specifically projection of the female other and projection *as* female other, appears to bring to bear. This is part of its unpredictable, affirmative project. Hence my definition of Germain's project(ion) as quasi-Levinasian, rather than merely Levinasian. God, for Germain, is 'the emptiest of all words and can never embrace, master or retain the meaning it dares thus designate. . . . The word God is a flagstone of bronze set on a bottomless pit, a door between eternity and us, between infinity and us. Between the highest joy of loving and us' (*W* 125–6). God is thus that which separates us from love, from the love of the other; which is to say both our love for the other, and the love which the other projects. In this, Germain appears to resemble – albeit at a distance or oblique angle – the female voice which is projected at the end of Derrida's own response to Levinas, a response which incorporates the acknowledgement of the unacknowledged female's enunciation in Levinas's text, in the essay 'At this very moment in this work here I am' (Derrida 1991a, 11–51).

It is worth commenting on some features of this essay, albeit in passing, before concluding this chapter, as a way of opening up the gap between Germain's wholly other text and the (always implicitly masculine) philosophical discourse to which the weeping woman appears to address herself, and onto which she projects herself, her *other* female self (projection, once again, as resistance to the masculine project and as affirmation of the gendered trace of the other). Derrida's essay bears a tangential relationship to the current consideration of projection as female affirmation in the writing of Sylvie Germain inasmuch as Derrida is concerned with the ways in which Levinas's writing is marked by what Peggy Kamuf calls 'the altogether other' (Kamuf ed. 1991, 403). Following Kamuf's introduction, we can say that Derrida's reading demonstrates how the trace of the other in Levinas's work is not reducible to a single signature. Clearly, this is the case with Germain's text. Furthermore, there is a relationship between the female voice in Derrida's essay who raises the question of the jealous God in Levinas's writing and the figure of an equally jealous God in *La Pleurante des rues de Prague*, who stands between us and infinite love. The weeping woman is always before us, always before God in this text, always appearing ahead of identity and calling us before her. Because of what is untranslatable in 'la pleurante', which is nothing less than the question of difference as sexual difference, we must always bear in mind, and bear witness to the fact that, Germain's writing works through the relationship, in Derrida's words, between 'sexual difference – the other as the other sex, otherwise said as otherwise sexed – and the other as wholly other, beyond or before sexual difference' (1991a, 40).

More than this, Germain calls us to acknowledge the constantly reiterated or recited call to appear before this woman, this weeping figure marked with the trace of the other which is also the untranslatable affirmation of her gender as otherwise: a female projection, a female affirmation. Germain's writing, in announcing a wholly other history, a history of silences, tremors, aporias, absences, and in placing itself in the place from which projection obliges and summons us to respond to the exclamation 'Here I am!', affirms – and here resists Levinas, resists him *en passant* – the constant saying of the wholly other, marked *before* any economical mastery or definition, *as a female other*.[23] What is being affirmed in this projection is nothing less than a radical (in)version, which is read (otherwise) by Derrida (having read Catherine Chalier) in his reading of Levinas, but wholly appropriate here: 'The other as feminine (me), far from being derived or secondary, would become the other of the Saying of the wholly other . . . to make sexuality secondary with respect to a wholly-other that in itself would not be sexually marked . . . is always to make sexual difference secondary *as* femininity' (Derrida 1991a, 42–3). In Germain's (in)version the female is never a secondary other but always already the affirmative projection of the Female Saying (Saying marked by the trace of the female other) of the wholly other. She – the untranslatable in 'la pleurante' and not reducible to the hierarchisation of sexual economy – affirms the projection of the other within the wholly other, which is , in this case, the silenced, the erased, the obliterated, the mute. She, the mourner, allows the possibility of recitation.

And if these projections are recited, they are also re*sited*: the woman is always projected from an other place in the city, an other in the text ahead of the reader, ahead of the narrator, never in the same place twice, in order (as Derrida puts it) to 'make us (without making us) receive otherwise, and receive otherwise the otherwise' (1991a, 12). There is, to make the point once more then, the call of the serial appearances or projections of this wholly other female mourner, a number of appearances or apparitions which cannot be reduced to a single identity, but which announce or demand in the name of some wholly other uncodified and uncodifiable law – certainly not the Law of the Father – that we appear before her to bear witness, and so it is that we must negotiate with the 'marginal effects' (1991a, 12) of projection. Each appearance constitutes, without being reducible to the economy of repetition, the traces of what Derrida calls 'an absolutely singular seriality' (1991a, 22). The reiterative projection – which is the very condition of projection and of projected-ness itself, reiteration always marking projection as already other than itself – is not thematisable, not recuperable within any economy. You cannot keep the woman in the house. Out on the streets she resists all finite definition, all law, she affirms her being, as being wholly otherwise.

Thus there occurs without end in *La Pleurante des rues de Prague* what Derrida has described (again with reference to Levinas) as '... a saying unreduced to silence although no longer *said in language*' (1991a, 19; emphasis in original):

> The singular textuality of this series does not enclose the Other but on the contrary opens itself up to it from out of irreducible difference... (1991a, 22)

This is always inscribed in the disturbing, dissonant *récits* of the text: in the narrator's narration, her narration of her self as other self, her narrated narration of the serial apparitions, the narratives of countless others within the appearances; and in that projection of female difference which traverses the reader in both the time of reading and the time of re-reading, the time of memory, where projection affirms the female other and that other's disruption of (resistance to) any dream or desire of 'my self'.

Which leaves us to recognise that, in the other's words

> Toute reste à dire, tout reste à faire. A récrire. Ou peut-être, plutôt, tout reste à lire, – car ce sont les autres, les vivants et les morts, qui constituent déjà le livre, tout livre.
>
> (P 125)

> All remains to be said, all remains to be done. To be rewritten. Or perhaps, rather, everything remains to be read, – for it is the others, the living and the dead, who already constitute the book, every book.
>
> (W 126)

Il y a là écriture: There is writing. Writing is *there*. The supplement of identity, marked forcefully in the written difference between 'dire' and 'lire'. Projected traces between, awaiting reading. Memory of the other before the event. We've not yet begun to read.

Notes

1. The definite article is signalled with quotation marks to acknowledge the problematic status of that article in relation to thinking concerning 'between'. Elsewhere in this collection of essays the 'the' is omitted. Briefly stated, the problem is that, when talking of 'the between', the definite article signals a locatable space or place, a location with definable parameters. Such a gesture calms down the radicality of 'between' as a non-locatable space. The term 'betweenness' is equally problematic, for different reasons, not least the sense it offers of 'between' as a quasi-concept, which can be defined through various abstract, theoretical, analogical commentaries, as though mapping out the terrain. This has also been largely avoided. Rather than placing the definite article *sous rature* with a cross to draw attention to its problematic status, thereby seeming to raise a moment in Derrida's *Of Grammatology* to the principle of a method or technique, I have chosen instead to omit 'the', even though this makes particular phrases including 'between' somewhat awkward. Also I have largely refrained from scare quotes marking the term, because these also seem like an effort to pin something down.
2. The term 'femininity' is marked by quotation marks as a sign of its problematic status in the above discussion. I have tried to indicate that the term is not to be thought of as referring to some essential quality or the marker of some objective referent.
3. There is an English language edition, *The Weeping Woman on the Streets of Prague*, trans. Judith Landry, int. Emma Wilson (1993). I have consulted this edition throughout, giving page references for readers to the English language edition as a reference source. However it is not always reliable; in the first page, the last part of the paragraph ('y trame des images ... de fins èchos de voix') is left out. I have therefore amended translations and supplied my own, erring on the side of inelegant literalism
4. In the original, Germain uses the term 'apparition', which has spectral connotations in both French and in its English counterpart. The translation as 'appearance' does not carry with it such an immediately other-worldly suggestiveness.
5. I use the German term here for its doubled connotations: of ghost, certainly, but also of spirit, as in the sense of spiritual identity, rather than merely ghostliness. Also haunting this term is Derrida's reading of 'spirit' in Heidegger.
6. Or, at least, 'Heideggerian', 'quasi-Heideggerian', from the perspective of Levinas.
7. Derrida's discussion, which is now well known, deals with the operation and place of titles in relation to what we can call, for convenience' sake, the body of the text and the law.
8. On preparing for the coming of the Other, see Jacques Derrida, 'Psyche: Inventions of the Other', in *Reading De Man Reading* (1989b, 60).
9. I would like to read a possible play in the French text here, a play resounds on the ear and tongue, and which, like the ink-trace, is

also a visual play. The phrase 'dans ses pas' clearly has the immediate meaning of 'in her footsteps'. However, 'pas' registers part of
a negative construction, such as 'n'est pas'. Where we follow, where
ink traces in the text those places where the weeping woman has
been but no longer is; this is where, in numerous places, she is not.
Thus we read the sites of her prior presences, we sight both these
and the words which mark, cite, her absence.

10. The question of the other heading, and the heading of the other,
the other's heading, is discussed with regard to questions of European and national identity, by Derrida in his *The Other Heading:
Reflections on Today's Europe* (1992c).

11. The gift of the name, giving a name, is of the order of an economic
fixing of the meaning of the other by the one who names. Naming
seeks to damp down the various dissonances of the other by providing a signature-limit.

12. We may consider this as being nowhere more forcefully foregrounded
than in Joseph Conrad's *Heart of Darkness*, with its insistent reiterative saying of the unsayable, culminating in the words of Kurtz,
'the horror, the horror', possibly the affirmative epigraph of the
aporia in art.

13. Celan's poem 'In Prag', from *Atemwende*, pursues the projective trace
of the other through the cityscape in relation to a certain unnameable
destruction (Paul Celan, *Selected Poems*, [1990, 248/249]).

14. This phrase, as well as being interpretable by the simple phrase,
'she was going away' (which I have given above), also has other
idiomatic senses which are pertinent in the context of the text as a
whole: she moved away (from one dwelling to another), she died,
she passed away, she stole away.

15. The verb 'ressasser' means to brood over or to dwell on, to keep
rehearsing or turn over, to keep trotting out or go over again and
again. 'Constant' is a poor translation here, but to suggest another
phrase, such as 'constantly reiterated', seems to force the translation too far (this problem takes us back to the introduction of this
chapter, the double question of idiom and identity, and the untranslatable between). The phrase seems to suggest that there was a
murmuring or whispering which she had brooded over and over,
or dwelt on repeatedly. Coincidentally, the verb 'ressasser' suggests
the words 'ressaut' and 'ressayer' or 'réessayer', meaning 'projection' in its architectural sense (a signification of projection with which
Heidegger plays constantly) and 'to try [on a garment] again' respectively. Thus, given the focus on projection in this essay and
the projection of murmuring from the folds of garments and other
materials in which the weeping woman is shrouded, there appears
to be a certain fortuitous chance in the use of the verb 'ressasser',
which is readable as weaving together certain threads of some
importance.

16. 'l'inaudible rumeur': the immediate logic of the sentence seems to
dictate the translation of this phrase as 'the inaudible murmur'. Other
senses are, however, available, which seem appropriate to the text.

Within certain contexts 'inaudible' can be translated as 'unbearable', while 'rumeur' can most obviously be translated as 'rumour'. It should be almost immediately apparent why a phrase such as 'the unbearable rumour in the blood' is so poetically appropriate, given the various spectres, whispers, and enunciations of the other which come to be projected through, and from, the weeping woman.

17. I have suggested both awareness *and* conscience because of the repeated presence of the discourse on the Holocaust as being coterminous with the projection of the weeping woman.

18. 'Comparution' implies a legal injunction to appear, as in a court appearance; at the same time the English 'appearance' is one possible translation of the French 'Apparition'; hence my choice of 'appearance' here with its implied double sense of legal obligation and apparition, rather than the more obvious 'summons' used in the English translation. The summons calls one to appear before the law. Again, Germain's text appears to be an indirect projection and affirmation of other texts, specifically this time, Franz Kafka's *vor dem Gesetz* (appropriately enough) and Derrida's *'Devant la loi'*.

19. I have translated the phrase 'du pas au-delà' as 'the step [not] beyond', rather than following the English translation's 'the step beyond' because this phrase seems to invoke Maurice Blanchot's text of the same name (Blanchot, *The Step Not Beyond* [1992]). This translation seems dictated by the shared themes of Blanchot's and Germain's work concerning limits, such as the limit between the philosophical and the literary, death, writing, the Holocaust, transgression. Similarly, both acknowledge, and use, the fragmentary, the aphoristic, as modes of expression; indeed, Germain, in the final pages, describes *La pleurante* as 'le livre en fragments/The book in fragments' (126/127; see Ch. 7 below, where I quote Nicholas Royle, who describes Derrida's *The Post Card* as philosophy in fragments). More than this, Germain, it could be argued, appears to adopt Blanchot's ideas concerning writing being a game of chance, a play of limits or multiplied terms and images without transcendental privileging. This is yet another of the possible dissonant oscillations of affirmative projection which it is possible – and even necessary – to discern, which I can only indicate for now in this cursory fashion. On the untranslatability of the title of Blanchot's work, see Lycette Nelson's introduction to that text (v–xxii), where she points out how the *pas* in the phrase points to a step that is also a false step, how the trace effaces itself even as it is written (xvi). This seems particularly pertinent to the wandering steps of the weeping woman. If the step beyond is never completed, as Nelson suggests (xvii), then the weeping woman never finishes walking the streets of Prague; we are always before her injunction to respond, to bear witness.

20. On the *mysterium tremendum*, the frightful mystery which makes you tremble, see Derrida (1995a Ch. 3, 53 ff.).

21. I have translated 'Très-Bas', for which there is no direct translation, as 'Outcastes', this being suggested by that group in Indian

society depicted by Mulk Raj Anand, in his novel *Untouchable*, (1986), the title of which would also suggest an appropriate term.

22. In the French *propre* obviously suggests property and what is proper to one, so that the line might read: 'How could she have a face which was proper to her?' The point that the narrative makes clear is that the weeping woman's identity is *improper*, there is no proper identity as such. This is resisted, as the impropriety of the weeping woman affirms all its traces of the other. Identity – known from another point of view, from that of the reader or narrator – is founded on a certain question or premise of translatability. As the introduction to this chapter concerning the untranslatability of the title and the idiom of identity suggests, any identity always retains that which resists interpretation; what is retained is the other's affirmation.

23. See Derrida (1991a, 38–44 passim).

7

The place between: sending love and resisting identity or, between Derrida, Deronda and Deguy

We recognise the alphabet; we are not sure of the language

George Eliot

... car chacun est celui qui vient de *perdre la face* en l'autre ... oublier l'unité

... for everyone is the one who has just *lost face* in the other ... forget unity

Michel Deguy

When I write 'what interests me', I am designating not only an *object* of interest, but the place that *I am in the middle of*...

Jacques Derrida

rehearsing the preliminaries

What is the place, the 'taking place', that the idea of the 'between' designates? What event does the figure of the 'between' acknowledge, for example in the act, in any act of writing, so that the subject finds himself or herself, positioned, albeit momentarily and in an instance which is both unique and iterable? Can we legitimately talk of '*the* between' when no place exists as such, other than as the necessary and provisional correspondence *between* identities (which space exists as the taking place of identity)? Why might love name otherwise the place of 'between', not in some abstract fashion, but in the event of taking place?

This essay concerns a certain number of betweens: particularly it concerns an imagined 'taking place' or 'between' which is readable in the work of Jacques Derrida and Michel Deguy, and in George Eliot's last novel, *Daniel Deronda*. To the anglophone world, Derrida's relationship to 'between', and his constant involved investigation of 'between' (with many names) is quite well-known: between philosophy and non-philosophy, between philosophy and literature, between writing and voice, between a restricted economy and a general economy. Between myself and the other.

The work of Michel Deguy is not so widely known in English-speaking countries, and this is perhaps a sign of that 'between' which his writing inhabits, between translatability and untranslatability, between French and English; however, his poems embrace many of these concerns, particularly that movement between self and other, its momentary flickering into being, or what we might designate as the becoming-between of the event of any relationship which is wholly unpredictable, unprogrammable. It is in a certain way the most fundamental of relationships, and signifies relationship as such, as the place where love might be said to 'take place'. This is a frequently troubled relationship, fraught with likely misinterpretations, open to misreading. It is, in one way at least, the relationship always taking place between reader and writer, between the writer as writer and the writer who reads in order to write. Already this type of sentence – the one just written, just read – will have annoyed some for the way in which it comes between them (you) and the me 'I' am presumed to be, as though 'I' was an origin. Or a source.

Daniel Deronda is a novel which challenges the very idea of source and origin through an open-ended narrative concerning identity. It seeks to work through the problem of *between* directly and indirectly, in a series of narrative strands which weave between one another, in terms of personal identity, ideological, racial, cultural and ethnic identity; and it does so in a fashion which opens out the enigma of identity and knowledge concerning one's identity as a constant taking place between fictions of stable identity, with which fictions one supposedly identifies (or not).

What can be suggested is that the figure of *between* names the certain staging or performance of, the acknowledgement of, the way in which identities come to be constructed. The identities, let us say, of Jacques Derrida, who in *Points, The Post Card*, and *Jacques Derrida* (to name only the most obvious places where these identities take place) writes of himself, of his identities – and he makes this plural plain, let's not forget this – as identities which take place between: most immediately between France and Algeria, between a passive affirmation of Jewishness and a resistance to that. There is also the question of a certain philosophical identity for Derrida which some try to establish, of which more below. These are well known, and not something we intend to pursue at any length here, except to acknowledge how crucial the (taking) place of *between* is in Derrida's writing to identity. Between is hymeneal, and, again as is well known, the hymeneal has concerned Derrida throughout his writing. We might say that he has written about nothing else over the last thirty years. The hymeneal is the trait, the trace which Derrida acknowledges in his relationship to 'French' writing, to 'German' philosophy (to a certain French reading of German philosophy), as though writing and philosophy could have, unequivocally, national identities, which were not somehow contaminated by their relationship to other identities, as though a certain between were not *always already* inhabiting their identities. The hymeneal is the trait which Derrida pursues and retraces between French literature and its others. This is clearly seen in his returns to Mallarmé, and particularly in the problematising relationship he establishes and folds back for our inspection in his entry on Mallarmé for the *Tableau de la littérature française* as a *French* writer whose identity is constructed by his resistances to and his being-folded-within French identity. The hymeneal then, as one possible figure for between.

I am also concerned with pursuing acts of 'amateur reading'. Amateur, not so much in the sense of that which is opposed to the 'professional'; although, indirectly, that is also my concern here, a concern over which others have been concerned to accuse Derrida: He's not a professional enough philosopher, for instance. Why doesn't he get on with philosophy, you hear muttered anytime in the last quarter-century with increasing annoyance; or, what is Derrida's theory of literature? why doesn't he come right out and state what his position is, why can't he be more professional? Why can't he profess what he does (when in fact he has done nothing else, as the quotations at the end of this chapter show), speaking about what he does, rather than just doing it? Why can't Derrida be more responsible to Marxism, why can't his response to Marx be more codified, more professional in its nature? Yet, what else has Derrida ever been except an involved professor who finds himself in the middle, in between what *interests* him, as the epigraph from *Points* makes plain? No, 'amateur' here for me is the reader who loves, the amatory reader. 'Amateur' in the sense of one who loves or is fond of something. This then is a 'loving' reading in which I will offer an *amateur* reading of a post card or two. This is not so much a reading; rather it should be considered more as an extended amatory note, *un écrit naïf*, a naive writing (Bennington and Derrida 1993, 8/4),[1] for reasons which will reveal themselves. A note on a post card then, and a note about a note on a post card.

There is also a concern here, albeit a concern approached obliquely and already questioned above, with that desire to 'know' Jacques Derrida, to have knowledge of Derrida, a knowledge without limits about 'who he is'. This desire for knowledge involves critics in seeking to know who he is, to comprehend his identity through those texts that are signed in his name, as though the signature and identity were the same; and the desire to search out identity through the game of seeking out those seemingly 'autobiographical' post-cards and fragments which some of us would like to believe Derrida is sending in his texts. Did I call this desire? Obsession is a better term.

And, lastly, I am concerned with love: sending love, addressing love, naming love, thinking about love as that which undoes both the promise of, and obsession with, a stable identity. This is a loving reading in that it explores texts which explore love, are written out of love, or which express love. Love is also the place from which this essay is generated as an expression between identities, love being one possible signature for the place of *between*. It's a question of being faithful to etymology (amongst other things) and what one loves, of loving the trace, rather than merely playing on chance resemblances in some nihilistic freefall (as some have accused Derrida and others who read him responsibly). Loving Derrida then, rather than knowing Derrida. Projecting Love through acts of reading and writing Love, which Derrida – or someone called Derrida – sends and discusses often enough in *The Post Card*, and frustrates identity itself.

The frustration of identity is often marked by the play with identity that is set in motion by the proper name and the 'fig-ure', the event of love, which figure or event, as Nicholas Royle suggests, is a 'condition of any deconstructive reading' (Royle 1995, 56). Before we go any further, it is perhaps best to say that that which is 'between' Derrida, Deronda, and Deguy is nothing other than 'love'. And if love as the figure of *between* is what amounts to a condition of any deconstructive reading, decon-structive reading is inevitably, very much an affair between iden-tities, *un amour propre* which remains in play and is untranslatable; which leaves in play its *traits* in any translation, as the sign of love between one identity and another, between French and English for example, or, in the case of *Deronda*, between the so-called English and Jewish parts of the story. Such a play sets off reso-nances, dissonances, oscillations both percussive and repercussive; in short, nothing less than aural apparitions. I shall attempt to signal these reverberative spectres throughout as they play in the non-place of the in-between, between, let's say for now, Derrida, Deronda, and Deguy. But let me ask two questions.

Who is writing? To whom?

(Derrida 1987b, 5)

Despite the absence of quotation marks this remark will have been identified, by some or by many perhaps, although this is undecidable. The remark having been applied, having been ap-plied to, its purpose or function remains open, even though the parenthesis offers a certain identity. You may think you recognise in these words, in what in other words is sometimes called a quotation or citation, the announcement of certain 'themes'. 'Themes', that is, if you are rushing ahead in order to pin down the 'themes' of this chapter, ahead of their arrival, ahead of their possible communication; or, if you assume the destination of these words I am giving to you as a given. You may even think you detect the possibility of reproduction, of parody, of pastiche, or some other form of imitative pantomimickry, or even ventrilo-quism, apparently being an academic imitation of a certain type of critical playfulness which will no doubt irritate. The antagonised reader will even detect in such a strategy and such rhetoric the imitation, the impersonation of a 'style', so as to fix an identity. Someone, not me,[2] comes to speak through me, to you, to some-one, all of which comes to take place 'between'.

Or this is how it might seem. The problem of course is that, already, 'I' have become, not the source, but the medium for a ghost writer. 'I' becomes, the between, the in-between, of the sender and the addressee, the unmappable *in medias res*[3] of apparent locations, locations which are themselves undecidable. 'I', in this case, is always already marked, not as a unified identity but as a between which cannot be located *as such*. As Derrida suggests 'the "I" constitutes the very form of resistance . . . Identification is a difference to itself, a difference with/of itself' (1995b, 340). 'My' identity, what I call 'my identity', is subject to events of resonant transference from incomprehensible addresses to unknowable destinations which leave their trace or mark on 'identity', and which determine the structuring of identity, while revealing that no identity is ever simply *there* but is always manifestly unstable and contingent on alterity. This general problem of the knowability of identity is further complicated by texts such as those we call Derrida's. And this is not necessarily because they are obscure, complex or difficult, as some have suggested. Contrary to such a thought, J. Hillis Miller reminds us, '[t]he chief obstacle to a complete cartography of Derrida's topographies . . . is not the extent and complexity of the terrain but the presence within any place on his map . . . that cannot be mapped' (Miller 1995, 296). *Between* takes place but has no place that is proper to itself. A non-place, it *takes place* as the chance or event *between* different identities, and as the affirmative difference of identities.[4]

And if a place cannot be mapped, how do we know where a post card has come from, how can we decide on the address? how could we even trust the words, 'wish you were here'? Where 'here' is remains undecidable precisely because nothing so far has arrived. As Nicholas Royle points out, if we are talking about Derrida's work, that work 'has not yet been received . . . [his] work precisely *resists* being received' (1995, 56; emphasis in original). Derrida's writing is, precisely, between. Unmappable, it remains between, affirming itself and resisting reception.

But more on the subject of 'themes': What might these 'themes' be? communication, the subject, the identity of the author, the impossible place of the other, the undecidable. But this would be to decide on the undecidable, creating a paradox already; like Stephen Daedalus, I love paradoxes, or can be accused of being a paradoxist. There is also a certain question of biography or autobiography perhaps, or even love. Certainly what connects all these issues is the space between them, where it is possible that communication takes place. And questions therefore arise: have I announced these themes in this possible citation? Is that what you think? Or do you wish to read them there? Is there a desire, between the Said and the Saying, and on the part of the auditor or what, in other circumstances, might be called the 'amateur' reader? is there a desire to decide on an interpretation? Do we, do you, desire the good reader, the professional reader, to step forward, announcing a meaning or identity?

Everything being announced here requires, for the moment, an answer which is another possible citation: I don't know, I do not know (Derrida 1987b, 5) or, as Rimbaud might have put it otherwise, 'I' does not know'. What is being indicated here is that this is not a beginning but the 'in-between', I have already given up the 'make-believe of a beginning' (Eliot 1967, 35) as part of a gesture which affirms strategic undecidability, mobility, strategic affirmation beyond thematisation, and simultaneously resisting thematisation *en passant*, while resisting the desire for absolute knowledge on the subject, resisting (en)closure and foreclosure; an affirmation, therefore, which resists, rather than acquiesces; an affirmation which resists through side-stepping, skirting round, circumscribing, loving, an affirmation which affirms and resists by posit(ion)ing questions, and questions concerning questions.

There is a certain apparent degree of application going ahead here, a certain play on the question of application, as in the sense of both applying to (some thought, some concept) and applying: adding, laying on, bringing into contact, administering, coming into contact with or, as the *Oxford English Dictionary* suggests, putting to use, giving a specific reference to (a general, theoretical, or figurative statement), using as relevant or suitable, bringing to bear, having relevance, applying the breaks. And certainly, what else should one love to do in the face of the professional reader but apply the breaks, in this case chiefly through the proliferation of questions and undecidables as a strategic means of affirming undecidability and thereby resisting fixing meaning and identity in place.

But there are other meanings for the term 'apply': to attend assiduously to, to devote one's energy to, to bend or direct one's thought, one's self (an intriguing proposition, bending one's self,

which I shall have to give up for the moment). All of these meanings, these definitions, seem to have come into play through the
opening two questions which, it seems to me, require (a further)
repetition at this point:

Who is writing? To whom?

I am of course, with or without quotation marks, citing a line
from *The Post Card*, from 'Envois', a line which seems to be announcing the difficulties involved in communication. In citing
it, I am also reciting and re-sounding. And, if no longer simply
citing, if not naming, then questioning something else, which so
far has yet to be addressed.[5] The citation comes from one of several possible signers who are signed themselves, addressed, by
the proper name 'Jacques Derrida', but who, this 'Jacques Derrida'
assures us – who is this Jacques Derrida? – are 'not always vis-
ibly and necessarily identical from one *envoi* to another... the
signers are not to be confused with the senders, nor the addressees
to the receivers, that is with the readers' (1987b, 5). And what
am I writing about? A post card, or two. The post card will seem
to be one of those which a certain 'Jacques Derrida' admits is
signed by possibly other 'Jacques Derridas', a 'wholly otherwise'[6]
Jacques Derrida perhaps; one of those post cards where a certain Derrida – which one? as a Derrida says 'doubtless we are
several' (1987b, 6) – writes about identity, love, and discussing,
for instance, what is called love, who one calls love, while, all
the while, and on a given day, desiring the possibility of 'erasing all the traits, even the most inapparent ones, the ones that
mark the tone, or the belonging to a genre (the letter for example, or the post card) ... somewhat in order to "banalize" the
cipher...' (1987b, 11). Derrida's desire for 'banalization' announces
a writing the status of which he has described elsewhere as being, 'in a certain way, impossible to assign' (1995b 117). The writing
of post cards or love notes for instance. This desire, in the name
of love, a name otherwise than love, traces on the post card the
impossible assignation of lovers, their dis-appointment, the writing
of which serves to announce the space between. How, then, shall
we name that which sets the tone?[7]

  This gives us pause to consider the proper name or signature.
In the face of what Michel Deguy calls '*l'excessive promesse des
noms*', (102) the excessive promise of names, who is this Jacques
Derrida, and how should we write this proper name? In imitation

of a signature, merely as a proper name? a presumed *telos*-as-addressee or addressee-as-*telos*? or can we imagine this proper name as the title of a text, co-authored by someone of the same name, and with that person mistaken – desired – as the subject of this text named *Jacques Derrida*, rather than those texts written by Jacques Derrida? And, furthermore, in which language is this text *Jacques Derrida* to be read, French or English? I cannot help but laugh every time I see the title page of the English language edition, which proudly bears the inscription 'Jacques Derrida translated by Geoffrey Bennington', as though Jacques Derrida – as opposed to *Jacques Derrida* – had been rendered other than himself by Geoffrey Bennington. Which, of course, may also be true in part, although we would have to acknowledge that there would be that 'in' 'Jacques Derrida' which exceeds and escapes Bennington's translation. There is that in the name of Jacques Derrida which remains untranslatable, which resists translation and thus affirms the otherness of its identity. In response to this, Bennington himself might say that translation means we have 'a very clear if not very simple, relation between two texts and two signatures' (Bennington and Derrida 1993, 166/156). Two signatures then, the same and not the same, one in French, one in English. Acknowledging all this, we would then have to write, conventionally, in various ways, this name: within quotation marks, without such marks, in italic script or not, as the law dictates. And there seems to be a similarity in the name of Daniel Deronda/*Daniel Deronda*, which is the name of both subject and text, subject as text and text as subject, which has already been cited and to which I shall return shortly.

There seems to be what Louis Kaplan, drawing on the work of Peggy Kamuf, refers to as totalising demands on the signature and the signature effect (Kaplan 1995, 7); it is the case that such totalising demands on the signature are often, especially in the case of 'Jacques Derrida', demands upon biography and autobiography also, often in the face of Derrida's arguments in *Glas* and 'Signature Event Context', where it is explained, particularly in the former, how the writing of the signature exceeds structure and definition.[8] So the signature both resists and affirms. So many possibilities, and none, despite the resonance between them, equivalent to the others. Doubtless they are several. And as you know, if there are resonances, there are also dissonances, disturbing oscillations and solicitations between imagined poles. So, in order to open up the space of the in-between to enquiry, let me ask another question, then:

What am I going to be able to write on a post card?

I have to ask this question because it involves, equivocally, in two places at least, a writing, a double writing or a ghost writing, the status of which, is, once again, impossible to assign. What am I going to be able to write? A signature perhaps, or a proper name. My own or another's. Or both. Perhaps an aphorism. The proper name is, after all, the absolute aphorism, as Derrida has suggested in the context of disappointed love (Derrida 1992a, 433); or, even, 'a few aphorisms, bits of postcards and other fragments' (Royle 1995, 124).

Or, I might write my love: that is to say, the communication of my love, of what I call 'my love', to someone who I call 'my love', someone who, in any case is already hovering around the pages of this essay, and who is other than the one who sends love, the one who signs the name at the bottom of the card. In writing (to) my love, I might send poetry, because poetry, like love, risks everything on signs, suggests Michel Deguy: *La poésie comme l'amour risque tout sur des signes* (60). In the very act of writing love, in writing of my love, to my love, and signing my name to this, I announce the destabilisation of what I call 'my identity', writing to one who is not to be captured but who is – again in Deguy's words – *l'autre, l'autre que cet autre que je suis*, the other, the other than that other that I am (170). Something of this is unfolded in a post card dated 3 June 1977:

> and when I call you my love, my love, is it you I am calling or my love? You, my love, is it you I thereby name, is it to you that I address myself? . . .
>
> (Derrida 1987b, 8)

Folding itself over, into and upon itself, the post card continues:

> when I call you my love, is it that I am calling you, yourself, or is it that I am telling my love? and when I tell you my love is it that I am declaring my love to you or indeed that I am telling *you*, my love, and that you are my love. I want so much to tell you.
>
> (1987b, 8)

The poignancy of this last line, which echoes – as does the entire post card – with the possibility of a line of Michel Deguy's – *Et je voudrais t'aimer deviendrait je t'aime* . . . (18); And I would like to love you would become I love you – this poignant expression announces the in-between which is between us, and which will lead, towards the end of this essay, to a short text of Deguy's which might fit on a post card, *c'est entre nous*, it's between us.

But for the moment, Derrida's post card, a post card we have been assured has been signed by a 'Jacques Derrida', maps out before us the unmappable regions of the in-between of love, that in-between played out in-between the names at the edges of the card, that in-between, that in-between-us which is between us and so destabilises all identities. It is this very question, concerning love, poetry and the question of the idiom, which Derrida discusses in response to the question, *Che cos'è la poesia* (Derrida 1995b, 288–300). Derrida is responding to the other, of course. To an other tongue, in the only tongue he has, as he attempts to address this question concerning translatability, considering the *hérisson, istrice*, the hedgehog, and responding once again to Heidegger in the negotiations of the amateur reader between French and German thought, between questions of translatability. Languages abound as Derrida places himself *between* at any number of crossroads, innumerable betweens or meeting points which make the gesture of *sous rature* where traces from unknowable locations intersect. What marks *between* for Derrida? the heart 'between paths and autostradas' (Derrida 1995b, 295). More than the biological thing, the heart, says Derrida, pulses with the difference of rhythm, the heartbeat itself the movement of difference, 'like a rhythm spacing out time' (Derrida 1995b, 295). Or like any one of countless post cards, spaced out between, sent and not yet received.

This is all quite well known, of course. One might even say that it is a given, although exactly what is given, what is being given, a given which is also a giving,[9] is clearly given over to the equivocation of the in-between, in the give and take of language.

Equivocation abounds. There is, for instance, the equivocation of the title: a note on a post card; whose note? mine? or another's? mine concerning the other's? Then there is the equivocation of the question with which I made a second start. This equivocation is locatable in the preposition 'on', in the question 'what am I going to be able to write on a post card'? Most immediately this might be taken – or given – to refer to the writing on the surface of a post card, as if to say, 'what am I going to be able to write *on* a post card, what am I going to be able to inscribe on its blank surfaces'? Or 'on' might be taken to mean, or to be approximately equivalent to, 'about'. As in, 'what am I going to be able to write *about* a post card (is this what I am going to do?). What subject, concept, context, idea, discourse concerning a post card am I going to be able to write on or about? It might be assumed, you might be forgiven for assuming, that such a meaning, such an identity, is a given.

So the ghost of the earlier question is raised: What am I going to able to write on a post card? It is difficult to say, but what I might be able to write on a post card is (about) a certain attempt to establish a communication between us, the continuous event of saying between us. It's between us, *c'est entre nous*, this text of *between*, between two names, top and bottom, between self and other, between the other other and the other that I am, between sender and receiver, between writer and reader. But, for now, let's acknowledge at least in the face of uncertainty, in the face of the in-between, and with the figure of the ghost writer in our mind's eye, that, as Hamlet says in a quibble over identities, 'we must speak by the card, or equivocation will undo us' (V. 1. 136).

absolute aphorisms

Nicholas Royle has stated that '[t]he "Envois" in *The Post Card* constitute perhaps Derrida's most provocative "self portrait" and most obvious affront to the conventional requirements and expectations of philosophical discourse. This is philosophy in fragments, on post cards' (Royle 1995, 133). If these are a 'self-portrait' the sender is not giving himself away. The 'envois', the post cards, might then be said to have been sent – are still being sent, having yet to arrive, *finally* – from one of those unmappable places spoken of by Hillis Miller. If their senders are some of the possible Jacques Derridas whom you might think you could pin down then it is worth bearing in mind another scene concerning 'Jacques Derrida', a scene involving the question of where Jacques Derrida comes from, who he is, what constitutes his identity. Allow me a detour, a circumscription.

In an interview entitled 'There is No *One* Narcissism (Autobiophotographies)' (1995b, 196–216) which deals with, amongst other things, identities, addresses, destinations, another Jacques Derrida makes the following remark concerning his writing and teaching. Of these activities, he has said, 'I have this feeling I am doing it from another place that I do not know: an exteriority based on a place that I do not inhabit in a certain way, or that I do not identify' (1995b, 206). Derrida, this Derrida, who seems to be locating himself in a manner similar to the way 'I' locate myself above – 'I' locates itself – acknowledges the unknowable other of identity; he is responding to a question aimed at finding cultural and intellectual determinants for the signature and proper name 'Jacques Derrida' and what 'Jacques Derrida' does (1995b, 205), being and doing momentarily conflated in the question in what seems to be a moment of Sartrean *mauvais fois*. Uncertain yet noticing the spectre of between, the interviewer has the feeling that Derrida's 'intellectual and cultural heritage is Greek and German' but asks whether there might not also be 'a sort of Judaic intrusion, difficult to define' (1995b, 205). This Judaic intrusion, itself calling on the other here, might come along, suggests the interviewer, to undo, deconstruct, the line of traditional division between German and Greek, referring also to this deconstruction as an inscription (1995b, 205–6). Thus the question involves a certain mark, a trace which is also a cut, a one-time incision to be reiterated over and over again, a circumcision, if you will, which signs the name 'Jacques Derrida'. So, circumcision as signature, the moment of inscription. This is admitted to elsewhere, in response to a question concerning *Circumfession* (and what that text turns around), that internal margin written by Jacques Derrida for *Jacques Derrida*:

> Circumcision means, among other things, a certain mark that, coming from others and submitted to in absolute passivity, remains on the body, visible and no doubt indissociable from the proper name which is likewise received from the other. It is also the moment of the signature (the other's as well as one's own) by which one lets oneself be inscribed in a community or in an ineffaceable alliance: birth of the subject . . . rather than "biological" birth. Every time there is this mark and this name . . . the *figure* at least of a circumcision is imposed on me.
>
> (1995b, 341)

Circumcision: the moment of the double signature, the mark of the other, as well as the naming of the self by the other and the communication between the two or, at least, the announcement of a possible *between*; nothing less than the application of the name, public and private. Circumcision is then the *partage*, the sharing and dividing of identity. The other applies to identity. Circumcision is, recalling the earlier definitions of application, administered, brought to bear. Perhaps, even, we can say that circumcision is, in a certain way, an *envois* from an unknown location, the arrival of which promises each time to determine the identity of the self as the place between, in-between the other and an 'ineffaceable alliance'. For example, there is the birth of the subject 'Jacques Derrida', 'Jacques Derrida', this proper name, is applied. Circumcision is an act of giving; 'Jacques Derrida' is given. What can this arrival, this delivery, this imposition, this given giving mean? Perhaps you hear the following answer, in two languages:

– He will have obligated (*il aura obligé*)[10]

But who speaks this? From where has the postcard or aphorism been sent? From where does it arrive, if at all? Or, to put this another way, in the way of the other – that is to say in the voice of the other and not as an obstacle – Who is writing? to whom? We cannot yet assume with any certainty that we know. As Eve Tavor Bannet has suggested, it is possible to hear the other and the affirmation of the other 'in Derrida's writing', but we also have to be aware that this other, whom we think we hear, is never unequivocally identifiable as simply or wholly other (Bannet 1993, 80–7).[11] There is always the chance of not hearing correctly, of the delivery going astray, of the other being mistaken, in certain circumstances, for Derrida. Is this someone named 'Derrida', someone to whom we apply, someone who is applied (to), merely reporting the reception of the other's address? is he merely re-iterating, reciting, as Tavor Bannet surmises? There is here a question of tonality and the undecidability of setting the tone, as you will recall, and this tone has much to do with the other's affirmation, the other's amatory transmission which, to paraphrase Jean-Luc Nancy, can be missed (Nancy 1991, 82–110); missed by, in this case, the professional reader. The amateur reader already loves, already awaits the coming of the other's delivery, which has yet to arrive. But this is to lose myself in love, from where

'I' cannot return except as other than I am. Identity is both marked and lost, hidden in its very inscription.

So far the detour which I shall curtail. However, why this detour? The detour, this circumscriptive trace as passing remark, can lead us to a post card, almost as if by chance. Nicholas Royle, as I have already pointed out, identifies the *envois* as Derrida's 'most provocative "self-portrait"'. Yet how sure can we be that what we read is indeed self-portraiture? None of the fragments are signed in the 'proper place' and the possible names of the addressees, the potential receivers, are never present; or they are, at the very least, not obviously where one might believe they should be. Peggy Kamuf has pointed out that these names are 'censored or cut out' (Kamuf ed. 1991, 485). Even as circumcision marks the proper name, the signature, it can also be said to hide identity by cutting it away. As I inscribe the name 'Jacques Derrida' I apply it, I make it into a work, I make it work, transforming the name into a thing, an application.[12] Yet there is that in the name, the other in the identity which is located in the giving of the name, which resists both monumentalisation and equipmentality. The other in the name applies the breaks. This is complicated further because names are never simply there or not there. As Derrida remarks in an interview from 1983, 'all the names of the family are encrypted, along with a few others, in *The Post Card*, sometimes unreadable even for those who bear these names; often they are not capitalised' (1995b, 120). So while the good reader, the polite or professional reader, goes off in search of such monuments and the family (en)crypt(ion), we, or at least I, the amateur reader, confronts a moment when I must bear witness to the fact that the structure of identity is inhabited in a certain way by non-knowing.[13] This non-knowing, I want to suggest is marked by the 'absolute aphorism' of the proper name which comes between identity and being, and between knowing and non-knowing as the signature of *between*.

And all that I have suggested so far can be applied to a certain moment in George Eliot's last novel, *Daniel Deronda* and its eponymous protagonist whose is *between*, between the knowable and the unknowable, between knowledge and ignorance, between Englishness and Jewishness.

between identities: sending, posting, writing

In one of the *envois* one of those proliferating Jacques Derridas mentions Daniel Deronda/*Daniel Deronda*. I insist on doubling the proper name here because this name is marked by equivocation and enigma, double reading no less, both within itself, *amongst itselves*, and in the post card/*The Post Card*.[14] Two proper names, two titles: Jacques Derrida/*Jacques Derrida*, Daniel Deronda/*Daniel Deronda*, all concerned with identities, cultural, national, inherited, personal, public and private; all bearing the marks of circumcision; all scintillating and ringing with undecidability, resounding with the repercussions of the desire 'to know' the truth of identity. Even the family names bear a fortuitous resemblance: Derrida/Deronda. If we are to believe, as Derrida tells us, that the family names are encrypted in *The Post Card* (1995b, 120) – it being a given that Derrida plays with his name and initials elsewhere: *J'accepte, déjà, derrière le rideau, débris de* – why might we not read in a moment of speculation the inscription of 'Deronda' as one of those encryptings? Of course we might, but this will tell us little or nothing about Derrida's identity, anymore than it will give us to understand Deronda's. We will not know him any better. We truly find ourselves ensnared in affirmative, resistant meshes, in what is described elsewhere as 'this net of the first name and family name' (1995b, 365).[15] This long envois, dated 6 June 1977, speaks of, amongst other things, that which cannot be dispatched; also about couriers, returns, detours, giving, and the memory of a failed delivery concerning *La différance*. Just over half-way through the following remark and parenthesis appears (a note within a post card):

> While we walk, she tells me about her work projects (18th century correspondence and libertine literature, Sade, a whole plot of writings that I cannot summarise, and then Daniel Deronda, by G. Eliot, a story of circumcision and of double reading) and we turn into the labyrinth between the colleges.
> (1987b, 15)

The 'she' is Cynthia Chase, as is known, the work on *Deronda* being referred to being an essay first published in 1978, and entitled 'The Decomposition of the Elephants: Double-Reading *Daniel Deronda*' (Chase ed. Newton 1991, 198–218).[16] It is not my intention, nor, indeed, is this the place to pursue any sustained reading of Chase's essay, or to counter at length any of her arguments concerning circumcision and the novel; this is more than adequately and expertly done in an essay by K. M. Newton.[17] I'm not concerned to engage in a professional debate on this matter; I do, however, want to pick up on a thread in Chase's text, in relation to Derrida's post card and the 'themes' of identity, undecidability, circumcision and love. This seems to dictate the return of the detour, the circumscription.

Chase writes that Daniel's 'circumcised phallus, proof of origin and identity, is more than exemplary metonymy, though it is certainly that. It is distinctively significant, not as a rhetorical structure but as a referent. . . . The scandal of the referent calls attention to the scandal . . . of rhetoricity' (Chase ed. Newton 1991, 210). Chase goes on to call the circumcised phallus the 'exemplary signifier' (Chase ed. Newton 1991, 212). I cannot help but feel that Chase, in limiting the 'appearance' of circumcision to the instance of Deronda's absent circumcised penis, and in seeing it as a referent, an exemplary signifier, is, in fact, rhetorically constructing a desired metaphysical presence, rather than finding the signs of it. If we step back from the obsession with the phallus to enquire after the mark of circumcision as 'exemplary metonymy' of identity's contingency, a mark, then, which is traced on the body of the text in other words, we find in Eliot's circumscription the trace of circumcision powerfully remarked; to borrow a line from a remark cited earlier, the *figure* at least of a circumcision is imposed. And it is in this that this note on a post card on Derrida's part resounds and produces interesting repercussions between the commentary on circumcision elsewhere and a particular line in *Daniel Deronda*, for which I have been heading.

The line, employing the proper name and the equivocacy of identity, is itself an aphoristic post card, a fragment providing a redoubled double reading of the novel.[18] It names Daniel's secret and his being between identities and cultures. It is spoken by Daniel Deronda, and has a quite startling importance for the questions I have raised. The line occurs in Chapter 42 (575–99), when Daniel is taken by Mordecai to a public house, *The Hand and Banner*, to be introduced to a small club of working men, who call themselves 'The Philosophers'. When introduced by Mordecai, and asked whether he is anonymous, Daniel replies:

My name is Daniel Deronda. I am unknown . . .

(Eliot 1967, 581)

In this response to a call for identity, Deronda marks himself as being, to borrow a phrase from 'Tympan', '[b]etween the proper of the other and the other of the proper' (Derrida 1982a, xii; emphasis mine). Daniel's response is governed by a referential pun on the part of one of the group to Shelley's 'Prometheus Unbound' and the 'Great Unknown'. However, the remark takes on the status of an aphorism in the context of the novel and its double narrative – conventionally referred to as the English and Jewish parts – which redoubles the numerous oscillations across the text between these so-called parts, at the limits of both, and which refuses to be settled in either one. Daniel's aphorism strikes a chord. The line marks the text, it is the intrusion or incision, the circumcision, the giving and determining of *Daniel Deronda*/ Daniel Deronda. On the one hand, Daniel names himself, announces himself publicly, giving out his name in response to the query concerning anonymity and the great unknown. In doing so he marks himself as other, his identity as something other than itself and so is written by that ghostly inscription from the other which named him at the time of his circumcision. He redoubles the public and private name.

On the other hand he admits to the unknowable in his identity, that which is other than the proper name, and beyond naming, at the very limit of the nameable. This aphoristic fragment, announcing within itself the absolute aphorism of the proper name, marks the birth of the subject 'Daniel Deronda' as other than he was. And this is precisely a circumfessional remark, a circumcisive utterance, because the words are a 'mark of belonging and exclusion' (Derrida 1991c, 67). It is the circumcisive act on Daniel's part – an act he does not wholly control, the other coming to address the 'philosophers' through him – which cuts him from his English identity, and which 'grants access', to quote 'Shibboleth', on the circumcised word, 'to the community, to the covenant or alliance' (Derrida 1991c, 67). Daniel's self-naming simultaneously cuts and traces the location of identity between fixed locations. Entering the philosopher's circle, he incisively marks the meeting and himself; if you'll allow me a certain play here his last name echoes with/in another language, French, with both the idea of the circle and a circumcisive cut, *ronde* meaning both circle and slice. Deronda cuts himself from himself in an act of Jewish inscription, albeit non-knowingly, for he has this feeling – does he not? – that he is doing it from another place that he does not know: his identity is determined by exteriority based on a place that he does not inhabit in a certain way, or that he does not, cannot, identify. Daniel's name, this double name of first and family name, the known and the non-known – Daniel does not know his 'family', he knows neither his parental nor his cultural identity, the identity called the 'Jewish family' by Derrida in *Glas* (Derrida 1986a, 41) – acts as a key, an intercession. His second remark re-marks the name and Daniel's identity, the *in medias res* between Englishness and Jewishness, as the in-between, even as he is between, between two cultures, two identities, 'at once both readable and secret' (Derrida 1991c, 67). And it is from this moment of naming, of marking his identity as other, that Daniel moves towards an identity, Jewish identity, at which neither he nor the novel ever arrives, but are always being sent towards, toward which they are directed, posted, destined. As Barbara Hardy puts it, Daniel is left 'poised on the edge of a future' (Eliot 1967, 29). Deronda, having been addressed by the other, finds himself sent, directed, but never delivered finally. The novel has no closure. There can never be a final identity, this is the chance the novel takes. It is the chance which loves the dissonant within identity. Circumcision is thus written onto the body, the body of the subject Daniel Deronda, and the body of the text *Daniel Deronda*, leaving it open. Daniel's cutting re-mark thus marks the un/remarkable connection to his unknown father, his family, his nation, all of whom he desires to know, with the amateur's passion.

Cynthia Chase is right to suggest that there is that in the text which undermines 'the authority of the notion of identity' and that the 'deconstruction of this identity has radical implications for the concept of the subject in general' (Chase ed. Newton 1991, 204), if, by identity, she means 'stable' or 'fixed' identity. But, in turning the absent circumcised phallus into a transcendental signifier of metaphysical proportions, Chase misses the very mark of circumcision, the mark of affirmative resistance, on the body which comes from the other to mark both subject and text, and to mark identity as always inhabited by the other, never fixed. If Daniel Deronda is unknown, he is also, to a degree, unknowable. What is at stake in George Eliot's work is, like the work of

Jacques Derrida, the effort to show how any 'system must remain essentially open' (Bennington and Derrida 1993, 1). This is what is often missed in both Jacques Derrida and *Daniel Deronda*, the latter's Jewish plot found by a professional critic such as F.R. Leavis to be a failure. It is important to observe that 'Daniel Deronda' is, like 'Jacques Derrida', what a certain Jacques Derrida has called 'a semi-fluid name/*un nom à demi-fluide*' (Bennington and Derrida 1993, 4/8); and Daniel like Jacques, has 'never loved anything but the impossible' (Bennington and Derrida 1993, 3/7).

But what of love?

This is also missed by the professional reader, though not the *amateur* reader, whose act of reading is already marked by love. Love is missed, it escapes identification; love is the figure for the in-between, a figure that is not to be captured. *There* – in-between, on the post card – is something secret [*il y a là du secret*] (Derrida 1992c, 5). Love is also a mark on identity, a trace or cut which determines the self as never wholly itself. Indeed, Derrida's reading of Hegel in *Glas* connects at a certain point circumcision and love (1986a, 39–41). As Jean-Luc Nancy suggests, love is such that 'one is shared and traversed by that which does not fix itself in any subject or signification . . . Whatever my love is it cuts across my identity' (Nancy 1991, 101). Furthermore, love is always arriving, Nancy informs us, love always arrives, it is the arrival of the other, so much *other*, in fact, 'that it is never *made* (one makes love, because it is never *made*) and so much *other* that it is never *my* love (if I say to the other "my love," it is of the other, precisely that I speak, and nothing is "mine")' (Nancy 1991, 102). Love, like Daniel's quest for Jewish identity, is never completed, never finished, never done with. Daniel is marked by love. Deronda comes to trace a trajectory in the space of the between precisely because his desire to know his identity, his obsession with identity, comes to coincide with his desire to know and love the other, to know and love Mirah.

However, allowing the ghost writer Geoffrey Bennington to seep through for a moment, it is no doubt easy to suppress love, deny it, ignore it, to imagine a scenario which would appropriate Deronda for a Jewish identity in some way opposed to the tyranny of English identity (Bennington and Derrida 1993, 293/271), even as there are those who desire to appropriate Derrida for similar purposes, in relation to other identities. After all, this is what the professional reader paradoxically desires, attempts and fears; hence, in the case of *Daniel Deronda*, the dismissal of the Jewish plot as inferior, it being read as the debased, exteriorised other to the 'proper' English plot and identity. Yet Mirah's effect upon Deronda cannot be explained away by reference to the two plots.[19] From their first encounter (Eliot 1967, 225–42), Daniel is enamoured, his desire to know Mirah interwoven with his musings on his (then) unknown mother and the obscured origins of his own identity. What passes between them, an initial glance 'but a couple of moments . . . a long while for two people to look straight at each other' (Eliot 1967, 227–8), announces what will become a correspondence between the two.[20] Daniel and Mirah address one another with the exchange between their eyes, and it is through this, and the inability to capture the other, that Deronda becomes haunted. Love arrives to inform Daniel that he is not himself; it comes to haunt his identity, and he finds himself obligated. And so do we, finding ourselves asking

– what happens in the blink of an eye?[21]

Between marks everywhere, not least the gaze of the loved one(s). And yet it is nowhere as such, as the blink of an eye reveals. Consider: The dispatch which is also a return: *envoi* as *renvoi*. And what is sent (*envoyer*), what is well-aimed (*envoyé[e]*), is also exchanged, between the blinking of eyelids (*s'envoyer des clins d'oeil*), the intercourse (*s'envoyer*) of the in-between.[22] But that's between us.

copulative correspondence[23]

Donnant donnant: I've taken up your time, given you mine in return. But then, as Jean-Luc Nancy reminds us, love 'consists as much in taking as in giving' (Nancy 1991, 101). Were you to spend your time with Daniel and Mirah, you would see the truth of this, in what passes between them. However, we are involved, between us, in a paradox, if we bear in mind, that commentary on love by Jacques Lacan, of which Derrida reminds us, in a note from *Given Time*.[24] We do not have love, love is not ours to give; nor does the other possess love. Love is not yours, not mine. Not Jacques Derrida's, not Nicholas Royle's, as he admits (Royle 1995, 140). And, furthermore, 'Love', writes Nancy, 'is addressed to one alone singularly and infinitely . . . it always flies to pieces as soon as it is sent' (Nancy 1991, 109). This is, it would appear, acknowledged implicitly throughout *The Post Card*, with its numerous sendings, dispatches, fragments even in the perplexity over the question of how love should be addressed. Yet love appears, in different guises, throughout.

Love – the French *amateur* – appears again, throughout 'Aphorism Countertime'. I've no intention of pursuing a 'reading' of such appearances, such apparitions, except to note, along with Nicholas Royle, that love is ghostly (Royle 1995, 139); it is, noting as we must what has already been said, nothing other than that; it is 'traced by the radically other (by death, in short)' (Royle 1995, 139). Returning to or sending the proper name, let us ask, in the name of love or the name of the other: who, or what, might come to speak in the name of love, yet wholly otherwise? Do we hear a voice, a name, do we believe we glimpse a 'spectrogrammatical' trace in love, as a series of singular reiterations or multiple singularities? Can we help but acknowledge our responsibility to such a ghostly figure, each time it comes, returns or is sent to us, each time the first and the last? What might we hear?

– I am thy father's spirit (I. v. 9)

You know this line, no doubt; and it calls to mind, to the mind's eye once again, as Hamlet might say, numerous texts that are signed in the name of 'Jacques Derrida', such as *Specters of Marx*, or, even, in a certain way, the opening line of *Of Spirit*, where someone comes to speak of the *revenant* and of flames.[25] There is no certain(ty concerning) identity here; and, as Derrida tells us, 'we must fall back on the voice, since we cannot identify the speaker in all certainty... The one who says "I am thy Father's Spirit" can only be taken at his word' (Derrida 1994b, 7). We feel ourselves addressed, obliged to respond. There is *there*, occurring, both in and through the words, and exceeding the words, being more, *other*, than the words, what a certain Derrida might call the 'spectral errancy of words. The spectral return does not befall words by accident... The spectral return is partaken of by *all* words' (Derrida 1991c, 58). I am thy father's spirit. He will have obligated. But why do I write of ghosts and love, and the ghost of a love in language? There is that which returns to haunt Derrida every time he comes to write love, to write of love, in French at least. This is his obligation, he cannot avoid it;

it is a given. Every love note, every note or aphorism, every post card, reverberates, someone, someone wholly other, an other Derrida, coming to speak, speaking through Jacques Derrida, tracing Jacques Derrida in the name of love, as the in-between, in ghostly whispers. For every time Jacques Derrida writes in French 'love', 'of love' and what it means 'to love', every time the verb *aimer* is conjured, *Aimé*, the name of the father, the beloved, seems to appear, as if dictating while standing over Derrida's shoulder. I say 'appears', 'seems to appear', deliberately, in the face of what may be a spectral writing, or what may be merely a simulacrum. I do not take this appearance as certain, of course; I am not presuming to take this to be a given. It is not only – ever – a question about fathers, the question of the father. Despite the resemblance affirmed by Marcellus, Bernardo and Horatio, even Hamlet cannot know for sure the identity of the spirit. But I am putting a certain name on the line here if only to open up, and cut into, any certainty concerning identity, and to recall a particular remark of Derrida's, which is that 'a name . . . cannot be summed up in a *self*' (Derrida 1985, 7). There is that in a name which has nothing to do with what you know by this name (Derrida 1985, 8). Do you think you catch a glimpse of a certain identity? If we think of Hamlet for a moment, we must recall, in this particular context which I am putting on stage at this moment, a desire, no, an *obsession*, with identity. And as if to confront this obsession, nowhere is the obsession more thoroughly brought into question than in *Jacques Derrida through* and *between* the play, the projection, and the aporia which is opened by that play, the play of the in-between, the 'between us', between the remarks of Geoffrey Bennington and Jacques Derrida's remarks, remarks which, as Derrida admits, are traced by love (Bennington and Derrida 1993, 13/14). I am also putting this name, these names, on the line so that it can be seen how love marks, and is marked by, the other of/in identity, love is traced – and traces – in the space between identities. Identity is never self-identical. Deronda's mother may well say to her son, 'there is something of your own father in you' (Eliot 1967, 696), but this something 'in Derrida' is not everything, this something is something other, in excess of the proper name, which may be the ghost of an image, even a biographical post card. But we can never tell.

This 'amateur reading', this amatory note, has sought to be responsible to those issues – I will not, even now, call them 'themes'

– of the in-between. A 'responsible reading', Timothy Clark reminds us, 'is one attuned to affirm whatever in a text exceeds
the closures of representation' (Clark 1992, 186). That which exceeds, that which is always responsible, cannot be pinned down,
cannot be named as some identity. Love calls on us to be responsible in coming to map the unmappable, that which is
between us. We might see this responsibility, an other responsibility at work or at play in Michel Deguy's *c'est entre nous*; which
I have already sent you in fragments, through various citations
and indeterminate references. And which I am sending you as
an *inter*-ruption, which comes between and breaks and marks,
in David Wood's words, 'the *between* by which we relate to the
other' (Wood 1990, 127).

C'est entre nous	It's between us
C'est entre nous	It's between us
L'air entre les mains salut	The air between the hands a greeting
Et la main entre les saluts	And the hand between the greetings
Et le salut pur intervalle	And the greeting pure space/interval
Rien avec rien jouant à	Nothing with nothing playing at
S'envoyer la belle apparition	exchanging with the beautiful apparition

In a certain manner, everything which I have so far noted is
here, between us now, between reader and reader, but never named
as such. In its gestures which mark the indefinable space of the
between as the space where the difference of identities announce
the spectre of love, that beautiful apparition between us. This
seems to appear, and is affirmed, in passing, between the female
hand and the masculine salute or greeting. The greeting itself is
both spatial and temporal, marked by a difference which cannot
be reduced to a moment as in a snapshot. 'I' remains undecided
in the verse above. There is no position which 'I' could take up,
with regard to what might be called a 'subject position' properly speaking. No making safe or domestication. What's between
us is not proper; it is no more my property, than it is yours.

Exchange without reserve, in this aphorism, this post card of between, perhaps, even, *from between*, wholly other than identity, *as such*. No beginning, no closure. Only the space between us, the interval between *envois* and *renvois*, in which is sent, sent back, without any final delivery, without arrival, ghostly love. It's between us. A given giving given.

One must pretend to close a lecture, and to have *encompassed* one's topic (Derrida 1991c, 56; emphasis mine).[26] I do not desire to 'know' Jacques Derrida. There are too many and, anyway, I might have the wrong address. I do, however, dream of being the amateur reader; to be, in relation to what we call Derrida's texts, and to the other in the texts of Jacques Derrida, 'radically amateur', in Nicholas Royle's words (Royle 1995, 56), in my acts of reading and writing, awaiting the post with eagerness and expectation. 'Amateur', as Royle suggests, 'here involves not only a sense of the lover and of that love which is a deconstructive reading, but also a deconstruction of the professional as such' (Royle 1995, 56). The professional reading cannot help but give way to the amateur reading in its fondness for its subject. Reading as affirmative resistance loses itself in the space between. A 'radically amateur writing', Royle continues, implies 'a 'dream of passion' (in Hamlet's words), which precedes ego, subject or identity' (Royle 1995, 57). How could I write this amateur writing, except perhaps by the ghost of a chance? Certainly I couldn't set out to pursue an amateur reading, even though I might announce this as a desire. Any amateur reading which might have emerged would be between us as a chance which I cannot control. What else could I do except allow a certain sending of notes and post cards – from the other? – a sending which is also a sending back, a ghostly return even – again the *envois* as *renvois*, as *revenant*/revenant; this doubled, redoubling word, the ghost of one language appearing in the figure of the other – a 'multiplicity of *renvois*' (Derrida 1982b, 324), without the make-believe of a beginning and without return addresses. Post cards and aphorisms. Fragments . . .

– That which exceeds?

Perhaps. Other voices. The other voices 'me'.

– I love very much everything that I deconstruct in my own manner; the texts that I want to read from a deconstructive point of view are texts I love, with that impulse of identification which is indispensable for reading ... my relation to these texts is characterised by loving jealousy ... (Derrida 1985, 87)

– Never will I have loved so much (Derrida 1987b, 176)

– I don't feel I'm in a position to choose ... (Derrida 1985, 87)

As Colette Soler confirms, 'the Other precedes the subject. The Other as the locus of language ... precedes the subject and speaks about the subject before his birth. Thus the Other is the first cause of the subject' (1995, 43). This speech, this writing which precedes the subject and any identity, is that which Derrida acknowledges in acknowledging his debt to love, in locating his *inter-est*, his being between, where his identity is already not his but signed in the name of love. Never in a position which is his, never in a position of his own making Derrida writes. And here, in so many betweens, so many becoming-betweens where the other affirms identity's dissonance, and where we read Deguy's 'it's between us' as nothing other than the between which dislocates any possibility of a single identity; this is where we might read the rhetoric of affirmative resistance.

Notes

1. All parenthetical citations to this *Jacques Derrida* are followed by two numbers, the first being the reference to the English-language edition of *Jacques Derrida*, the second to the French.
2. This is a play on the sentence 'Someone, not me, comes and says the words: "I am interested in the idiom in painting."', which opens Jacques Derrida's *The Truth in Painting* (1987c, 1). There is also a play on the opening line of Derrida's *Specters of Marx: The State of the Debt, the Work of Mourning, and the New International* (1994b, xvii: 'Someone, you or me, comes forward and says: *I would like to learn to live finally*'). Both of Derrida's sentences invoke an unknowable identity, unknowability as the premise of identity. In imitating two different texts, in placing my own writing *between* these two others, not only am I opening up the space of between, but also pointing to the instability of identity, in drawing on two texts which articulate their concerns in the contexts of aesthetics and Marxism: two different identities. In every place that I invoke and rewrite a phrase of Derrida's there is an acknowledgement of the dissonance

of identity and the other within any pretence of identity's unity.

3. Although a common Latin phrase, I am drawing it with conscious reference from George Eliot, *Daniel Deronda* (1967, 35), where Eliot uses it to designate a condition of narrative, and to dismiss the idea of origins, sources, points of beginning and departure. Here we see how even the identity of citation can be problematic.

4. See Derrida's reading in *Khôra* (Paris: Galilée, 1993) of Plato's *Timaeus* and the non-figure of *khora* (as opposed to 'the khora', as Derrida makes the distinction), which might be another name for 'between'.

5. This commentary is doubled inasmuch as it calls upon, applies, the opening lines of another essay of Derrida's 'Before the Law' (1992a, 181–221).

6. This phrase is taken from the title of an essay by Emmanuel Levinas, 'Wholly Otherwise' (1991, 3–11).

7. This question echoes a line from 'Les jours ne sont pas comptes' by Michel Deguy (1984, 60). All references to Deguy are taken from this edition, the page number following quotation being a reference to the French text. I have followed Eshelman's translation but have altered silently where the need seemed to dictate.

8. *Glas* (1986a); 'Signature Event Context'(1977) in *Limited Inc* (1988, 1–25). See also Geoffrey Bennington, (Bennington and Derrida 1993, 104–14/100–10 and 148–66/140–56).

9. This is a reference to work by both Derrida and Deguy, particularly Derrida's *Given Time: I. Counterfeit Money*, (1992b) and Deguy's collection *Donnant Donnant* (Paris: Gallimard, 1981) which is excerpted in *Given Giving* (1984). Although in *Given Giving* Clayton Eshelman translates 'Donnant Donnant' as 'Given Giving', it can be seen from the phrase itself that no such certainty concerning translation lies in the phrase, a current idiom in French, which might be approximated, however roughly and inaccurately, by the English 'you scratch my back, I'll scratch yours'. The problem of translation is clearly marked here as a problem of what is lost between identities; language is marked by cultural and national identity, which identity – the identity of the other – is rendered otherwise, while remaining at least partly unknowable. 'Donnant Donnant' can be equ(ivoc)ally translated as 'giving giving', 'given given', 'giving given'. I play amongst all these possible translations in this essay as a way of announcing the other that always inhabits identity, while also alerting the reader to the ways in which such radical otherness always already undermines (the desire for a) stable identity and problematises communication. Derrida alludes to Deguy's *Donnant Donnant* in the final footnote of *Given Time*, (172) discussing briefly Deguy's reading of Baudelaire and citing Deguy's poem 'Donnant Donnant' (1981, 57). I acknowledge gratefully both Peggy Kamuf and Ruth Robbins's willingness to get involved in telephonic discussions concerning the matter of translation in general, and the translation of 'donnant donnant' in particular.

10. This line is spoken by an unidentified voice at the beginning of an essay by Derrida, 'At this Very Moment in this Work Here I Am', (1991a, 11–51).

11. Eve Tavor Bannet, *Postcultural Theory: Critical Theory after the Marxist Paradigm* (New York: Paragon House, 1993), 80–7.

12. In this sentence I am echoing a comment of Derrida's from one of the interviews in *Points* . . .: 'When a proper name is inscribed right on the text, within the text, obviously it is not a signature; it is a way of making the name into a work, of making work of the name, but without this inscription of the proper name having the value of any property rights so to speak. Whence *the double relation of the name and the loss of the name*: by inscribing the name in the thing itself . . . by inscribing the name in the thing, from one angle, I lose the signature, but, from another, angle, I monumentalize the name, I transform the name into a thing' (1995b, 365–6; emphasis mine). It is precisely this double relation which I believe to be at stake in circumcision, and which is certainly at stake in *Daniel Deronda*.

13. On non-knowing as opposed to secrets, see Derrida's discussion in *Points* . . . (1995b, 201).

14. In the 'envoi' Derrida appears to write Daniel Deronda as the proper name of a subject and not a work. The name is not italicised as is 'proper' in the citation of novel titles. Of course the 'envoi' is not supposed to be a 'properly constructed academic text, with full bibliographical details, notes, and so on. Is this some form of mistake? And, if so, whose fault is it? The one who writes? the translator? the editor? the typesetter or compositor? From internal evidence we cannot tell. Certainly, other titles are italicised: *Limited Inc* (1987b,14); *Beyond the Pleasure Principle* (22); *Le facteur de la verité* (53); *The Interpreter's Dictionary of the Bible* (73). This inexplicable issue seems to connect equivocation with identity (one is tempted to say unequivocally).

This particular 'envoi' also ends equivocally, with the phrase *Je me trie* (16; 'I sort myself'). A note on the line is appended to the foot of the page which comments that could be *Je me tue* (I kill myself). This internal note, on the equivocation of identity with which the two lines toy, points out that 'the writing makes it impossible to distinguish between the two impossibilities' (16). In the English language edition of *The Post Card* there is no conventional abbreviation with this note, such as '[trans.]' or '[ed.]', to suggest that this is a commentary by Alan Bass, so it would appear to be some other voice. Curiously, this line is left open, there being no punctuation following 'possibilities'. This picks up the absence of 'final' punctuation throughout the 'envois'.

Also, it is worth noting, in passing, the equivocal slippage introduced by translation from French to 'American English', rather than 'British English'. In phrases such as 'I am finishing writing you in the street', 'I will continue to write you', and 'I write you all the time, that is all I do' (16). In British English such lines would be written 'I write *to* you', the preposition indicating trajectory, destination, posting, address. The American English form, while carrying the same connotation for American readers as 'I write to you' does for British readers, also suggests that 'I', in writing, actively construct 'you' your 'identity'; the other here always marks the self.

15. See Peggy Kamuf's comments on Derrida, the proper name and the spider's web in her 'Introduction: Reading Between the Blinds', (Kamuf ed. 1991, xiii–xlii).
16. See also, in the same volume, a counter-argument to Chase by the volume's editor, K. M. Newton, '*Daniel Deronda* and Circumcision', (Newton ed. 1991, 218–32).
17. Cynthia Chase's argument is drawn in part from Steven Marcus's discussion of *Daniel Deronda* ('Human Nature, Social Orders and 19th Century Systems of Explanation: Starting in with George Eliot', *Salmagundi*, 28 [1975]). Her reading of the narrative is premised on Daniel's apparent ignorance of his Jewishness, his being circumcised, and the fact that he never seems to 'look down'. She argues further that *Daniel Deronda* presents itself 'to be read in two conflicting ways' (199). Chase suggests that the novel's narrative is at odds with itself, its identity divided, due to the tension between its realist and idealist trajectories; furthermore, this tension is never acknowledged, and this absence of acknowledgement is indicated by the absence of any apparent reference to circumcision in general or Daniel's circumcised phallus in particular. Although using what is conventionally recognised by many today as 'deconstructive' discourse to interpret the tensions and the absence, Chase is indebted – as she acknowledges – to critics such as F. R. Leavis, Barbara Hardy and David Kaufmann, who have traditionally divided *Deronda* into two parts, the 'English' and the 'Jewish' parts.

Chase argues that the narrative insistence on the hero's identity as, specifically, a Jewish identity, disrupts the narrative's coherence and that this reference to identity leads 'relentlessly' to the 'hero's phallus, which must have been circumcised . . . Deronda must have known, but he did not: otherwise there could be no story. The plot can function only if *la chose*, Deronda's circumcised penis is disregarded; yet the novel's realism and referentiality function precisely to draw attention to it (209–10). The 'hero's circumcised phallus [is] proof of origin and identity' (210). The circumcised penis is both the 'unacknowledged mark' of Jewishness and, simultaneously, the 'exemplary signifier' (210).

Chase's argument that circumcision is synonymous solely with Jewish identity is countered significantly by a historico-medical reading by K. M. Newton which challenges Chase's assertions concerning identity and circumcision on the grounds of her 'use of historical discourse and her implicit assumptions about the author's intentions' (220). He pursues a reading of the historical and cultural contexts of circumcision and the medical conditions which would lead to circumcision of non-Jews as a form of hygienic precaution, or as a cure for phimosis (222–23). Newton's fascinating counter does more than merely offering a historicist riposte, however, for he turns the tables on Chase, employing the various documentary and medical sources to explore and ultimately 'deconstruct' Chase's essay, arguing that circumcision may well be 'part of the theme of the ambiguity of signs' (226). Newton moves from this cautious, conditional remark, to the idea that circumcision 'becomes a sign of difference' (228); he concludes with a commentary – no more than an allusion really – on the highly allusive and indirect nature of Eliot's imagination (230). This, for me, remains too centred on the author, but the movement of Newton's thought can lead to a more general movement away from the idea of authorial intentionality – that Eliot encrypted circumcision within the text as an ambiguous or equivocal allusive mark – to the possibility that we may be able to glimpse in *Daniel Deronda* the trace of the other coming to Eliot, coming to us, on the way to arriving, but not having yet been received.

On the subject of the novel's 'English' plot and its realism, this seems a misreading, for, as I argue elsewhere, there is much evidence to suggest a self-reflexiveness, a general level of self-conscious allusion to the theatrical and performative nature of this plot in relation to the subject of English national identity which 'deconstructs' the illusion of realism (Wolfreys, *Being English: Narratives, Idioms, and Performances of National Identity from Coleridge to Trollope* [1994, 129–51]).

18. The idea of the redoubled doubling is taken from the beginning of an essay by John Sallis, 'Doublings', in David Wood, ed., *Derrida: A Critical Reader* (1992, 120–37).

19. When introduced to Mrs Meyrick by Deronda, Mirah says, 'I am a stranger. I am a Jewess' (241). This remark ghosts Daniel's later comment 'My name is Daniel Deronda. I am unknown', but appears also to acknowledge to a greater degree that otherness is a structural condition of Jewish identity. One is never at home within such an identity, this identity cannot be fixed or determined, given its radical alterity.

20. Eliot emphasises Mirah's beauty and the impression it makes on Daniel's mind in these paragraphs. Deronda, on returning Mirah's gaze and seeing the sorrow written into her expression, speculates on the 'probable romance that lay behind that loneliness and look of desolation'. There is a certain irony in the tone which remarks 'there was no denying that the attractiveness of the image made it likelier to last' (228). It may be worth speculating on the fact that Daniel encounters both Mirah and Mordecai on bridges, Kew and Blackfriars respectively. Bridges mark 'between', in the act of spanning the watery margin of the Thames (interestingly, in connection with this, Deronda meets Mirah in the book entitled 'Meeting Streams').

21. This question echoes a similar question in *Specters of Marx* (119).

22. I am playing here on the various meanings of *s'envoyer*, which will come up again in the poem *c'est entre nous*, by Michel Deguy. *S'envoyer* means to exchange, but in idiomatic phrases such as *s'envoyer des clins d'oeil* and *s'envoyer des baisers*, the meaning is 'to wink at one another' or 'to blow each other kisses' respectively. Furthermore, *s'envoyer* is slang for sexual intercourse, 'having it off', for example.

23. This phrase is taken from 'Tympan' (xvi) to suggest the sexual – or, at least, erotic – aspect of all correspondence, whether postal or human.

24. *Given Time* (172 n.32). The works to which Derrida refers are Jacques Lacan, *Ecrits* (1966) and *Feminine Sexuality: Jacques Lacan and the 'école freudienne'*, ed. Jacqueline Rose and Juliet Mitchell (1985).

25. 'I shall speak of ghost [*revenant*], of flame, and of ashes'. *Of Spirit: Heidegger and the Question* (1989a, 1).

26. The term 'encompassed' has a particular resonance with regard to the theme of circumcision. Even as this essay is marked by the arbitrary *tranche* of citation, there is an attempt constantly to fold it back on itself, itself doubling and folding itself as other than itself.

Works Cited

Anand, Mulk Raj. *Untouchable* (1935). Preface E. M. Forster. Harmondsworth, 1986.

Anderson, Perry. 'Modernity and Revolution'. *Marxism and the Interpretation of Culture*. Ed. Cary Nelson and Lawrence Grossberg. Urbana and Chicago, 1988. 317–34.

Attridge, Derek. *Peculiar Language: Literature as Difference from the Renaissance to James Joyce*. Ithaca, 1988.

Bannet, Eve Tavor. *Postcultural Theory: Critical Theory after the Marxist Paradigm*. New York, 1993.

Barker, Francis, Peter Hulme, Margaret Iversen and Diana Loxley, eds. *Literature, Politics and Theory: Papers from the Essex Conference 1976–84*. London, 1986.

Barker, Francis. *The Tremulous Private Body: Essays on Subjection*. London, 1984.

Baudrillard, Jean. *America* (1986). Trans. Chris Turner. London, 1988.

Bennington, Geoffrey and Jacques Derrida. *Jacques Derrida* (1991). Trans. Geoffrey Bennington. Chicago, 1993.

Bennington, Geoffrey. *Legislations: the Politics of Deconstruction*. London, 1994.

Bernauer, James. *Michel Foucault's Force of Flight: Toward an Ethic for Thought*. New Jersey, 1990.

Bhabha, Homi K. 'The Other Question: Difference, Discrimination and the Discourse of Colonialism.' Barker *et al.* 148–73.

Bhabha, Homi K., ed. *Nation and Narration*. London, 1990.

Bishop, John. *Joyce's Book of the Dark*. Madison, 1986.

Blamires, Harry. *The New Bloomsday Book: A Guide through Ulysses: Revised Edition Keyed to the Corrected Text*. London, 1990.

Blanchot, Maurice. *The Infinite Conversation* (1969). Trans. and Foreword Susan Hanson. Minneapolis, 1993.

Blanchot, Maurice. *The Step Not Beyond* (1973). Trans. Lycette Nelson. Albany, 1992.

Bloomer, Jennifer. *Architecture and the Text: The (S)crypts of Joyce and Piranesi*. New Haven, 1993.

Boone, Joseph A. 'Staging Sexuality: Repression, Representation, and "Interior" States in *Ulysses*'. *Joyce: The Return of the Repressed*. Ed. Susan Stanford Friedman. Ithaca, 1993. 190–225.

Brannigan, John, Ruth Robbins and Julian Wolfreys, eds. *Applying: To Derrida*. London, 1996.

Budick, Sanford, and Wolfgang Iser, eds. *The Translatability of Cultures: Figurations of the Space Between*. Stanford, 1996

Butler, Judith. *Bodies That Matter: On the Discursive Limits of "Sex"*. New York, 1993.

Cache, Bernard. *Earth Moves: The Furnishing of Territories.* Trans. Anne Boyman. Ed. Michael Speaks. Cambridge, Ma., 1996

Carroll, Lewis. *The Annotated Alice* (1960). Ed. Martin Gardner. Harmondsworth, 1987.

Celan, Paul. *Selected Poems.* Trans. Michael Hamburger. Harmondsworth, 1990.

Chambers, Iain. *Border Dialogues: Journeys in Postmodernity.* London, 1990.

Chase, Cynthia. 'The Decomposition of the Elephants: Double-Reading *Daniel Deronda*' *PMLA*, 93 (1978), 215–27.

Cheng, Vincent J. *Joyce, Race, and Empire.* Foreword Derek Attridge. Cambridge, 1995.

Cheyette, Bryan. *Constructions of 'the Jew' in English Literature and Society: Racial Representations, 1875–1945.* Cambridge, 1993.

Cixous, Hélène. 'Joyce: the (r)use of writing' (1970). *Post-Structuralist Joyce: Essays from the French.* Ed. Derek Attridge and Daniel Ferrer. Cambridge, 1984. 15–31.

Cixous, Hélène. *L'Exil de James Joyce ou l'art de remplacement.* Paris, 1968.

Clarke, Timothy. *Derrida, Heidegger, Blanchot: Sources of Derrida's notion and practice of literature.* Cambridge, 1992.

Clément, Catherine. *Syncope: The Philosophy of Rapture* (1990). Foreword Verena Andermatt Conley. Trans. Sally O'Driscoll and Deirdre M. Mahoney. Minneapolis, 1994.

Cook, Pam. 'The Point of Self-Expression in Avant-Garde Film'. *Catalogue of British Film Institute Productions 1977–1978.* London, 1978.

Corlett, William. *Community without Unity. A Politics of Derridean Extravagance.* Durham, 1989.

Cowie, Elizabeth. '*Underworld USA*: Psychoanalysis and Film Theory in the 1980s'. *Psychoanalysis and Cultural Theory: Thresholds.* Ed. James Donald. Basingstoke, 1991.

Davison, Neil R. *James Joyce, Ulysses, and the Construction of Jewish Identity: Culture, Biography, and "the Jew" in Modernist Europe.* Cambridge, 1996.

de Bolla, Peter. *The Discourse of the Sublime: Readings in History, Aesthetics and the Subject.* Oxford, 1989.

Deguy, Michel. *Donnant Donnant.* Paris, 1991.

Deguy, Michel. *Given Giving: Selected Poems of Michel Deguy.* Trans. Clayton Eshleman. Int. Kenneth Koch. Berkeley, 1984.

Deleuze, Gilles. *Difference and Repetition* (1968). Trans. Paul Patton. London, 1993.

Deleuze, Gilles. *The Logic of Sense.* (1969). Trans. Mark Lester, with Charles Stivale. Ed. Constantin V. Boundas. New York, 1990.

Deren, Maya, with Alexander Hammid, dirs. *Meshes of the Afternoon.* 14 mins. *Experimental Films 1943–1959.* Mystic Fire Video, 1990. Videocassette.

Deren, Maya. 'Cinematography: The Creative Use of Reality'. *The Avant-Garde Film: A Reader of Theory and Criticism.* Ed. P. Adams Sitney. New York, 1978.

Deren, Maya. 'Cinema as an Art Form'. *The Avant-Garde Film: A Reader of Theory and Criticism.* Ed. P. Adams Sitney. New York, 1978.

Deren, Maya. 'Letter to James Card'. *Women and Cinema: A Critical Anthology.* Ed. Karyn Day and Gerald Peary. New York, 1977.

Derrida, Jacques. *Of Grammatology* (1967) Trans. Gayatri Chakravorty Spivak. Baltimore, 1976.

Derrida, Jacques. 'An Interview with Jacques Derrida'. *Literary Review*, 14 (1980): 21–2.

Derrida, Jaccques. *Dissemination* (1972). Trans. Barbara Johnson. Chicago, 1981a.

Derrida, Jacques. *Writing and Difference* (1967). Trans. Alan Bass. London, 1981b.

Derrida, Jacques. *Margins of Philosophy* (1972). Trans. Alan Bass. Chicago, 1982a.

Derrida, Jacques. 'Sending: On Representation'. *Social Research*, 55 (1982b).

Derrida, Jacques. *Signéponge/Signsponge*. Trans. Richard Rand. New York, 1984.

Derrida, Jacques. *The Ear of the Other: Otobiography, Transference, Translation* (1982). Trans. Peggy Kamuf. Ed. Claude Levesque and Christie McDonald. Lincoln, 1985.

Derrida, Jaccques. *Glas.* (1974). Trans. John P. Leavey, Jr, and Richard Rand. Lincoln, 1986a.

Derrida, Jacques. *Parages.* Paris, 1986b.

Derrida, Jacques. *Schibboleth: pour Paul Celan.* Paris, 1986c.

Derrida, Jacques. 'L'aphorisme à contretemps'. *Psyché: Inventions de l'autre.* Paris, 1987a. 519–533.

Derrida, Jacques. *The Post Card: From Socrates to Freud and Beyond* (1980). Trans. Alan Bass. Chicago, 1987b.

Derrida, Jacques. *The Truth in Painting* (1978). Trans. Geoffrey Bennington and Ian McLeod. Chicago, 1987c.

Derrida, Jacques. *Ulysse gramophone.* Paris, 1987d.

Derrida, Jacques. *Limited Inc.* Ed. Gerald Graff. Trans. Samuel Weber and Jeffrey Mehlman. Evanston, 1988.

Derrida, Jacques. *Of Spirit: Heidegger and the Question* (1987). Trans. Geoffrey Bennington and Rachel Bowlby. Chicago, 1989a.

Derrida, Jacques. 'Psyche: Inventions of the Other'. Trans. Catherine Porter. *Reading de Man Reading.* Ed. Lindsay Walters and Wlad Godzich. Minneapolis, 1989b.

Derrida, Jacques. 'Some Statements and Truisms about Neo-Logisms, Newisms, Postisms, Parasitisms, and other Small Seismisms'. *The States of "Theory": History, Art, and Critical Discourse.* Ed. and int. David Carroll. New York, 1990. 63–95.

Derrida, Jacques. 'At this moment in this work here I am'. Trans. Ruben Berezdivin. *Re-Reading Levinas.* Ed. Robert Bernasconi and Simon Critchley. Bloomington, 1991a. 11–51.

Derrida, Jacques. *Cinders* (1987). Trans., int. and ed. Ned Lukacher. Lincoln, 1991b.

Derrida, Jacques. 'Shibboleth for Paul Celan' (1986). Trans. Joshua Wilner. *Word Traces: Readings of Paul Celan.* Ed. Aris Fioretos. Baltimore, 1991c. 3–75.

Derrida, Jacques. ' This is Not an Oral Footnote'. trans. Stephen A. Barney and Michael Hanly. *Annotation and its Texts.* Ed. Stephen A. Barney. Oxford, 1991d.

Derrida, Jacques. 'Before the Law' (1984). Trans. Avital Ronell, with Christine Roulston. *Acts of Literature*. Ed. Derek Attridge. London, 1992a. 181–221.

Derrida, Jacques. *Given Time: I. Counterfeit Money* (1991). Trans. Peggy Kamuf. Chicago, 1992b.

Derrida, Jacques. *The Other Heading: Reflections on Today's Europe* (1991). Trans. Pascale-Anne Brault and Michael B. Naas. Int. Michael B. Naas. Bloomington, 1992c.

Derrida, Jacques. 'Passions: 'An Oblique Offering''. Trans. David Wood. *Derrida: A Critical Reader*. Oxford, 1992d. 5–36

Derrida, Jaccques. *Aporias* (1993). Trans. Thomas Dutoit. Stanford, 1993.

Derrida, Jacques. 'The Spatial Arts: an Interview with Jacques Derrida'. Trans. Laurie Volpe. *Deconstruction and the Visual Arts: Art, Media, Architecture*. Ed. Peter Brunette and David Wills. Cambridge, 1994a.

Derrida, Jacques. *Specters of Marx: The State of the Debt, the Work of Mourning, and the New International* (1993). Trans. Peggy Kamuf. Int. Bernd Magnus and Stephen Cullenberg. London, 1994b.

Derrida, Jacques. *The Gift of Death* (1992). Trans. David Wills. Chicago, 1995a.

Derrida, Jacques. *Points . . . Interviews 1974–1994* (1992). Ed. Elizabeth Weber. Trans. Peggy Kamuf and others. Stanford, 1995b.

Derrida, Jacques. 'Deconstruction and the Other'. Kearney, 107–26.

Derrida, Jacques. 'Desistance.' Lacoue-Labarthe. 1–43.

Dollimore, Jonathan. *Radical Tragedy: Religion, Ideology and Power in the Drama of Shakespeare and his Contemporaries*. Brighton, 1984.

Duffy, Enda. *The Subaltern Ulysses*. Minneapolis, 1994.

Eagleton, Terry. 'Nationalism: Irony and Commitment'. *Nationalism, Colonialism and Literature*. Terry Eagleton, Fredric Jameson, Edward Said. Int. Seamus Deane. Minneapolis, 1990. 23–43.

Eagleton, Terry. 'Text, Ideology, Realism'. *Literature and Society*. Ed. Edward Said. Baltimore, 1978.

Eagleton, Terry. *Ideology: an Introduction*. London, 1991.

Easthope, Antony. *British Post-Structuralism since 1968*. London, 1991.

Elam, Diane. *Feminism and Deconstruction: Ms. en Abyme*. London, 1994.

Eliot, George. *Daniel Deronda* (1874–6) Ed. Barbara Hardy. Harmondsworth, 1967.

Eliot, George. *Middlemarch*. (1871–72). Ed. W. J. Harvey. Harmondsworth, 1965.

Empson, William. *Some Versions of Pastoral*. London, 1935.

Feldstein, Richard, Bruce Fink, and Maire Jaanus, eds. *Reading Seminar XI: Lacan's Four Fundamental Concepts of Psychoanalysis*. Albany, 1995.

Feldstein, Richard. 'The Phallic Gaze of Wonderland'. Feldstein *et al.*, 149–75.

Fenves, Peter. *'Chatter': Language and History in Kierkegaard*. Stanford, 1993.

Forrester, John. *The Seductions of Psychoanalysis: Freud, Lacan and Derrida*. Cambridge, 1990.

Foucault, Michel. *Histoire de la sexualité*. Paris, 1976

Foucault, Michel. *The Archeology of Knowledge and the Discourse on Language.* (1969) Trans. A.M. Sheridan Smith. New York, 1979.

Fraiberg, Allison. 'Of AIDS. Cyborgs. and Other Indiscretions: Resurfacing the Body in the Postmodern'. *Essays in Postmodern Culture.* Ed. Eyal Amiran and John Unsworth. New York, 1993.

Frey, Hans-Jost. *Studies in Poetic Discourse: Mallarmé, Baudelaire, Rimbaud, Hölderlin.* (1986) Trans. William Whobrey. Stanford, 1996.

Genesko, Gary, ed. *The Guattari Reader.* Oxford, 1996.

Germain, Sylvie. *La pleurante des rues de Prague.* Paris, 1992. Translated as *The Weeping Woman on the Streets of Prague.* Trans. Judith Landry. Int. Emma Wilson. Sawtry, 1993.

Gidal, Peter. *Understanding Beckett: A Study of Monologue and Gesture in the Works of Samuel Beckett.* London, 1986.

Gifford, Don, with Robert J Seidman. *Ulysses Annotated: Notes for James Joyce's Ulysses.* 2nd ed. Berkeley, 1989.

Gilman, Charlotte Perkins. 'The Yellow Wallpaper'. *Four Stories by American Women.* Ed. Cynthia Griffin Wolff. Harmondsworth, 1990. 39–59.

Greenacre, Phyllis. *Swift and Carroll.* New York, 1955.

Grotjahn, Martin. 'About the Symbolization of Alice's Adventure's in Wonderland'. *American Imago.* 4 (1947): 32–41.

Guattari, Pierre-Félix. 'Toward a New Perspective on Identity'. (1992) Trans. Joseph-Anton Fernández. Genesko, 215–18.

Guignon, Charles B. 'Authenticity, Moral Values, and Psychotherapy'. *The Cambridge Companion to Heidegger.* Ed. Charles B. Guignon. Cambridge, 1993. 215–240.

Haraway, Donna. 'A Manifesto for Cyborgs: Science, Technology and Socialist Feminism in the 1980s'. *Feminism/Postmodernism.* Ed. Linda J. Nicholson. London, 1990.

Heath, Stephen. *Questions of Cinema.* Bloomington, 1981.

Heidegger, Martin. 'The Origin of the Work of Art' (1960). Trans. Albert Hofstadter. *Basic Writings,* revised and expanded edition. Ed. David Farrell Krell. London, 1993. 139–213.

Heidegger, Martin. *Being and Time* (1927). Trans. John Macquarrie and Edward Robinson. New York, 1962.

Henke, Suzette A. *James Joyce and the Politics of Desire.* London, 1990.

Herr, Cheryl. *Joyce's Anatomy of Culture.* Urbana, 1986.

Irigaray, Luce. *je, tous, nous: Towards a Culture of Difference* (1990). Trans. Alison Martin. New York, 1993.

Jabès, Edmond. *The Little Unsuspected Book of Subversion* (1982). Trans. Rosmarie Waldrop. Stanford, 1996.

Jameson, Fredric. 'Modernism and Imperialism'. *Nationalism, Colonialism and Literature.* Terry Eagleton, Fredric Jameson, Edward Said. Int. Seamus Deane. Minneapolis, 1990. 43–69.

Joyce, James. *Letters of James Joyce.* Vol. 1. Ed. Stuart Gilbert. New York, 1966.

Joyce, James. *Stephen Hero.* Ed. Theodore Spencer. New En. John J. Slocum and Herbert Cahoon. New York, 1955.

Joyce, James. *Ulysses.* (1922). Ed. Declan Kiberd. London, 1992.

Joyce, James. *Ulysses*. (1922). Ed. Hans Walter Gabler, with Wolfhard Steppe and Claus Melchior. London, 1986.

Joyce, James. *Ulysses*. (1922). Ed. Jeri Johnson. Oxford, 1993.

Kaite, Berkeley. *Pornography and Difference*. Bloomington, 1995.

Kamuf, Peggy, ed. *A Derrida Reader: Between the Blinds*. New York, 1991.

Kamuf, Peggy. 'On the Limit'. *Community at Loose Ends*. Ed. The Miami Theory Collective. Minneapolis, 1991.

Kaplan, Louis. *Laszlo Moholy-Nagy: Biographical Writings*. Durham, 1995.

Kearney, Richard. *Dialogues with Contemporary Continental Thinkers: The Phenomenological Heritage*. Manchester, 1984.

Kiberd, Declan. 'Notes'. *Ulysses: Annotated Student's Edition*. James Joyce. London 1992. 941–1196.

Kincaid, James R. *Annoying the Victorians*. New York: Routledge, 1995.

Kincaid, James R. *Child-Loving: The Erotic Child and Victorian Culture*. New York, 1992.

Klein, Scott W. *The Fictions of James Joyce and Wyndham Lewis: Monsters of Nature and Design*. Cambridge, 1994.

Krell, David Farrell. *Of Memory, Reminiscence, and Writing: On the Verge*. Bloomington, 1990.

Kristeva, Julia. *Tales of Love* (1983). Trans. Leon S. Roudiez. New York, 1987.

Lacan, Jacques. *The Four Fundamental Concepts of Psycho-analysis*. (1973). Ed. Jacques-Alain Miller. Trans. Alan Sheridan. Int. David Macey, London, 1991.

Lacan, Jacques. 'Le sinthome: *Séminaire du 18 novembre 1975*.' *Joyce avec Lacan*. Ed. Jacques-Alain Miller. Paris, 1987. 37–49.

Lacan, Jacques. *Écrits: A Selection* (1966). Trans. Alan Sheridan. New York, 1977.

Laclau, Ernesto. 'Totalitarianism and Moral Indignation'. *Diacritics* (Fall 1990, 20: 3): 88–95.

Laclau, Ernesto. *New Reflections on the Revolution of Our Time*. London, 1990.

Lacoue-Labarthe, Phillippe. *Typography: Mimesis, Philosophy, Politics*. Ed. Christopher Fynsk. Trans. Christopher Fynsk *et al*. Int. Jacques Derrida. Cambridge, Ma., 1989.

Larsen, Neil. *Modernism and Hegemony: A Materialist Critique of Aesthetic Agencies*. Minneapolis, 1990.

Lecercle, Jean-Jacques. *Philosophy of Nonsense: The Intuitions of Victorian Nonsense Literature*. London, 1994.

Lentricchia, Frank. 'Foucault's Legacy: A New Historicism'. *The New Historicism*. Ed. H. Aram Veeser. New York, 1989. 231–43.

Leonard, Garry M. *Reading* Dubliners *Again: A Lacanian Perspective*. Syracuse, 1993.

Levinas, Emmanuel. 'Ethics of the Infinite'. Kearney, 49–70.

Levinas, Emmanuel. 'Wholly Otherwise'. Trans Simon Critchley. *Re-Reading Levinas*. Ed. Robert Bernasconi and Simon Critchley. Bloomington, 1991. 3–11.

Levinas, Emmanuel. *Outside the Subject* (1987). Trans. Michael B. Smith. London, 1993.

Levinas, Emmanuel. 'Martin Heidegger and Ontology'. (1932) Trans. Committee of Public Safety. *Diacritics* (Spring 1996, 26: 1): 11–32.

Lippard, Lucy. 'Homage to the Square'. *Art in America* (55, 4). Cited in *Agnes Martin: Paintings and Drawings 1977–1991*. London, 1993.

Lukacher, Ned. 'Introduction: Mourning Becomes Telepathy'. Derrida, *Cinders*. 1–21.

Lyotard, Jean-François. *Heidegger and "the jews"* (1988). Trans. Andreas Michael and Mark Roberts. Int. David Carroll. Minneapolis, 1990.

Lyotard, Jean-François. *The Different: Phrases in Dispute*. (1983) Trans. Georges Van Den Abbeele. Manchester, 1988.

MacCabe, Colin. *James Joyce and the Revolution of the Word*. London, 1979.

Macherey, Pierre, *The Object of Literature* (1990). Trans. David Macey. Cambridge, 1995.

McGee, Patrick. *Telling the Other: The Question of Value in Modern and Postcolonial Writing*. Ithaca, 1992.

Miller, J. Hillis. *Topographies*. Stanford, 1995.

Moi, Toril. *Feminist Theory and Simone de Beauvoir*. Oxford, 1990.

Motzkin, Gabriel. 'Memory and Cultural Translation'. Budick and Iser, 265–281.

Mulhern, Francis. 'English Reading.' Bhabha. 250–65.

Nancy, Jean-Luc. *Le partages des voix*. Paris, 1982.

Nancy, Jean-Luc. *The Experience of Freedom* (1988) Trans. Bridget McDonald. Foreword Peter Fenves. Stanford, 1993.

Nancy, Jean-Luc. *The Inoperative Community*. Ed. Peter Connor. Trans. Peter Connor, Lisa Garbus, Michael Holland, and Simona Sawhney. Foreword Christopher Fynsk. Minneapolis, 1991.

Newman, Robert D. *Transgressions of Reading: Narrative Engagement as Exile and Return*. Durham, 1993.

Newton. K. M. '*Daniel Deronda* and Circumcision'. *George Eliot*. Ed. and int. K. M. Newton. Harlow, 1991. 198–218.

Nolan, Emer. *James Joyce and Nationalism*. London, 1995.

Olalquiaga, Celeste. *Megalopolis: Contemporary Cultural Sensibilities*. Minneapolis, 1992.

Pfeiffer, K. Ludwig. 'The Black Hole of Culture: Japan, Radical Otherness, and the Dissappearance of Difference (or, "In Japan, everything normal")'. Budick and Iser, 186–206.

Pfeil, Fred. 'Postmodernism as a "Structure of Feeling"'. *Marxism and the Interpretation of Culture*. Ed. Cary Nelson and Lawrence Grossberg. Urbana and Chicago, 1988. 381–405.

Rabaté, Jean-Michel. 'Joyce the Parisian'. *The Cambridge Companion to James Joyce*. Ed. Derek Attridge. Cambridge, 1993. 83–102.

Rabaté, Jean-Michel. *James Joyce, Authorized Reader* (1984). Baltimore, 1991.

Rabaté, Jean-Michel. *Joyce upon the Void: The Genesis of Doubt*. New York, 1991.

Ronell, Avital, *The Telephone Book: Technology, Schizophrenia, Electric Speech*. Lincoln, 1989.

Ronell, Avital. *Finitude's Score: Essays for the End of the Millenium*. Lincoln, 1994.

Royle, Nicholas. *After Derrida*. Manchester, 1995.

Sallis, John. 'Doublings'. *Derrida: A Critical Reader*. Ed. David Wood. Oxford, 1992. 120–37.

Sellers, Susan, ed. *The Hélène Cixous Reader*. Foreword Jacques Derrida. London, 1994.

Silverman, Kaja. *The Threshold of the Visible World*. New York, 1996.

Simons, Jon. *Foucault and the Political*. London, 1995.

Sinfield, Alan. *Faultlines: Cultural Materialism and the Politics of Dissident Reading*. Oxford, 1992.

Sitney, P. Adams, ed. *Film Culture Reader*. New York, 1970.

Skinner, John. 'Lewis Carroll's Adventures in Wonderland'. *American Imago*. 4 (1947): 32–41.

Soler, Colette. 'The Subject and the Other' (I and II). Feldstein *et al.*, 39–44, 45–54.

Somer, John. 'The Self-Reflexive Arranger in the Initial Style of Joyce's *Ulysses*'. *James Joyce Quarterly*. 31, 2 (Winter 1994): 65–81.

Soper, Kate. *Troubled Pleasures: Writings on Politics, Gender and Hedonism*. London, 1990.

Spanos, William V. 'The Detective and the Boundary: Some Notes on the Postmodern Literary Imagination'. (1972) *Early Postmodernism: Foundational Essays*. Ed. Paul A. Bové. Durham, 1995. 17–40.

Stratton, Jon. *Writing Sites: A Genealogy of the Postmodern World*. Ann Arbor, 1990.

Suzuki, Tomi. *Narrating the Self: Fictions of Japanese Modernity*. Stanford, 1996.

Taminaux, Jacques. *Heidegger and the Project of Fundamental Ontology*. Trans. and Ed. Michael Gendre. Albany, 1991.

Thomas, D. M. *The White Hotel*. Harmondsworth, 1981.

Tsukamoto, Shinya, dir. *Tetsuo: The Iron Man*. 67 mins. ICA Projects. 1993. Videocassette.

Visker, Rudi. *Michel Foucault: Genealogy as Critique*. (1990) Trans. Chris Turner. London, 1995.

Ward, Ian. *Law and Literature: Possibilities and Perspectives*. Cambridge, 1995.

Weber, Samuel. *Return to Freud: Jacques Lacan's Dislocation of Psychoanalysis* (1978). Trans. Michael Levine. Cambridge, 1992.

White, Eric. ' "Once They Were Men, Now They're Land Crabs": Monstrous Becomings in Evolutionist Cinema'. *Posthuman Bodies*. Ed. Judith Halberstam and Ira Livingston. Bloomington, 1995.

Williams, Linda Ruth. *Critical Desire: Psychoanalysis and the Literary Subject*. London, 1995.

Wolfreys, Julian. *Being English: Narratives, Idioms, and Performances of National Identity from Coleridge to Trollope*. Albany, 1994.

Ziarek, Ewa. 'The Female Body, Technology, and Memory in "Penelope"'. *Molly Blooms: A Polylogue on "Penelope" and Cultural Studies*. Ed. Richard Pearce. Madison, 1994. 264–287.

Ziarek, Krystof. *Inflected Language: Towards a Hermeneutics of Nearness: Heidegger, Levinas, Stevens, Celan*. Albany, 1994.

Index of Proper Names